Francesca Arnavas
Lewis Carroll's "Alice" and Cognitive Narratology

Narratologia

Contributions to Narrative Theory

Edited by
Fotis Jannidis, Matías Martínez, John Pier,
Wolf Schmid (executive editor)

Editorial Board
Catherine Emmott, Monika Fludernik, José Ángel García Landa, Inke Gunia,
Peter Hühn, Manfred Jahn, Markus Kuhn, Uri Margolin, Jan Christoph Meister,
Ansgar Nünning, Marie-Laure Ryan, Jean-Marie Schaeffer, Michael Scheffel,
Sabine Schlickers

Volume 73

Francesca Arnavas

Lewis Carroll's "Alice" and Cognitive Narratology

Author, Reader and Characters

DE GRUYTER

Revisions for this book were supported by the European Regional Development Fund (Mobilitas Pluss, MOBJD491) and the Estonian Research Council (Grant 1481).

ISBN 978-3-11-110406-5
e-ISBN (PDF) 978-3-11-068927-3
e-ISBN (EPUB) 978-3-11-068930-3
ISSN 1612-8427

Library of Congress Control Number: 2020946506

Bibliographic information published by the Deutsche Nationalbibliothek
The Deutsche Nationalbibliothek lists this publication in the Deutsche Nationalbibliografie; detailed bibliographic data are available on the Internet at http://dnb.dnb.de.

© 2022 Walter de Gruyter GmbH, Berlin/Boston
This volume is text- and page-identical with the hardback published in 2021.
Printing and binding: CPI books GmbH, Leck

www.degruyter.com

Acknowledgements

First and foremost, I would like to thank immensely the three people this book, which is the final product of my PhD years, would not have been possible without: my parents, who have given me all kinds of possible support, as they have always done throughout my life, and my PhD supervisor, Professor Richard Walsh. Richard has been everything a good supervisor can be, and more: his precision, his accurate and intelligent suggestions, his detailed revisions, his always prompt and helpful support, alongside his kind and good-natured character, have made the three years and a half of working with him a great honour and pleasure – and I honestly do not know what I would have done without him.

I owe a debt of gratitude to my TAP member, Professor Hugh Haughton, who has always provided me with excellent advice and sympathetic support.

I thank my internal and external examiners, Professor Matthew Campbell and Professor Jan Alber, for their precious feedback and suggestions.

I thank the University of York and its resources, for having offered me the means to carry out my research and a friendly, stimulating academic environment. I thank the academic associations and societies which are a constant source of ideas and intellectual stimuli, like the Lewis Carroll Society UK, the BAVS, the International Society for the Study of Narrative, the International Association for the Fantastic in the Arts, and the FLS. I am grateful for the intellectually enriching experience I had at the Summer School in Narrative Studies organised by the University of Aarhus.

I will always remember how my friend Dr Manal Atesh Omabdulaziz escorted me to my viva voce and waited outside the door for two hours: I am still moved by her affection and kindness. I thank my friend Dr Emily Bell (otherwise known as the Queen of Referencing) who has patiently assisted me every time I needed advice on all the tricky formal aspects. I am grateful to my friend and children's book author Daisy Johnson, who was there with me to hold my hand while I was trying to last minute print my work. My first friend in York, Dr Agata Frymus, deserves a special mention, for all the funny moments together during our PhD years. Last but by no means least, thanks to Hannah, whose luminous and warm presence acted as my personal shiny rainbow throughout all my years in York.

I would finally like to thank Professor Tom Stoneham, from the Philosophy Department of the University of York, for having shared with me his brilliant insights on the cognitive nature of dreams, and Professor David Herman, whose suggestion to contact Richard Walsh for a possible PhD opportunity has been the best academic advice I have ever received.

Contents

List of Illustrations —— XI

List of Abbreviations —— XIII

Quotations in Headings —— XV

Preface
Pictures and Conversations —— XVII

Chapter 1
Why the *Alices*? —— 1
1.1 Cognitive Narratology: Conceptual Framework —— 1
1.2 Lewis Carroll and the Mysteries of the Mind —— 9

Chapter 2
Virtual Alice —— 25
2.1 "The Question Is – Said Humpty Dumpty – Which Is to Be Master – That's All": The Author —— 26
2.1.1 The Rabbit Hole, Humpty Dumpty, and other Metaphor-Related Images —— 27
2.1.2 Wonderland and the Looking-Glass World as Blended Spaces —— 34
2.1.3 Cognitive Features of Carroll's Creative Inventions —— 36
2.2 "He Was Part of My Dream of course – but then I was Part of His Dream, too!": The Character(s) —— 40
2.2.1 A Curious Child —— 42
2.2.2 The Dreamchild Dreaming —— 48
2.3 "The Magic Words Shall Hold Thee Fast: / Thou Shalt not Heed the Raving Blast": The Readers —— 54
2.3.1 A Cognitive Approach to Fictional Worlds —— 55
2.3.2 The Visual Aspects of Alice's Worlds —— 61

Chapter 3
Mirrored Alice —— 68
3.1 "The More Head-Downwards I Am, the More I Keep Inventing New Things": The Author —— 68
3.1.1 Magic Mirrors and Lewis Carroll —— 70

3.1.2	The Cognitive Significance of Carroll's *Mise en Abymes* —— 77	
3.1.3	The Looking-Glass Land: A Multi-Faceted Narrative Dimension —— 80	
3.1.4	Carroll's Own Literary Doubles —— 84	
3.1.5	Language Is Not a Mirror: Looking-Glass Insects —— 86	
3.2	"So You Are Another Alice": The Character(s) —— 89	
3.2.1	Queen Alice —— 91	
3.2.2	Two Sides of the Same Coin? Mirrored Characters —— 94	
3.2.3	"Impenetrability! That's What *I* Say!": *Here* Minds Are Not Mirrors —— 97	
3.3	"Which Do You Think It Was?": The Readers —— 99	
3.3.1	Mirror Neurons: Caveats and Carroll's "Bright Silvery Mist" —— 101	
3.3.2	Mind Games and ToM in Alice's Worlds —— 103	
3.3.3	Worlds Upside Down and Meta-Representations in Trouble —— 106	

Chapter 4
Emotional Alice —— 112

4.1	"Is This an Extempore Romance of Yours, Dodgson?": The Author —— 114
4.1.1	The "Discovery" of Emotions in Victorian Literature and the Rhetoric of Nonsense Vs Victorian Sentimentality —— 114
4.1.2	"The Poignant Love Song Beneath the Invented Nonsense Words" —— 117
4.1.3	"Still She Haunts Me" —— 120
4.1.4	"Lolita Has Been Safely Solipsized" —— 122
4.2	"What Are Little Girls Made of? Sugar and Spice and All That's Nice": The Character(s) —— 127
4.2.1	Alice's Emotions —— 127
4.2.2	Alice's Actions —— 131
4.2.3	Alice's Body —— 133
4.3	"What Is the Use of a Book, without Pictures or Conversations?": The Readers —— 138
4.3.1	The *Feel* of Nonsense: Do We Weep for Alice? —— 139
4.3.2	"Tut, Tut, Child! Every Thing's Got a Moral, if only You Can Find It" —— 144

Chapter 5
Unnatural Alice —— 147
5.1 "You May Call It 'Nonsense' if You Like [...] but *I*'ve Heard Nonsense, Compared with Which That Would Be as Sensible as a Dictionary!": The Author —— 148
5.1.1 Is Nonsense Unnatural? —— 148
5.1.2 Carroll's Interest in the Supernatural, Unnatural, Hypernatural —— 153
5.1.3 The "Unnaturalness" of the Carrollian Worlds —— 154
5.1.4 Creating the Unnatural: Authorial Strategies and Scientific Connections —— 158
5.2 "... But There's one Great Advantage in It, That One's Memory Works Both Ways": The Character(s) —— 161
5.2.1 Unnatural Minds in the Alices: It's Always Tea-Time —— 162
5.2.2 "... And the Rule Is, Jam Tomorrow and Jam Yesterday – Never Jam Today" —— 168
5.2.3 What Happens in the Minds of Flowers, Cards, Chess Pieces —— 170
5.3 "It Always Makes One a Little Giddy at First": The Readers —— 172
5.3.1 How Do We Grasp the Unnatural? —— 172
5.3.2 The Slippery Nature of the Impossible: Unicorns, Little Girls and Other Fabulous Monsters —— 176

Conclusion —— 182

Bibliography —— 184

Authors Index —— 198

Index of Subjects —— 200

List of Illustrations

Fig. 1 Maxim Mitrofanov, illustration for *Alice Through the Looking-Glass*, 2010. Moscow: Rosman, 2014 —— XVII

Fig. 2 Harry Furniss, illustration from *Sylvie and Bruno*, 1890. New York: Dover Publications, 1988 —— 15

Fig. 3 Max Ernst, *Pour Les Amis D'Alice*, 1957. Painting, oil on canvas. Fondation des Treilles, Tourtour —— 22

Fig. 4 Maggie Taylor, *These Strange Adventures*. Illustration for *Alice's Adventures in Wonderland*. San Francisco: Modernbook Editions, 2008 —— 41

Fig. 5 Lewis Carroll (under his real name, Charles Dodgson), *Alice Liddell Asleep*. Spring 1860. Photograph. National Media Museum, Bradford —— 48

Fig. 6 Kenneth Rougeau, *The Red King Sleeping*, 2007. Digital collage —— 56

Fig. 7 John Tenniel, illustration for *Through the Looking-Glass and What Alice Found There*, 1871 —— 62

Fig. 8 Lewis Carroll, illustration for *Alice's Adventures Underground*, 1862–64 —— 66

Fig. 9 Kenneth Rougeau, *The Garden of Live Flowers*, 2007. Digital collage —— 67

Fig. 10 John Tenniel, illustration for *Through the Looking-Glass and What Alice Found There*, 1871 —— 69

Fig. 11 Lewis Carroll (under his real name, Charles Dodgson), *Annie Rogers and Mary Jackson as Queen Eleanor and Fair Rosamund*. July 3, 1863. Photograph. Museum of the History of Science, Oxford —— 71

Fig. 12 Lewis Carroll (under his real name, Charles Dodgson), *Reflection*, 1862. Photograph. Princeton University Library —— 72

Fig. 13 John Tenniel, illustration for *Through the Looking-Glass and What Alice Found There*, 1871 —— 76

Fig. 14 Kenneth Rougeau, *Alice Through the Looking-Glass*, 2007. Digital collage —— 78

Fig. 15 John Tenniel, illustration for *Through the Looking-Glass and What Alice Found There*, 1871 —— 81

Fig. 16 "Acheta Domestica" (Budgen, Louise), illustration for *Episodes of Insect Life*. London: G. Bell and Sons, 1879 —— 89

Fig. 17 Screenshot from Walt Disney's *Alice in Wonderland*, 1951 —— 90

Fig. 18 David Delamare, *Caterpillar No. 2*. illustration for *Alice's Adventures in Wonderland*. Ed. Goodacre, Selwyn and Wendy Ice, 2015 —— 100

Fig. 19 Arthur Rackham, *Pig and Pepper*. Illustration from *Alice's Adventures in Wonderland*. London: William Heinemann, 1907 —— 108

Fig. 20 Trevor Brown, *The Pool of Tears*. Illustration from *Alice*. Tokyo: Editions Treville, 2010 —— 112

Fig. 21 Lewis Carroll (under his real name Charles Dodgson), *Open Your Mouth and Shut Your Eyes*, July 1860. Photograph. National Portrait Gallery, London —— 115

Fig. 22 Lewis Carroll (under his real name Charles Dodgson), *Alice Liddell As a Beggar Maid*, 1858. Photograph. Private collection —— 123

Fig. 23 Dominic Murphy, *The Queen Cutter*, from his *Alice in Wonderland Art* series. dominicmurphytarot.com —— 130

Fig. 24 Trevor Brown, *Eat Me*, Illustration from *Alice*. Tokyo: Editions Treville, 2010 —— 135

Fig. 25 Andrea D'Aquino, illustration from *Alice's Adventures in Wonderland*. Beverly, Massachusetts: Rockport Publishers, 2015 —— 149

Fig. 26 Salvador Dalí, *The Mad Tea Party*, 1969. Painting, as shown in *Alice's Adventures in Wonderland*. Princeton: Princeton University Press, 2015 —— 161

Fig. 27 Max Ernst, *Alice in 1941*, painting, 1941 —— 173

Fig. 28 Maxim Mitrofanov, illustration for *Alice's Adventures in Wonderland*, 2013 —— 177

List of Abbreviations

AAIW Lewis Carroll. [1865]. 2001. "Alice's Adventures in Wonderland". *The Annotated Alice: The Definitive Edition.* Edited by Martin Gardner. London: Penguin Books.
TTLG Lewis Carroll. [1871]. 2001. "Through the Looking-Glass and What Alice Found There". *The Annotated Alice: The Definitive Edition.* Edited by Martin Gardner. London: Penguin Books.
SAB Lewis Carroll. [1889]. 1988. *Sylvie and Bruno.* New York: Dover Publications.
SABC Lewis Carroll. [1893]. 2010. *Sylvie and Bruno Concluded.* Charleston, South Carolina: NabuPress.
SPR Society for Psychical Research.
ToM Theory of Mind.
CMT Cognitive Metaphor Theory.

Quotations in Headings

1. (2.1) "The Question Is -Said Humpty Dumpty …" (*TTLG*, 224) —— 26
2. (2.2) "He Was Part of My Dream …" (*TTLG*, 285) —— 40
3. (2.3) "The Magic Words Shall Hold …" (*TTLG*, 139) —— 54
4. (3.1) "The More Head-Downwards I Am …" (*TTLG*, 254) —— 68
5. (3.2) "So You Are Another Alice" (M. Cohen 1989b, 196–197) —— 89
6. (3.2.3) "Impenetrability! That's What *I* Say!" (*TTLG*, 224) —— 97
7. (3.3) "Which Do *You* Think It Was?" (*TTLG*, 285) —— 99
8. (4.1) "Is This an Extempore Romance …" (M. Cohen 1995, 91) —— 114
9. (4.1.2) "The Poignant Love Song …" (Rackin 1982, 38) —— 117
10. (4.1.3) "Still She Haunts Me" (*TTLG*, 287) —— 120
11. (4.1.4) "Lolita Has Been Safely Solipsized" (Nabokov 2000, 60) —— 122
12. (4.2) "What Are Little Girls Made of? …" (Collingwood 1898, 381) —— 127
13. (4.3) "What Is the Use of a Book …" (*AAIW*, 11) —— 138
14. (4.3.2) "Tut, Tut, Child! …" (*AAIW*, 95) —— 144
15. (5.1) "You May Call It 'Nonsense' …" (*TTLG*, 171) —— 148
16. (5.2) "But There's one Great Advantage in It …" (*TTLG*, 206) —— 161
17. (5.2.2) "And the Rule Is Jam Tomorrow …" (*TTLG*, 206) —— 168
18. (5.3) "It Always Makes One a Little Giddy …" (*TTLG*, 206) —— 172

Preface
Pictures and Conversations

Fig. 1: Maxim Mitrofanov, illustration for *Through the Looking-Glass*, 2014. The general topics of the main four chapters in this book can be found summarised in this image: the idea of entering a virtual reality; the presence of a mirror; the complexities of emotions (Alice has three faces with different expressions on them); the unnaturalness of Alice's worlds. The chess and the clock highlight two other important elements: the metaphor of the playground and the relevance of the bizarre representation of time in the *Alices*.

> 'And what is the use of a book,' thought Alice, 'without pictures or conversations?'
> (*AAIW*, 11)

This book follows Alice's advice, using pictures and conversations as its framing devices: pictures formally, by juxtaposing the argument with illustrations from the rich illustrative history of the *Alice* books; and conversations thematically, by considering the *Alice* books in dialogue with a cognitive narratological approach. The word "dialogue", from the Greek *dialogos*, is a compound word which combines together *dia* (through) and *logos* (word, speech, reason, thought). This means that a dialogue entails navigating through words, speech and thought: as David Bohm writes,

> The picture or image that this derivation suggests is of a stream of meaning flowing among and through and between us. This will make possible a flow of meaning in the whole group, out of which may emerge some new understanding. It's something new, which may not have been in the starting point at all. It's something creative. (2004, 6)

In this sense, the dialogue between the *Alice* books and cognitive narratology staged in this book is intended to be a mutual exchange of meaning, fostering new connections and conceptual ramifications and encouraging a far-reaching interdisciplinary perspective upon both theory and Carroll's texts.

The application of interpretative methods from cognitive narratology to the *Alice* books has to be seen in dialogic terms, then, and has two complementary aims in view: on the one hand, to produce new insight into the construction and meaning of the *Alice* books; on the other hand, to make a contribution to the field of cognitive narratology, furnishing an extended practical example of the application of cognitive narratology's tools to a relevant literary work. These two main objectives are balanced, and an equal weight is given to them, so as not to make cognitive narratology overshadow the *Alices*, nor the other way around, to let the *Alices* impose themselves, making the conceptual framework of interpretation less relevant. In other words, a cognitive-narratological viewpoint should not force the content of the *Alice* books into its own mould, while the idiosyncratic narrative nature of the *Alices* should not foreclose the possibility that cognitive narratology can offer a new way of looking at them. This pursuit of synthesis is at the very core of my research, manifesting itself in a number of different ways: balancing the *Alices* with cognitive narratology, cognitive studies with narrative theories, science with art, Lewis Carroll with Charles Dodgson, "natural" with "unnatural" texts, Alice Liddell with her fictional counterpart ... my approach does not seek to abolish contradictions or oppositions in favour of an artificial theoretical unity, but to refuse the hypostatisation of rigid dichotomies and to aim instead for a richer and more fruitful approach that gives to each element its right relevance in the equal and balanced dialogue of an interdisciplinary framework.

I take the *Alice* books as a case study in order to illuminate the working of cognitive narratology as an interdisciplinary field, drawing upon both classical narrative studies and concepts taken from the cognitive sciences. The complex and heterogeneous theoretical corpus of cognitive narratology is elucidated by practical application in the interpretation of a literary text, establishing a fertile reciprocity between theory and interpretation. As Peter Stockwell emphasises:

> Concerned with literary reading, and with both a psychological and a linguistic dimension, cognitive poetics offers a means of discussing interpretation whether it is an authorly version of the world or a readerly account, and how those interpretations are made manifest in textuality. In this sense, cognitive poetics [....] is a radical evaluation of the whole process of literary activity. (2002, 5)

Moreover, a hermeneutics grounded in cognitive narratology has much to gain from the insights of previous studies on the *Alice* books, so that the encounter between theory and text provides for a mixture of new interpretations and new ways of looking at old interpretations. Such a negotiation has also been, indeed, essential to cognitive narratology itself, the emergence of which has crucially involved a combination of the revaluation of classical narratology and its reinvigoration through the introduction of a new conceptual paradigm.

Regarding my use of pictures, I would like to insist upon their relevance to the theoretical space of my argument. The *Alice* books have been conceived as illustrated books since their very first elaboration (Carroll himself illustrated the first manuscript of *Alice's Adventures Underground*) and they have continued to inspire countless artists through all the subsequent years. It is not even possible to think about the *Alice* books without an insurgence of images into our minds: Alice and her adventures are always associated with visual representations, whether the black and white, slightly grotesque original illustrations by Tenniel, or Dalí's surrealist version, or more recent, innovative interpretations. In order to remain faithful to this important aspect of the *Alices*, I have conceived this book as an interplay of words and images, for the conceptual framework of the dialogue is again a useful model. The choice of images ranges from Victorian illustrations (by, for example, Tenniel, Arthur Rackham and photographs by Carroll himself) to contemporary, provocative ones (by artists such as Trevor Brown, Kenneth Rougeau, Andrea D'Aquino).

Given the diverse elements contributing to the book, my combination of different overlapping approaches can be usefully grounded in the idea of the *Alice* books as a cognitive playground; a huge mental landscape in which multiple intellectual suggestions and speculations coexist with experientiality, visual representations and emotions. The enigmatic world of the *Alice* books, continuously gives us this sense of a playground, whether a croquet ground or a chessboard, where disparate characters meet each other, new rules are continuously invented, old rules are revised, and experiences, emotions and mental games all happily mix together in a wonderfully open cognitive space: "It's a great huge game of chess that's being played – all over the world – if this *is* the world at all, you know. Oh what fun it is!" (*TTLG*, 172).

The idea of the *Alices* as cognitive playground helps to tie together the range of perspectives generated by the intellectual encounter between the *Alice* books and cognitive narratology. Another useful metaphor informing the structure of the book is the conceptualisation of the *Alice* books as the encounter of different minds. In fact, whose minds they might be, how these minds are depicted and how they related to each other, is the point of departure for my cognitive approach. The minds centrally concerned are those of the readers, of the author and of the characters. I divide each chapter into three sections dealing with these different minds and perspectives. The different kinds of mind involved are treated in turn, within each chapter, as a focus for the application of a specific aspect of cognitive narratology. Wonderland and the Looking-Glass Land, as fantastical cognitive playgrounds where different minds interact, are an ideal literary and aesthetic space within which to apply and examine cognitive-narratological ideas.

For what concerns the specific content of each chapter, after a first introductory one in which I highlight why Lewis Carroll's *Alice* books offer such an appropriate literary ground for a cognitive narratological perspective, the second chapter, "Virtual Alice", explores the creation, the internal features and the reception of virtual worlds and virtual minds: the basic idea underlying this chapter's approach is the vision of the realities depicted in fictions as privileged tools for exploring the mind and as exemplifications of cognitively necessary elements of our mental equipment. The third chapter, "Mirrored Alice", invokes the conceptual metaphor of the mirror as related to the mind and the image of the mind to inquire into different narrative aspects of the *Alices* and their reception. As its title suggests, "Emotional Alice", the fourth chapter, focuses on emotions in literary texts, and it considers them as inextricably linked to thoughts and actions, and as connected to the idea of the mind as embodied; the specific emotional tissue of nonsense narratives is another important topic of this chapter. The last chapter is called "Unnatural Alice", and it is the final development of the cognitive approach to the *Alices*, considering them as unnatural fictions and discussing a cognitive reading of the unnatural as a way to overcome rigid dichotomies.

The sequential development of the chapters follows a *crescendo* of cognitive complexity, firstly dealing with the most basic cognitive processes connected to the elaboration and reception of literary texts, such as how we access the virtual space of a narrative, using as conceptual tools notions like cognitive deixis, conceptual metaphor, blending, storyworld (chapter two, "Virtual Alice"). The following step further elaborates on our cognitive involvement with narratives, taking into account more complex mental activities, invoking concepts such as mirror neurons, double embedded narratives, meta-representations, ToM and specific linguistic implications of mirror-related mental processes (chapter three, "Mirrored Alice"). After having considered the more purely cognitive aspects of the relationship with a literary world, chapter four, "Emotional Alice" introduces the idea that cognitive mechanisms never work alone, but are deeply entangled with emotional components, expanding in this way the considered mental scenario. The final step involves more extreme cognitive challenges, the ones entailed by mentally approaching an unnatural, anti-mimetic storyworld (chapter fifth, "Unnatural Alice"). The chapters are interconnected, as thought processes are always interlinked, but their unfolding can be pictured as an expanding and increasing progress of cognitive complexity.

Chapter 1
Why the *Alices*?

> Ultimately, Alice's adventures offer something much more
> interesting: the opportunity to explore a world that exists only
> in the space between our ears. (Douglas-Fairhurst 2015, 126)

This introductory chapter is divided into two sections: in the first, I briefly survey the main concepts from cognitive narratology that I use in the book and make explicit their link to my analysis of the *Alices*; in the second, I further explore the significance of Lewis Carroll as an author for a cognitive approach, elucidating his own theoretical interests and background. These two sections are foundational for the rest of the book, since they provide the theoretical framework necessary to navigate through the subsequent chapters.

1.1 Cognitive Narratology: Conceptual Framework

If "most basically, cognitive science is an interdisciplinary form of study aimed at understanding human cognition" (Hogan 2003, 29), the field of cognitive narratology seems to be a further complication of the picture, with its attempt to approach literary texts with a non-systematic application of cognitive theories taken from various and heterogeneous tendencies and schools. Nonetheless, what seems to be its main weakness is actually its fundamental strength: in fact, it is precisely this still-in-formation status and this multiplicity of inspirations and perspectives that makes cognitive narratology a particularly stimulating and extensive field of study, rich in possibilities.

The "cognitive turn" has affected a wide range of different disciplines (besides the neurobiologists and psychologists, also social scientists, linguists, philosophers, anthropologists, computer scientists, and many scholars in other fields have begun to enrich their theoretical domains with cognitive influences). For literary theorists to ignore this significant "cognitive revolution" would be "clearly short-sighted" (Hogan 2003, 1). As Judith Duchan et. al. emphasise,

> The path to truth is not defined by a single discipline, nor by a single methodology. Cognitive science takes its topic – cognition – and tries to understand it from a variety of knowledge bases and basic methodologies. (2005, 3)

Any full study of the mind, necessarily, involves the arts in general and literature in particular – since art explores the mind, stimulates it, feeds it, describes it, even *changes* its structures. Poetry, novels, music and paintings reveal specific aspects of our mental experiences and functioning which are not accessible by other means. Jonah Lehrer puts it like this: "By expressing our actual experience, the artist reminds us that our science is incomplete, that no map of matter will ever explain the immateriality of our consciousness", and "any description of the brain requires both cultures, art and science." (2008, x)[1]

Moreover, "literature and the arts pose specific problems for cognitive study; they raise specific issues; they present specific challenges" (Hogan 2003, 3); in this sense, cognitive narratology presents itself as both a relevant contribution to mind studies and a beneficiary of new, refreshing theoretical paradigms.

This development in literary theories obviously is not free from risks, as well underlined by Hans Adler and Sabine Gross in a 2002 article titled "Adjusting the Frame: Comments on Cognitivism and Literature": there is a "fundamental question about the compatibility of two different value systems" (2002, 214). The ambitious aim of cognitive narratology is to establish a bidirectional exchange between cognitive studies and literary theories: as David Herman points out "cognitive narratology has fostered the expectation that there is indeed a positive, reciprocal influence, a basic synergy, between research on intelligent behaviour and detailed analysis of narratives of all sorts" (2003, 20). Many critical remarks have been directed against a too easy merging of the two disciplines, and some of cognitive narratogy's directions of study have deserved these censures, since they have indulged in one or other of the possible irresponsible attitudes listed by Mark Bruhn: disciplinary imperialism, in which literature becomes just a branch of cognitive science (Adler and Gross 2002, 225–244), or the other way around; or "tinkering" with the terms of mind science by literary theorists, without a clear awareness of what these terms actually signify in their original disciplinary context (Bruhn 2011, 404–460).

Much of the perplexity and difficulty related to cognitive narratology arises from the idea of the incommensurability of the two disciplines: on the one hand the empirical method, the seeking for regularity and the urge for simplification, on the other hand the representation of the subjective, the creative approach and the emphasis upon the exceptional. From one point of view, cognitive science and literary theory *are* indeed incommensurable, but this is because the mind itself is incommensurable: as Ellen Spolsky (1993) rightly says, "the gaps in the interpretative systems, far from being accidental, are necessary and innate

---

[1] What Lehrer, as a neuroscientist, affirms, is that the complexity of our minds can't be reduced to "a loom of electrical cells and synaptic spaces" (2005, x), and that art offers an essential collaboration in the investigation of the elaborated form of the human mind.

aspects of our genetically inherited epistemological equipment" (192) – different perspectives coexist because the mind cannot be reduced to one perspective: our cognitive apparatus is reflected in the way we try to study it. From another point of view, however, it is possible to find "temporarily satisfactory connections" between the different perspectives (192),[2] which overcome rigid dichotomies and show how different theoretical fields can benefit from a productive and well-informed mutual exchange of knowledge.

Since cognitive narratology is not a well-defined, unitary theoretical position, it is problematic to trace its outlines clearly: as Isabel Jaén and Julien Jacques Simon have pointed out

> There is no such thing as a cognitive literary method, but there is a willingness to leave our comfort zone, our discipline's shell, for the sake of contributing to the construction of a more complete and coherent image of the human mind and its manifestations. (2012, 4)

Maintaining this attitude, I would nevertheless propose to briefly mention some of the basic concepts and themes that I use in my subsequent analysis of the *Alice* books, in order to provide a general sketch of the theoretical framework of my research. It is nonetheless always necessary to keep in mind the problematic status of these concepts, since they are all still in a phase of elaboration and they are implicated in several different accounts and different connected perspectives.

The idea of *storyworlds*, as more cognitively oriented versions of mental models referred to a textual universe (see Herman 1997, 2005, 2013; Gerrig and Egidi 2003; Stockwell 2002) is theoretically significant in my description of Alice's worlds, Wonderland and the Looking-Glass Land, as complex mental spaces – a cognitive combination of literary creation, universe per se and readerly re-creation. The different and controversial relations a story world can have with the "actual world" are explored throughout the book, in connection with the composite substance of the *Alices*, focusing on a cognitive re-elaboration of Marie-Laure Ryan's (1991) principle of minimal departure and of possible world theory, also expanding the analysis to the impossible worlds of unnatural fictions.

Similarly, *cognitive deixis*, understood as a mental device used by readers to position their frame of reference inside the textual scenario, works as an important tool in order to deal with the multi-layered deictic projections implied by reading the *Alices*. Due to their frequent presenting of dreams within dreams,

---

[2] Spolsky (1993) insists upon the non-permanent essence of every interpretation and cultural perspective, since our system of knowledge is characterised by a "categorical instability" (201).

tale within tale, and even genre within genre, Carroll's masterpieces require a persistent fictional re-centering, an imaginative effort which stimulates the reader's cognitive skills, in order to be able to grasp a reality more and more complex and multifaceted.

Another cognitive integration and expansion to the possible world theory as used in narrative studies is the *conceptual metaphor theory* (see Turner 1996; Lakoff and Turner 1989; Fludernik 2011) and the related concepts of *conceptual blending* and *parable* (Turner 1996; Lakoff and Johnson 1980; and, more recently: Freeman 2012; Sinding 2012). My utilisation of these approaches in the context of the *Alice* books offers a new way of conceptualising Carroll's creation of metaphors, emphasising how he expanded and even deconstructed our so-called "basic embedded metaphors", and how he invented new metaphorical structures which are now part of our daily lives (the Rabbit-Hole being the most famous example). Conceptual blending and parable, in turn, help defining the construction and meaning of Wonderland and of the Looking-Glass Land, as more elaborated products of metaphoric thinking.

Being a third of each chapter focused on the author, I explore Carroll's poetical inventions with the aid of *creative cognition*- related theories (Smith et al. 1992; Hogan 2003; Bernini and Caracciolo 2013), paying particular attention to "cross-domain borrowings" (Hogan, 70) and child-like structures of thought (Hogan 2003, 75–86) as relevant aspects involved in the generation of the *Alices*. Elements of creative cognition are also part of the reader's receptive imagination. If in literary writing textual generation and storyworld exploration are "mutual and bidirectional" (Bernini 2014, 358), for readers, too, the mental imagery is continuously affected by, on the one hand, the sequence of words and the images they carry with them and, on the other hand, by their own pre-existent mental constructions, thought structures and cognitive apparatus. As Porter Abbott (2008) points out, there is an obvious "cognitive gap" (471) between the mind of the author, with its unique complex interplay of intentions, creative inputs and ideas, and the mind of the reader, located in another space, often also in another epoch, and constituted by a quite distinct amalgam of cognitive parameters. Nevertheless, we can focus on the textual site on which these two minds meet; where the imaginary landscapes generated on both sides come alive. In this sense, approaches such as the one proposed by Elaine Scarry in her *Dreaming by the Book* (1999) provide us with a detailed and appealing analysis of how writers activate our creative imagination in a unique way, instructing us in the construction of vivid mental compositions. How the *Alice* books foster and push the reader's imaginative acts is always an integrative part of the reader section of my chapters.

In choosing the *Alice* books as ideal texts for a dialogic interaction with cognitive narratology, an important element has been the role that emotions play in them, and the ways of dealing with the emotional components of our mind as diversely expressed in literary texts proposed by cognitive narratologists. The emotional engagement of both author and reader and the eminent role of emotions in characters' development, have been the object of study of scholars such as Suzanne Keen (2007, 2011), Alan Palmer (2005), Kay Young (2010). What has been somehow neglected by this integration of emotion into the hermeneutics of narratives is the peculiar role emotions can play in the context of a nonsense text. In my fourth chapter, "Emotional Alice", I address the issue of how theory of emotions as integrated within theories of cognition can enrich our understanding of the meaning, construction and reception of Carroll's *Alices*.

Another essential, if still controversial, concept for explaining cognitive involvement with novels is *Theory of Mind* (abbreviated as ToM). Cognitive narratology is importantly concerned with how our minds are stimulated by reading, the peculiar quality of attention reading requires and the cognitive endowment resulting from the reading experience – "how various kinds of narrative practice vehiculate intelligence in various ways" (Herman 2003b, 152). Recent developments in cognitive studies and their application to the narrative field show that fictions always involve a kind of "mind-game", and that ToM is a useful tool in novel hermeneutics (see Zunshine 2006). However, there is not universal agreement among scholars about how exactly ToM works, for instance in relation to autistic people or schizophrenics (see for example Langdon et al. 2005), or in relation to child development (Korkmaz 2011, Bruner 1986), or in connection with the role of mirror neurons (Gallese 1998, Rizzolati 2006, Goldman 2007).

Mirror neurons in particular have been a controversial area of theoretical discussion. They have been defined as neurons which "fire" when observing other persons doing a certain action, i.e., nervous cells that are activated not only when we do a particular action, but also when we merely witness others performing that action (Ramachandran 2003). It is therefore clear the importance of this neurological mechanism for the process of *imitation* and its complex implications. In addition to language emergence, behaviours acquisition, empathy and abilities in "reading others' minds" are all phenomena connected in some way with the work of mirror neurons, since they all involve the processes of imitation and of simulation of virtual realities. The imaginative make-believe thus plays a central role in our cognitive archaeology; the fact that our mind reacts in the same way with an effective action and with a mental simulation of that action, underlines the importance of the mental construction of possibilities: possible worlds and virtual realities appear as a fundamental part of the brain 's activity. The ways in which ToM and related mental activities are interconnected with the work of mirror neurons are multiple, and, as said, no universal agreement has been reached among neuroscientists. Moreover, the alternative approaches of "theory theory" and "simulation theory" claim to better account for the concerns addressed by ToM and offer another theoretical framework to approach its controversies.

Notwithstanding these unresolved debates, ToM has significant implications for narrative analysis and for this research. With respect to the reader-text relationship, focusing on, as Lisa Zunshine puts it, the way "literature pervasively capitalises on and stimulates our Theory of Mind mechanisms" (2006 10), I inspect how the *Alice* books engage our minds in processes of thinking and rethinking, challenging our ToM and our meta-representational abilities (for this latter concept, see again Zunshine, 150; Cosmides and Tooby 2000). This mental tool enables us to distinguish the source of a sentence, a thought, or some information; we are thus able to relativise it according to its origin. Meta-representations can be assumed to inform our discourse about the world fundamentally, since no truths without a source are to be found; if we want to question the meaning of reality, to rethink notions or to reshape beliefs, we need to use our meta-representational capability. In this sense meta-representational competence is a powerful instrument of relativisation.

The use Carroll's books make of ToM and meta-representational skills is peculiar, on the one hand ToM being inapplicable to the reading of Wonderland and Looking-Glass Land's characters' minds, on the other hand Alice's failure in reading them inspiring reflections on children's mental reading abilities, notwithstanding our own, as readers, meta-representational skills being continuously challenged and questioned by the *Alices*' narrative scenarios. In this sense the *Alice* books reveal themselves to be among those fictions where our mental source-monitoring is continually forced to reshape itself; we are obliged to reassess our truth attributions again and again.

I would like to conclude this excursus on some of the basic concepts of cognitive narratology and their connection to Carroll's *Alice* stories by introducing the notion of *unnatural texts* and the specific concerns they raise. Alber, Iversen, Nielsen and Richardson, in their "manifesto" for an "unnatural narratology" (2010) propose to extend the "standard cognitive narrative theory" (114) in order to give prominence to texts dealing with "unnatural" scenarios; that is, narratives subverting mimetic models of temporal order, duration and frequency, or depicting physically impossible worlds, or unnatural minds, or events violating the logical principle of non-contradiction. The peculiar challenges posed by unnatural texts invite a re-thinking of the standards of narrative analysis, in order to provide a more comprehensive account of both possible and impossible fictional worlds.

The *Alice* books as nonsense narratives present also, I argue, the features of unnatural texts, questioning our real-world frames, our ToM, our stored cognitive schemata, using innovative literary devices to stretch the limits of our minds. A full cognitive analysis of texts involving unnatural elements has to take into account the claims made by unnatural narratologists, but also the critical reactions and controversies arising from those claims, so identifying their limits and the extent to which they may be integrated with other approaches. The most basic objection to unnatural narratology is that it is founded upon a questionable dichotomy between the natural and unnatural and so hypostasises the rigid boundary it proposes to overcome. This opposition makes it difficult to understand the connections between the two domains and, moreover, makes the unnatural definitional subordinate to its opposite, the natural. Monika Fludernik, in an article about the strengths and weaknesses of the unnatural model ("How Natural Is 'Unnatural Narratology'; or, What Is Unnatural about Unnatural Narratology?" 2012) suggests,

> The spirit of "unnatural" narratology would need a term that signifies a third space or position from which to analyse the negotiations between the mimetic and its various contraventions. (Perhaps *impossible* or *phantasmal* narratology could work.) (366)

There are several other issues with the unnatural approach to narrative, including: its blurring of the two distinct concepts of conventionalisation and naturalisation (see Fludernik 2012, 367–368 and Alber et al. 2012, 378–380); the absence of consensus about the exact scope of the "unnatural" (unnatural narratologists differ in what they claim to be unnatural: see Alber and Heinze 2011, 1–20 and Klauk and Köppe 2013, 78–86); and the need to clarify the supposed cognitive consequences of "dealing with the unnatural." Unnatural narratology, then, is an interesting and challenging approach, which nevertheless needs further exploration, clarification and ramification in the light of specific applications. Using the *Alices*, with their peculiar mixture of natural and unnatural elements, I highlight the limits implied in the "unnatural approach" and, after a comparison between nonsense and the unnatural, I try to propose the fantastic as a way of overcoming rigid boundaries.

The topics above are the main theoretical points of departure for this book, and they represent the diverse but complementary aspects of a cognitive narratological approach to narrative texts. Cognitive deixis, storyworlds/possible worlds, cognitive creation, emotional involvement, ToM and meta-representational abilities and, finally, unnatural narratives are all concepts that I explore and test in my subsequent analysis. As Stockwell (2002) emphasises talking about cognitive poetics "it is under application – the practical exploration of a cognitive framework – that approaches are tested and achieve any sort of value" (166).

Before proceeding with the second section of this introductory chapter, I would like to briefly deal with what can look like a theoretical gap in my approach: i.e., the almost complete omission of references to classical narratology. There are two main reasons behind this choice: firstly, cognitive narratology does not exclude and eliminate traditional narratological concepts: on the contrary, I take for granted the acknowledgement that many of the just surveyed notions have arisen as developments, or as questioning tools, in relation to classic narratological issues and debates. Herman provides us with a similar consideration, when, talking about the definition of cognitive narratology, writes that

> At issue are frameworks for narrative study that incorporate the ideas of classical, structuralist narratologists but supplement their work with concepts and methods that were unavailable to story analysts such as Barthes, Genette, Greimas, and Todorov during the heyday of the structuralist revolution. In the case of scholarship exploring the nexus of narrative and mind, analysts have worked to enrich the original stock of structuralist concepts with research on human intelligence either ignored by or inaccessible to the classical narratologists; they have thus built new foundations for the study of basic and general principles of mind vis-à-vis various dimensions of narrative structure, as well as the various uses to which stories can be put. (2013b, 5)

Despite the methodological changes and innovations, and a new multi-disciplinary focus, cognitive narratology, as well as other forms of post-classical narratology (see Alber and Fludernik 2010) retains, re-formulating and re-discussing them, fundamental theoretical inputs coming from the history of narratology.

For instance, reader-response theory was not born with cognitive narratology, but traces its origins to Wayne Booth's *The Rhetoric of Fiction* (1961), subsequently expanding and enriching it with the analysis and study of readers' cognitive reactions and emotional involvement. Similarly, basic and essential narratological concepts such as focalisation, unreliable narrator, defamiliarisation, which are part of the history of the field (with works by Genette, Todorov, Booth), all experience a re-elaboration in the context of a cognitively oriented narrative theory.

If this obvious tacit background is always there despite an explicit acknowledgement, it is also true (and this is the second point I would like to raise) that the structure itself of my work – the division of each chapter into three different perspectives, the author's, the reader's and the characters' – works as a recognisance of classical narratology's influence. Discussions on authorial intent, authorial primary and secondary audience (also referring to Alice Liddell as the first real target of the whole story), readers' responses to the Carrollian texts and character construction cannot even exist without the previous elaboration of these categories by classical and structuralist narratologists. This said, my attention to the *mind*s of author, reader, characters highlights the new cognitive approach and its attempt to explore and unravel the complex nexus of narrative and mind (see Herman 2009).

1.2 Lewis Carroll and the Mysteries of the Mind

'One side of *what?* The other side of *what?*' thought Alice to herself.
'Of the mushroom,' said the Caterpillar, just as if she had asked aloud;
and in another moment it was out of sight. (*AAIW*, 55)

A cognitive approach to the *Alice* books finds a contextual rationale in Lewis Carroll's own interest in exploring and understanding human mental processes. Throughout the books we find the exploration of specific mental activities (how do dreams work? How do children create meta-representations? How does memory form our self-identity?); they also continuously challenge our mental habits and demand the reconfiguration of our interpretative schemata through devices like the personification of linguistic attitudes and the creation of impossible worlds and nonsense scenarios.

Lewis Carroll's own personality is commonly conceived as a controversial one, a personality split in two: on the one hand the rigorous and conservative logician Reverend Charles Dodgson, on the other hand the witty, extravagant nonsense writer Lewis Carroll. However, the two parts of his "Janus-like identity" (Lecercle 1994, 201) converge at a certain point, which is their concern to lay bare the operations of the mind: Dodgson and Carroll are thus not so different from each other, they can be compared to communicating mirrors, flashing their signals back and forth (see Ranson-Pollizzotti 2011). Furthermore, it can be argued that the *Alice* books do not represent just one side of this "double personality", but are actually a synthesis between the logical, scientific approach and a more "irrational" subjectivity. Carroll's interest in the working of the human mind in some sense cuts across his dichotomous personality, attenuating its polarity; yet this is not to completely neglect its being "coupé en deux", nor an attempt to reduce its multi-facetedness to some kind of definitive resolution. My approach has the goal of being a step towards the elucidation of Carroll's composite character, taking into account its various components, without reducing its complexity on the one hand, and without losing sight, on the other, of my theoretical claim that the negotiation between these different interests is central to his deep and highly significant exploration of the human mind.

As many scholars have already observed, the *Alice* books are full of mathematical references, geometrical allusions, problems, logic games. They depict enigmatic and curious problems of logic, mathematics and even physics: the Mock Turtle mentions the possible existence of negative numbers (still a novel concept in Carroll's time); the Rabbit-Hole is a source of peculiar reflections about the nature of gravity; the passage through the Looking-Glass suggests speculations on anti-matter; the Unicorn is linked to the problematic realm of non-existent entities. Giving substance to the most intriguing and strange branches of logic, maths and physics, the *Alice* books seem to subvert the more traditional and conservative views Carroll expressed in academic contexts, by focusing on *exceptions*. Lecercle points out that the *Alice* books represent the impossible events to which traditional logic normally denies ontological existence:

> and the sorites, those protracted syllogisms that were one of the main objects of Carroll's interest (he suggested new methods for solving them) logicise the literary discourse of nonsense – each sorite is an incipient Wonderland. (1994, 201)

Carroll's fictional explorations of logical riddles, mathematical impossibilities and paradoxical scenarios, are all aspects of the subjects that intrigued him, but that he felt constrained to avoid in "official" contexts. The *Alice* books work as imaginary illustrations of the strange issues lurking in the scientific topics with which he was engaged. John Fisher writes that

> with a magician's instinct for tracking down the impossible, he was able to apply something more than the straightforward academic approach to his studies in mathematics and logic, sources of mystification no conventional magician had ever tapped ... (1973, 8)

Referring to the fact that Carroll, beyond academic contexts, in order to delight his sisters, when he was young, and his child-friends later, Carroll used mathematics and logic to create riddles, puzzles, mystifying tricks and illusionistic games. Like his literary counter-part, the White Knight, he was an inventor: he played with musical boxes, mechanical animals and distorting mirrors (M.N. Cohen 1995, 12; Taylor 1952, 2). In this way, mathematical speculations became wonderlands, mind games and magical experimentations – and the *Alice* books testify all this.

During Carroll's life, mathematics and logic were beginning to take a significant turn towards the exploration of different dimensions: symbolic algebra, four-dimensional mathematics, non-Euclidean geometries, speculations about the null class. It is well known that Carroll maintained a traditional position on these subjects, writing books and essays against the critics of Euclid's *Elements* and against the use of symbolic algebra. Yet, again, the *Alice* books seem to go in exactly the opposite direction; Taylor, for example, suggests that Fechner's speculations about the fourth dimension are one source for Carroll's *Through the Looking-Glass* (Taylor 1952, 89–90). Elizabeth Throesch's essay "Nonsense in the Fourth Dimension of Literature: Hyperspace Philosophy, the 'New' Mathematics, and the *Alice* Books" (2009) argues that "the bizarre linguistic logic of the inhabitants of the *Alice* books can be read as a critique of the new mathematics and the rationale that supports its quirky offspring, hyperspace philosophy" (39). However, Carroll was too fond of his *Alice* books and the alternative realities they represent, to make his "depiction of exceptions" just a polemical stance. It is true that the *Alice* books are full of satirical elements and parodies, but their fantastic dimensions are something more:[3] as Throesch herself writes, nonsense and the fourth dimension both show the meaninglessness of various accepted norms, putting in danger the notion of a stable, univocal reality and offering a phantasmagorical multiplication of associations and perspectives, "a giddying multiplication of possible realities and spaces" (50).

Conjectures on different dimensions of space and time, according to their first theorists Abbott (Carroll owned a first-edition copy of *Flatland* -Throesch, 43) and Hinton, have "consciousness-expanding implications" (2009, 47), their deep sense being an exploration of the depths and labyrinths of the human mind. The *Alice* books are, indeed, subtly revelatory:

> they stealthily instil into us a unique state of mind. Their jam – wild strawberry – is the powder – virgin gold-dust – though we may never be conscious of its cathartic effects. [....] The *Alices* lighten our beings like sunshine (De la Mare 1932, 56)

If Carroll refused, in academic contexts, to accept new interpretations of reality (which, by putting in danger the eternal truths of mathematics, threatened to undermine the stability of religion),[4] he allowed them to run freely in his fantasy

---

[3] Walter De la Mare (1932) states that "all satire and most parody in themselves are mortal enemies of true Nonsense, which is concerned with the joys of a new world" (13–14).
[4] On this topic, Joan Richards (1988) writes that the category of necessary truth grounded in mathematical ideas, as proposed by the philosopher William Whewell, "was critically important for the assurance that man really could come to know his world. This assurance in turn supported his basically conservative outlook in which there were certain immutable truths about God" (29). In a similar vein, Daniel Cohen (2007) maintains that Carroll "clung to the traditional idea that mathematics was a paradigm of simplicity and a conduit of absolute truth about the cosmos" (173).

life; he was far too clever and curious not to be interested in intellectual possibilities for mind expansion. The *Alice* books are not distant from his scientific interests, but represent the most innovative and captivating side of his mathematical mind, allowing him to be much more creative and visionary – and also, as Fisher puts it, a kind of magician. Helen Groth affirms the idea, saying,

> He retained, along with his fellow members of the Society for Psychical Research, a theological sense of the mind which coexisted quite comfortably alongside his enthusiastic embrace of modern scientific method and mathematical theory. (2013, 141)

Carroll was traditional in his official attitudes to mathematics and religion, but his narrative works show that his views on the relation between spiritual and scientific dimensions of mind were much more multifaceted and complex.[5]

Rudy Rucker (2014) suggests that the looking glass and the rabbit hole can be conceived as being like Einstein-Rosen bridges, i.e., hyperspace tunnels that, theoretically, following the theory of relativity, allow travel to different space-time universes: "if a massive star or black hole distorts space enough it is possible that an Einstein-Rosen bridge to another universe can be created. Flying into the right kind of black hole might pop you out into a different world" (120). This is precisely what happens to Alice who, through a hole and then through a mirror, arrives in different realities, experiencing in this way different conceptions of space: in Wonderland she often changes size, while in the Looking-Glass world she has the same height of a chess-piece (and the same perspective!), and numerous space paradoxes are depicted. Similarly, she experiences different conceptions of time: the eternal tea-time of the Mad Hatter and the March Hare; time going backwards in the looking-glass trials; the fact that she begins her Looking-Glass adventures in winter and finds herself in summer; the White Queen's memory of the future. Moreover, the mirror, the second means Alice uses to jump into another dimension, recalls Rucker's description of Einstein-Rosen bridges: in *The Fourth Dimension: Toward a Geometry of Higher Reality* (2014) he writes that an Einstein-Rosen bridge would have more or less the appearance of a spherical mirror with the strange property that the world inside the mirror would actually be different from the world outside the mirror

---

[5] In this sense, it is worth mentioning what Melanie Keene in her *Science in Wonderland* (2015) persuasively shows: the strong connection established in the Victorian Age between fairy tales and scientific topics: "reasoned scientific books", she writes, were "not easily distinguished from more imaginative or fantastical writings" (9).

(113–130). This, of course, is exactly what Carroll has imagined with his looking-glass world: an entire universe is trapped beyond the surface of the mirror.[6]

Alice is able to enter these new worlds of paradox and fantasy through *physical passages*, whereas in *Sylvie and Bruno* the access to other universes no longer requires a golden key, a door, a hole, or a mirror: the protagonist (Carroll himself) can reach the far-away regions of Outland and Elfland with just the power of his *own mind*. Yet, this is not exactly the truth: Carroll writes in *Sylvie and Bruno* that, in order to be able to go among fairies in Elfland, "it must be a very hot day" and "you must be just a little sleepy", and this is indeed what happens at the beginning of *Alice's Adventures in Wonderland* ("the hot day made her feel very sleepy", 11), just a moment before the sudden appearance of the White Rabbit. It may be worth reminding ourselves that one of Carroll's ideas about the title of his first Alice book was "Alice's Adventures in Elfland" (M.N. Cohen 1995, 299). In addition, Carroll describes peculiar "eerie states," very similar to Alice's feeling just before going through the looking-glass, at the beginning of *Sylvie and Bruno Concluded* [1893]: while conscious of his actual surroundings, he is also conscious of the presence of Fairies; or alternatively he refers to "forms of trance in which, while unconscious of actual surroundings, and apparently asleep, he (i.e. his immaterial essence) migrates to other scenes, in actual world or in Fairyland" (2010, xiii). Taylor comments on this, writing that "this is the state, a moment of trance, a falling from her, vanishing, which comes upon Alice as she stands musing before the looking-glass with the black kitten in her arms" (Taylor 1952, 82).

Rucker says that "Wonderland tales are very much like waking dreams" (2009, 60), and this takes us to the second influence on Carroll's interest in the peculiarities of the human mind, other than his exploration of the more innovative and intriguing branches of the exact sciences, which is his engagement with studies of "psychic phenomena", for instance through the Society for Psychical Research (SPR), of which he was a member from the moment of its foundation until his death (see Shaberman 1973, 4). Dreams were generally conceived by the SPR as vehicles of profound meaning and as revealing experiences which can often occur also in peculiar half-waking hypnotic conditions.[7] In this sense, the shifting of consciousness between dreaming to waking, the possibility of ex-

---

[6] About this connection between Alice's looking-glass and the Einstein-Rosen bridge, see also Rucker 2009, 54–55.

[7] The SPR was a very heterogeneous society, embracing different stances and interests, and thus it is difficult to describe a fixed perspective recognised by the whole society; yet, the strong power of dreams and mystic visions was one of the most shared and popular subjects among his members.

changing the two and the revealing power of dream states are topics central to the *Alice* books, but also present elsewhere in Carroll's writing: " 'so either I've been dreaming about Sylvie', I said to myself, 'and this is reality, or else I've really been with Sylvie and this is a dream!' " (*SAB* 1988, 19). In the *Sylvie and Bruno* books [1889, 1893] he relies explicitly on the SPR, putting, in the preface to *Sylvie and Bruno Concluded*, "a table of the incidents of abnormal psychic states that occur in both *Sylvie and Bruno* books (...) directly based on the statistical method of the SPR" (Shaberman 1973, 6), but the eerie states described by the SPR share the same features as Alice's mental dispositions when she goes to Wonderland and the Looking-Glass Land.[8] Dreamy states were recognised by the SPR as having profound connections to the disclosure of meaning and even to experiences of clairvoyance, and in Carroll's universes dream is "*the* sovereign element" (De la Mare 1932, 60), the basic mode of his narratives.

The Society for Psychical Research in some sense served to synthesise Carroll's longstanding interests in occultism, spiritualism[9] and waking dreams with his analytic interest in the mind's functioning. It was founded in England in 1882, and other famous members interested in mind studies were William and Henry James, Virginia Woolf and John Ruskin (who was also a close friend of Carroll); Freud was also a corresponding member and wrote for the Society's journal in 1912.[10] According to its own manifesto ("Objects of the Society" written in 1882 and printed in the *Proceedings*) the fundamental goal of the society was "making an organised and systematic attempt to investigate the large group of debatable phenomena designated by such terms as mesmeric, psychical, and Spiritualistic"; among the subjects most readily embraced by the Society were "thought-reading", hypnotism, clairvoyance, ESP and psychokinesis.

The Society presents itself, to contemporary eyes, as a peculiar mixture of obscure spiritualistic beliefs and the scientific methods espoused in its declared

---

8 One of the most well-known books edited by the SPR, *Phantasms of the Living*, written by the psychical researcher Frank Podmore and by two founding members of the SPR (Edmund Gurney and Frederick W.H. Myers) describes studies of telepathy divided into categories. As Charlie Lovett (2005, 138) has already underlined the category of Borderland, a special suspended mental condition between sleeping and waking, shares key features with the eerie states so accurately described by Carroll.

9 Carroll's interest in spiritualism should not be mistaken with his spirituality: the two can actually be connected, but, when mentioning spiritualism, I hint at the belief in spirits, communication with them through mediumship experiences, supernatural events. When dealing with Carroll's spiritual side, I connect it to a more general faith in an immaterial dimension.

10 I have listed here some later members of the SPR, such as Virginia Woolf and Freud, because I think they are significant for an overall evaluation of the society and underline its strong connection with psychological studies and interest in how the mind works.

Fig. 2: Harry Furniss, illustration from *Sylvie and Bruno*, 1890. The fairy world of Sylvie (who is a Fairy with no wings, "only a few inches high and dressed in green", *SAB*, 192) can be accessed by the main character on a hot day, being a little sleepy, and feeling a little "what one may call 'fairyish' – The Scotch call it 'eerie'" (191).

purpose to ascertain facts and collecting tangible evidence to put still inexplicable phenomena on solid empirical ground. The presence of several prominent intellectuals among the members of the Society shows that some of its research directions were connected to important studies on the nature of human mind. Investigations linked to the Society carried out by William James, for instance, touched such interesting subjects as continuous consciousness and the breach from one mind to another, "cosmic consciousness", the neurological basis for religious experiences, and the mediumship experience.[11] An interest in the substance of ghostly entities, which was a popular topic in the Society, can be found in *The Turn of the Screw* by William James's brother Henry, where the relationship between supernatural apparitions and mental hallucinations is deeply and interestingly explored in the form of a story of never-resolved ambiguity. George Johnson, in *Dynamic Psychology in Modernist British Fiction* (2006), ex-

---

[11] See James 1986; Murphy and Ballou 1960; Knapp 2001.

plores the influences of the Society on the representation of characters and narrative events in British fiction writers of the end of the nineteenth century and beginning of the twentieth and argues that "psychical research did lead to a more expansive mapping of the inner world even before Freud's identification of the id, ego, superego, and so on" (Kunka 2007, 906). In this sense, psychical research, the investigation into transcendental phenomena, can be thought of the initial method to look into the human psyche itself.[12]

While the Society was founded in 1882, and *Alice's Adventures in Wonderland* dates back to 1865 (the date of the first edition; Carroll first told the tale of Alice underground on the almost mythical date of 4 July 1862, during his golden afternoon with the Liddell sisters), Carroll was interested in psychic phenomena long before the SPR came into being. The first story about the fairy world of Sylvie, called "Bruno's revenge", appeared in 1867 in *Aunt Judy's Magazine*, and already contained all the "psychical elements" he would develop later in *Sylvie and Bruno*, such as the description of the "eerie states" that lead one into different dimensions and among fairies. As his nephew Stuart Dodgson Collingwood writes, "Mr Dodgson took a great interest in occult phenomena" (1898, 92); the catalogue of his books shows he owned a lot of texts about the occult, spiritualism, and psychic incidents, and this collection obviously began far earlier than the creation of the SPR. Charlie Lovett states, in the preface to his *Lewis Carroll Among His Books: A Descriptive Catalogue of the Private Library of Charles L. Dodgson*, that "his collection of works related to spiritualism and supernatural phenomena was significant, and his interest in this area is certainly ripe for further investigation" (2005, 11).

What is particularly significant with regard to this thesis is the fact that many of the texts in Carroll's library are about both the supernatural and psychology: Lovett divides Carroll's books into various categories, and many of them are listed under "supernatural" and *also* under "psychology", or "mind", or "mental diseases", or "dreams". Some of the titles can help in showing that the mental states Carroll was most eager to inspect were dreams, madness, telepathy, various kind of abnormal mental phenomena connected to supernatural experiences, clairvoyance, and nervous disorders.[13] What these collections

---

[12] As highlighted also by Sommer 2012 and 2013.
[13] These books (list to be found in Lovett 2005) include *Essay on the History and Reality of Apparitions* (1727) by Daniel Defoe, which conjectures about "the possibility of angelic communication through dreams" (Lovett, 546); *Lights and Shadows of Spiritualism* (1877) by Daniel Dunglas Home, a text about the experiences of mediumship and telekinesis; *The Other World; or Glimpses of the Supernatural. Being Facts, Records, and Traditions relating to Dreams, Omens, Miraculous Occurrences, Apparitions, Wraiths, Warnings, Second-sight, Witchcraft, Necromancy, etc*

show clearly is that Carroll's interest on the study of the mind was a mirror of the way this topic was treated in his cultural environment. The scope of the SPR's interest reflects the fact that psychological studies in Victorian England lay in a strange borderland between medical approaches and psychical conjectures, and the two perspectives often overlapped.

Carroll also contributed two articles ("A Logical Paradox", July 1894 and "What the Tortoise Said to Achilles", April 1895) to the journal *Mind: A Quarterly Review of Psychology and Philosophy* edited by George Frederick Stout. *Mind*, which has also counted among its contributors William James, Charles Darwin, Bertrand Russell and John Ellis McTaggart, is now concerned mainly with issues related to analytic philosophy, but in its beginnings it was above all engaged with the question of whether or not psychology was to be considered as a science. Carroll was also connected to the Ashmolean Society, for whom he lectured at a meeting in November 1860 on one of his favourite topics, the paradox of time and space, under the title "Where Does the Day Begin?". Elias Ashmole was both a man of science and a mystic interested in alchemy, and the Society bearing his name had "the purpose of reconstructing ancient Platonic and Gnostic mysticism" (Ackerman 2008, 12).

(1875) edited by Frederick George Lee; *Illusions. A Psychological Study* (1881) by James Sully, about the relativity of human perceptions; William Howitt's *The History of the Supernatural in all Ages and Nations, and in all Churches, Christian and Pagan, Demonstrating a Universal Faith* (1863); Edward Clodd's *Myths and Dreams* (1885) which deals with the theme of the birth of supernatural beliefs, conceived as having their roots in early interpretations of the world related to mythologies and dreams; Frank Seafield's *The Literature and Curiosities of Dreams: A Commonplace Book of Speculations Concerning the Mystery of Dreams and Visions, Record of Curious and Well-Authenticated Dreams, and Notes on the Various Modes of Interpretation Adopted in Ancient and Modern Times* (1865); Henry Holland's *Chapters on Mental Physiology* (1852), which tries to explain the relationship between mind and body; *The Physiology and Pathology of the Mind* (1867) by Henry Maudsley; two books by Daniel Hack Tuke, one being *Illustrations of the Influence of the Mind upon the Body in Health and Disease, Designed to Elucidate the Action of the Imagination* (1872), a text with the aim of illustrating the powerful actions of mind upon the body and the other being *Sleep-Walking and Hypnotism* (1884); Forbes Winslow's *On Obscure Diseases of the Brain and Disorders of the Mind; Their Incipient Symptoms, Pathology, etc* (1860), which some claim was the first psychiatric study written in English and which talks about new ways of treating insanity, including the use of psychoactive drugs; *Problems of Life and Mind* (1874–5), a series of books on various topics related to mind, philosophy and physiology by George Henry Lewes; *Footfalls on the Boundary of Another World* (1860) by Robert Dale Owen, an investigation of the physiological side of spiritualism dealing also with "psychology, sleep, hallucination, insanity" (Lovett 2005, 228) and many others on similar topics.

A topic which was to become very popular at meetings of the SPR was that of ghosts and the possibility of communicating with them. Carroll was animated by this theme, as is shown by the large selection of texts labelled "ghosts" in the catalogue of his books as well as by his membership of the Ghost Society (M. Cohen 1995, 368). He admitted the plausibility of the existence of supernatural entities, and wrote an entire poem, *Phantasmagoria*, about a ghost (the poem's tone is light and humorous, but this was Carroll's peculiar way of treating the topics of which he was most fond). On 23 April 1867 he recollected in his diary a visit he paid to the artist Thomas Heaphy, who was known for making paintings of ghostly apparitions he himself had seen. Carroll was very curious about the story of a ghost-lady who sat for Heaphy in his studio, and records that he had "a very interesting talk about the ghost, which certainly is one of the most curious and inexplicable stories I ever heard" (Wakeling 1993, 181).

The strong belief Carroll had in mysticism, spiritualism, and studies of psychic phenomena was recently investigated by Sherry Ackerman's *Behind the Looking-Glass: Reflections on the Myth of Lewis Carroll* (2008), which underlines the influences of esoterism and mystical faiths upon the *Alice* books and the *Sylvie and Bruno* books. She highlights many topics common to both, arguing that *Sylvie and Bruno* just put in more explicit terms what had already been evoked in the *Alices* (169–184). Ackerman provides historical context for Carroll's position in the contemporary cultural environment: in the Oxford debate (8–13) between reason and empiricism on the one hand, and faith and theosophical currents on the other, Carroll was evidently more at home with the latter orientation. Moreover, he had a poor opinion of the rigid ritualism of the Anglican Church, advocating instead a more spiritual attitude towards religion, which he conceived in overtly mystical terms, as a theosophical doctrine of pure love: "For I think it is Love, /For I feel it is Love, For I'm sure it is nothing but Love!" (*SABC*, 307). Ackerman stresses how Carroll

> yearned to explore the mysteries of interiority, of moods and motives, inner conflicts and contradictions, memories and dreams, to bring the unconscious into consciousness, to experience extreme and ineffable states of consciousness, and to know the infinite. (33)

Carroll's beliefs exhibit deep influences of Neoplatonism and Gnosticism, as in his conviction of the existence beyond the senses of a realm of Thought, capitalised as such in some of his poems, for instance *Three Voices* (Ackerman 2008, 15); or in his participation in the devotion to pure Beauty, and the concept of Platonic Love, which were highly diffused "in Victorian England's artistic and intellectual circles" (20). Platonic Love entailed that "writers, poets, philosophers and artists began associating erotic love with spiritual bonds, as reflective of the relationship between individuals and God" (20), and Carroll made such a mysterious icon of his Alice, his "ideal child friend", a kind of little perfect Beatrice. In this sense it is worth recalling that Carroll had many friends in the circle of the Pre-Raphaelites (like Dante Gabriel and Christina Rossetti, John Everett Millais, William Holman Hunt, Arthur Hughes and the critic who most encouraged them, John Ruskin), and was inspired by their work, full of spiritualism and idealism against contemporary currents of materialism, and permeated by ideal Beatrices and medieval muses.

Ackerman also argues that with the topic of dreams, "rather than employing a simple literary device, Carroll was introducing the problem of perception" (27); he was concerned with analysing the complex status of dreamy consciousness, the difficulty in distinguishing "the real" from "the unreal", and the problematic assumptions of this rigid distinction. "We often dream without the least suspicion of unreality: 'Sleep has its own world', and it is often as lifelike as the other", wrote Carroll in his diary on 9 February, 1856 (Wakeling 1993, 38). This was a theme highly debated by Plato and by Neoplatonists, who considered certain dream states as vehicles of knowledge (Ackerman 2008, 24–30). The obsessive dream-theme of the *Alice* books is developed in a more explicitly philosophical way in *Sylvie and Bruno* where, as Carroll explained to Ruskin (through a letter to his nurse Joan Severn), "what look like dreams are meant for trances-after the fashion of esoteric Buddhists" (M. Cohen 1995, 448).

Carroll's interest in alternative and theosophical philosophies is further corroborated in *Behind the Looking-Glass* by references to his connection with Fechner's studies on the fourth dimension, and to his reading of a defence of spiritualism on scientific bases, *Transcendental Physics, an Account of Experimental Investigations: From the Scientific Treatises* by Johann Carl Friedrich Zollner (a book also mentioned in Lovett's catalogue). As Ackerman points out, however, these intellectual tendencies only found a representation in his narrative works, while he maintained a traditional position in official academic contexts. Thus, the *Alice* and *Sylvie and Bruno* books stand "as unique points of conjunction between Carroll's intellect and spirituality" (Ackerman 2008, xiii): this claim, that, Carroll's narrative works function as a harmonious compendium of the different strands of his complex and often cryptic personality, is the perspective emphasised in this book as well.

Regarding the *Alice* books specifically, we can identify further examples of psychic incidents in the narratives (besides the major topics of dreams, time, space and memory, which will be developed in subsequent chapters). The strange essence of the Cheshire Cat, appearing and disappearing, suggests how we could possibly be perceiving phantasms: "Carroll's Cat personifies a perception which is taken cognizance of by the mind from impressions made upon the organs of sense by means other than material, external objects" (Ackerman 2008, 109). Or again, Carroll puzzles us with the ability of the Blue Caterpillar to read other minds: " 'One side of *what?* The other side of *what?*' thought Alice to herself. 'Of the mushroom,' said the Caterpillar, just as if she had asked aloud; and in another moment it was out of sight" (*AAIW*, 55). This is a literary figuration of the phenomenon of "thought-reading", a psychic phenomenon he was inclined to accept as being very likely. In this connection, Carroll wrote to his friend James Langton Clarke that

> all seems to point to the existence of a natural force, allied to electricity and nerve-force, by which brain can act on brain. I think we are close on the day when this shall be classed among the known natural forces, and its laws tabulated, ... the scientific sceptics will have to accept it as a proved fact in nature ... (Cohen M.N 1989, 471–472)

Groth, commenting on this letter, argues that the *Alice* books exemplify Carroll's use of "technological analogies to capture the phantasmagoric dynamism of dream-thought and the powers of imaginative process" (2013, 141). Here again the *Alice* books articulate the complex but still harmonious coexistence of two views (or, perhaps, the two complementary aspects of a single view) characteristic of Carroll's thinking on the enigmas of the human mind.

The famous nonsense poem *Jabberwocky* is a particularly interesting instance of Carroll's investigation of where the powers of the mind can lead us, for its significant location in the *Through the Looking-Glass* book, and the circumstances of its creation (his other magnificent nonsense poetical work, *The Hunting of the Snark* also raises this question of the mind's creativity). At the beginning of *Through the Looking-Glass and What Alice Found There*, there is a reference to the practice of automatic writing, conceived as writing down something guided by an external force – an activity highly debated among the members of the SPR: Alice holds the White King's hand while he is writing his memorandum, and immediately after that she finds the *Jabberwocky* poem, with all its ambiguous and cryptic style. Carroll wrote about his own creative process as something mysterious and out of his conscious control:

> I jotted down, at odd moments, all sorts of odd ideas, and fragments of dialogue, that occurred to me – who knows how? – with a transitory suddenness that left me no choice but either to record them then and there, or to abandon them to oblivion. Sometimes one could trace to their source these random flashes of thought – as being suggested by the book one was reading, or struck out from the 'flint' of one's own mind by the 'steel' of a friend's chance remark but they had also a way of their own, of occurring, a propos of nothing – specimens of that hopelessly illogical phenomenon, 'an effect without a cause.' Such, for example, was the last line of 'The Hunting of the Snark,' which came into my head (as I have already related in 'The Theatre' for April, 1887) quite suddenly, during a solitary

walk: and such, again, have been passages which occurred in *dreams*, and which I cannot trace to any antecedent cause whatever. (*SABC*, xxiv)

With the *Jabberwocky* Carroll plays with dream words in order to lead us to experience a special state of mind: as Alice herself comments, "It seems very pretty [...] but it's rather hard to understand! [...] Somehow it seems to fill my head with ideas – only I don't exactly know what they are!" (*TTLG*, 156). Taylor states that "it does powerfully affect some region of the mind akin to that which appreciates music" (1952, 80), while Martin Gardner writes that

> there is an obvious similarity between nonsense verse and an abstract painting. [...] the words Carroll uses may suggest vague meaning, like an eye here and a foot there in a Picasso abstraction, or they may have no meaning at all – just a play of pleasant sounds like the play of non-objective colours on a canvas. (2001, 158)

Recent research on neuro-aesthetics suggests that to attract the mind's attention powerfully a work of art needs to have a kind of unresolved ambiguity, a puzzling element, which elicits a strong aesthetic engagement. Carroll's nonsense poems have these ambiguous and particularly compelling features, and the aesthetic discernment they exhibit testifies to his deep intellectual interest in how the mind works, reacts and creates.

There is another aspect of Carroll's life which bears upon his peculiar narrative portraits of unusual mental states, which is his own possible brain pathology or pathologies. The most debated of these is his probable temporal lobe epilepsy. On this issue critics are divided: some never mention it, while others (like Eve LaPlante 1993, Ranson-Polizzotti 2011) think of it as a pathology revealing a lot about Carroll's personality, especially given that there exists a connection between epilepsy and artistic expression, as well as a link with religious fervour and hypergraphia (see Ranson-Pollizzotti 2011). Other typical symptoms of temporal lobe epilepsy also correspond with Carroll's life and behaviours: for example, a psychic life particularly intense in emotions and cognition; the already mentioned "half-mystical" dreamy states; the experience of distorted perceptions; and anomalies in sexual behaviour (one of the most widespread sexual consequences of temporal lobe epilepsy is hyposexuality, that is, a lack of sexual impulses).

Many readers of the *Alice* books have found in them the descriptions of an altered consciousness: they are frequently compared with the experience of psy-

Fig. 3: Max Ernst, *Pour Les Amis D'Alice*, 1957, watercolour on paper. The connection between Carroll's own creative process and the surrealists is manifest also through the presence of Carrollian references throughout surrealist artworks. Ernst's series on Alice in particular emphasises how Carroll's art, as surrealist art, inspires the mind of the readers / viewers, through ambiguity, puzzlement, uncertain boundaries.

choactive drugs (see Fensch 1970);[14] while some contemporary neuroscientists use the *Alice* books to explain certain brain diseases. Ramachandran has named a mental pathology involving the inability to distinguish between an ob-

---

14 Even Ackerman (2008) writes about the Caterpillar's mushrooms and hookah, comparing the episode to an initiation of the Eleusian Mysteries (121–122).

ject and its mirror image "the looking-glass syndrome", suggesting that maybe Carroll could have experienced it (2003, 111–126). Another mental disease associated with Carroll is the "Alice in Wonderland syndrome", which

> as described by Todd in 1955, denotes a variety of self-experienced paroxysmal body schema disturbances (obligatory core symptoms of the AIWS) which may co-occur with depersonalization, de-realization, visual illusions and disorders of the time perception (facultative symptoms of the AIWS). (Podoll et al. 2002, 287)

The "Alice in Wonderland syndrome" has been studied by various psychiatrists and neuroscientists, and some have conjectured that Carroll's own experiences of migraine, documented from 1856, could have inspired many of the descriptions of distorted perception that we find in the *Alice* books (see Ramachandran 2003, Blom 2016).

It is quite unlikely that Carroll had personal experience of hallucinogens, though he did own a copy of Francis Edmund Anstie's *Stimulants and Narcotics, Their Mutual Relations: With Special Researches on the Action of Alcohol, Aether, and Chloroform, on the Vital Organism,* and a couple of other books with references to psychoactive drugs. His own letters and diaries testify to his migraine episodes, and he was diagnosed with epilepsy by three different doctors in the course of his life – Dr Morshead, Dr Brooks, and Dr Stedman, who diagnosed him after two attacks during which he completely lost consciousness (Wakeling 1993, 52). It is perhaps useful to quote the "Report of Dr Yvonne Hart on Carroll's neurological symptoms, August 2008", included by Jenny Woolf at the end of her biography of Carrol (2010, 298–299): the doctor, having studied all the references to Carroll's probable pathologies in diaries, letters, and documents, concludes that

> I think it is very likely that he had migraine. I think it is possible that he also had epilepsy (and there is considerable debate in the medical world as to the extent to which these conditions may be linked), but without further evidence (preferably in the form of an eyewitness description of the episodes of loss of consciousness), I would have considerable doubt about this. (298–299)

While some clues to Carroll's mental disturbance can be found in the *Alice* books (in particular relating to migraine's distorting perceptive effects), and such pathologies can suggest hypotheses accounting for certain episodes, descriptions, and absurd scenarios, such connections must be treated with considerable caution, and mainly confined to the realm of the hypothetical.

In general, however, the thrust of this introduction to Carroll's mental preoccupations is to demonstrate why his *Alice* books are particularly suited for a narrative analysis of a cognitive kind; which is to say, their being a continuous representation and depiction of how our minds function, or misfunction. I have given a sketch of Carroll's interest, made evident mainly in his narrative works of fantasy, in the more speculative and "magical" aspects of mathematics and the sciences, and the link between such conjectures on space and time, and the "eerie" states of which Carroll was so fond. I have described Carroll's narrative and theoretical obsession with dream worlds and their revelatory nature, and their connections with the psychic phenomena studied by the SPR; I have given an account of Carroll's own study of psychic phenomena, spiritualism and theosophical beliefs, in the context of the general status of psychology in the Victorian period, drawing upon Ackerman's *Behind the Looking-Glass: Reflections on the Myth of Lewis Carroll*. Finally, I have discussed the possibility that Carroll experienced neural disturbances that might relate to the strange perspectives depicted in the *Alice* books. A cognitive interpretation of Carroll's *Alice* books, I suggest, is positively *suggested* by Carroll's own attitude towards the topic of the mysteries of the mind: he explored both scientific and speculative avenues to understanding how our minds work and how they can be activated and stimulated, and his literary works are an expression of this balance. Literature thus plays, for Carroll as well as for theorists of cognitive narratology, a revealing, investigative and enlightening role with respect to the mind.

Chapter 2
Virtual Alice

> "'What – is – this?' he said at last.
> 'This is a child!' Haigha replied eagerly, coming in front of Alice to introduce her [...]
> 'I always thought they were fabulous monsters!' said the Unicorn.
> 'is it alive?'"
> (*TTLG*, 241)

This first chapter's exploration and analysis of the *Alice* books will focus on their creative invention, their represented mind-internal features, and the reader's reception and mental re-creation of their virtual worlds and virtual minds. There have been claims in cognitive studies that "most of our experience, our knowledge, and our thinking is organised as stories" (Turner 1996, v). Accordingly, the investigation of cognitive structures related to the production and reception of storyworlds is central to a better grasp of how minds function. My discussion draws upon various cognitive concepts to describe the virtual realities associated with the three types of mind involved in the literary context of the *Alice* books: the author's mind, the characters' mind and reader's mind. I show how the study of these kinds of virtuality contributes to a new cognitive account of the *Alice* books, and develops the idea that in the creation and reception of storyworlds we "deal with central and indispensable aspects of our conceptual systems" (Lakoff and Turner 1989, 215). This chapter draws upon a number of concepts central to cognitive literary study, including cognitive metaphor theory (CMT), conceptual blending (and the related concepts of parable and projection), deictic shift theory (DST), and possible worlds theory. As explained in the introduction, these notions are not well harmonised with each other in all respects, and there are theoretical tensions between them.

For example, controversies have arisen between cognitive metaphor theories and possible worlds theories,[1] and between CMT itself and other narrative approaches to metaphor.[2] However my discussion aims to negotiate between these different theoretical inputs, which can all contribute to a coherent cognitive analysis of the fictional worlds represented in the *Alice* books.

---

[1] See for example Ryan 1991, 82–83; Sinding 2011, 239–257; Stockwell 2002, 135–149; Fludernik 2009, 109–128; Freeman 2000, 253–280; Schneider and Hartner 2012; Kimmel 2011, 199–238.
[2] See mainly the various contributions in Fludernik 2011.

2.1 "The Question Is – Said Humpty Dumpty – Which Is to Be Master – That's All": The Author

> I'm very much afraid I didn't mean anything but nonsense! Still, you know, words mean more than we mean to express when we use them: so a whole book ought to mean a great deal more than the writer meant. (Carroll [1884] in M.N. Cohen 1995, 243–44)

Cognitive metaphor theories and their adjustments and/or extensions have proved useful to inquiry about the meaning of literary texts, as well as to the study of our everyday cognition. Fludernik (2011) observes that in recent years "the gradual absorption and creative appropriation of this model in literary circles" has led to the formation of new theoretical approaches, all trying to take advantage of CMT's powerful insights, including its recognition and demonstration of the pervasiveness of metaphorical mechanisms of thought (5). These approaches have also sought to overcome the two main problems of its application to literary studies, namely "universality or reductivism in opposition to textual specificity" and "its theoretical position regarding the creativity or originality of metaphors" (6).

Lakoff and Johnson (1980) and Lakoff and Turner (1989) have underlined how metaphors structure our minds in deep and pervasive ways, their role being far more than an aesthetic literary device, since "most of our conceptual system is metaphorical in nature" (Lakoff and Johnson, 4). While *Metaphors We Live By* offers a detailed theory of how metaphors inform our everyday understanding of the world, our way of making sense of experience and our construction of meaning, *More Than Cool Reason* also attends to the specificity of poetic metaphor. This study points out some distinct features of poetic metaphors (such as their power of extending, elaborating, questioning and composing conventional metaphors, 67–70): "Poets can appeal to the ordinary metaphors we live by in order to take us beyond them, to make us more insightful than we would be if we thought only in the standard ways. Because they lead us to new ways of conceiving our world, poets are artists of the mind" (215). Nonetheless, literary critics are still trying to refine Lakoff and Turner's ideas, pointing out that a more accurate account of literary metaphors needs to pay closer attention to the individual text, to the cultural schemas operating behind the use of specific metaphors, and to the cognitive creativity of an author's use of metaphors.

Here I take a closer look at how a cognitive analysis of the virtual spaces of the *Alice* books can benefit from attention to metaphor and related aspects of literary creativity. I invoke then the notion of conceptual blending in order to show

how Wonderland and the Looking-Glass world function as examples of blended spaces, into which different elements of Carroll's cultural and personal background are projected and combined. Ultimately, I focus upon two theoretical ideas about creative cognition that characterise Carroll's poetical inventions particularly well: "cross-domain borrowings" (Finke et al. 1992, 70), and childlike ways of reasoning.

2.1.1 The Rabbit Hole, Humpty Dumpty, and other Metaphor-Related Images

In *Philosophy of Nonsense* Lecercle (1994) identifies what he calls "the rejection of metaphor" of nonsense texts as "a logical consequence of the avoidance of semantic anomaly" (63). He enumerates a number of strategies nonsense writers use in order to avoid metaphors: the use of tautologies as hypo-metaphors, and of coinage as hyper-metaphors; the literal interpretation of sentences and the circumscription of metaphors by substituting puns (63–66). However, Lecercle is here referring to specific verbal metaphors, not to more pervasive metaphors incarnated in characters or narrative situation. Moreover, neither linguistic play with metaphors, nor their exaggeration or literalisation, nor the other strategies Lecercle cites, are ways of *avoiding* metaphors. Rather, they are ways of reflecting upon metaphors, playing with their forces and weaknesses, and actually confirming their pervasiveness. Creative metaphors and their elaboration play an important role in shaping the virtual realities depicted in the *Alice* books, helping to expand and enrich the meaning of characters and narrative situations. Carroll explores how they do so in a number of different ways, playing with the metaphorical implications of the fictional scenario, drawing out their further ramifications, or literalizing them.

This last device, literalisation, is a rhetorical technique typical of satirical texts and involves "spatializing metaphors in storyworlds (sometimes called "realization" or literalization)" (Sinding 2011, 239), or "literalizing metaphors and turning them into narrative events" (Hunter, quoted in Sinding 2011, 239). The Caucus-Race is an example: it refers to a "system of highly disciplined party organization by committees", the meaning that "caucus" had for English politics at that time (M. Gardner 2001, 32), but Carroll ridicules the intricate and often absurd system by portraying a circular run of bizarre animals, with no order or sense, where everybody wins and the prize is a meaningless thimble. The metaphor of the Race thus becomes an active part of the narrative structure: the target domain of the "real" caucus has to be understood in terms of the narrative spatial representation of the Wonderland race, with the animals running in circle without a real goal or a logical development.

The use of metaphors as embedded elements of the storyworld, whereby "words referring to storyworld-metaphor elements are both literal – they refer literally to the storyworld – and metaphorical – they refer metaphorically to the target meaning" (Sinding 2011, 255) turns out to be a powerful rhetorical instrument in the nonsense genre, which is often characterised by satirical overtones. The Looking-Glass Insects, on the other hand, with their comically tragic destinies as incarnations of the principle of correspondence between names and things, function as metaphorical representations of the failure of the same literalizing principle, proving once again Carroll's polysemous and ironic use of figures of language.

A similar thing happens with Humpty Dumpty, as a metaphor for the failure of the nominalist philosophy of language.[3] but Humpty Dumpty is a more complex metaphor than that, being also the narrative manifestation of a nursery rhyme (so forced by this circumstance to perform an already decided destiny), as well as a symbol of human pride and its consequent fall, and an illustration of Carroll's idea of the power and weakness of the writer (he can invent new fantastical words and make them mean what he wishes, but he is also trapped by them, rigidly defined by his own name). In this sense, Humpty Dumpty serves as an example of how different metaphorical mappings may be operating in the same space, without being limited by each other. The coexistence of different metaphors can be accounted for without conflicts of meaning if we adopt "a reading that arrives at a more abstract level of metaphorical system mapping" (Freeman 2000, 265). In Humpty Dumpty's case this more conceptual level is the abstract idea of the paradoxical simultaneity of strength and weakness, operating at different levels of human existence. On the other hand, Humpty Dumpty can also be viewed as a meta-reflection on the nature of metaphor itself: after all, he is imprisoned by his existence as a living metaphor, showing the rigidity of fixed readings of metaphorical relations; at the same time, his polysemic figurative connotations demonstrate that metaphors are indeed alive, always changing, producing new interpretations, and "rearranging the furniture of our minds" (Kittay 1987, 314).

With Humpty Dumpty, and the various metaphor-related devices and linguistic games in the *Alice* books, Carroll plays with figures of language in order to show both their limits and their power. This kind of play is further manifest in his puns and literalisations of linguistic expressions. So, the fourth chapter of *Alice in Wonderland*, titled "The Rabbit Sends in A Little Bill", puns upon

---

[3] For an accurate description of the meaning that philosophical stance may have had for Carroll, see M. Gardner 2001, 224–227.

"the bill to pay" that the White Rabbit gives Alice for having invaded his house and a literal reference to the little lizard Bill, whom he sends into his house to get rid of her. Or, the totemic animal of nonsense, the Cheshire Cat, exists in the narrative as a living, moving and talking embodiment of a linguistic expression. Similarly, the character of the Mock-Turtle makes an expression referring to a culinary dish into a live and active agent in the storyworld.

Metaphor-related devices are also exploited by Carroll in order to highlight the peculiar working of abnormal minds. I address the topic of the representation of madness directly in my chapter on unnatural minds, but it is worth noting here that peculiar ways of using metaphors are often linked to the depiction of ill-functioning minds. As Lecercle (1994) says "the characters of nonsense indeed tend to be delirious – they go from eccentricity to raving madness" (204), and he shows how three characteristics of schizophrenic behaviour are well represented in the *Alice* books, namely possession, literalness and negation (207–208). Negation can actually function as the common denominator of these devices, since both possession and literalness in the *Alice* books deal with processes of reversal, negating common sense and common moral perspectives through the affirmation of their opposites. Negation, including possession and literalness, is characteristically related to the use of metaphorical structures in Carroll's writing. The logic of inversion rules over his use of verbal expressions: conceptual metaphors, and the basic orientation of their significance, are often subjected to a reverse logic, in which things "go the other way" (*TTLG*, 147).

Let us consider some examples: Carroll exploits the motif of possession every time Alice tries to recite a poem, and finds herself talking without knowing what she is saying.[4] In these moments Carroll parodies, through Alice's mouth, popular poems and rhymes well known to Victorian readers, while "poor Alice is reduced to the state of a tape recorder, a possessed mystic or a raving lunatic" (Lecercle 1994, 118). These parodies always present a reversal of the original metaphors in the poems, serving to reveal the dark side of traditional verses. Thus the laborious and industrious bee becomes the lazy and hungry crocodile (*AAIW*, 23); the wise and experienced old father William, symbolizing a sage and sound old age, becomes an eccentric and ridiculous character (*AAIW*, 52–54); the lullaby encouraging gentleness towards little children, linked to the common Victorian metaphor of children as little angels, becomes an exhortation to ill-treat and beat them (*AAIW*, 64); the little bright star, comforting trav-

---

4 The same happens to the White King, when Alice guides his hand in writing, which she does as in a kind of possessed state (*TTLG*, 153–154). Just as Alice guides the White King, Carroll guides Alice.

ellers with its light, becomes a dark bat, flying above the world (*AAIW*, 76–77). Thus, in the *Alice* books common metaphors traditionally used as didactic devices are turned into images with ambiguous, disturbing and ironic meanings through the possessed speech of characters. Through this device, "the secure domestic order of Alice's moral universe is exposed to reveal terror and appetite" (Haughton 2003, xiii).

It is broadly acknowledged that "since the first clinical descriptions of schizophrenia, clinical practitioners have been interested in the difficulties experienced by patients with schizophrenia in interpreting the meaning of metaphors" (Iakimova et al. 2006, 995). As we have seen, the characters of the Looking-Glass Land and Wonderland – where everyone is mad, as the Cheshire Cat remarks (*AAIW*, 68) – very often interpret expressions literally, giving concrete substance to an abstract metaphorical sentence. This continuous misinterpretation of metaphors, and literalisation of abstract concepts, is evidence of a strong connection between the world of nonsense and the world of schizophrenics. The negation and literalisation of figurative expressions in the *Alice* books enacts a typically schizophrenic disruption of our cognitive grasp of metaphorical conceptual structures. I return to this topic in more detail in my chapter on unnatural minds in nonsense texts; however, my argument will develop Schwab's claim (1996, 49–70) that the use of a sort of schizophrenic logic in the *Alice* books should by no means be interpreted in a way that reduces Carroll's texts to expression of schizophrenic discourse – an interpretation that would undermine the distinctive *anti-mimetic* quality of the texts.

Carroll explores common "metaphors we live by", as Lakoff and Johnson call them, through their extensions and negations in the lunatic scenarios of Wonderland and of the Looking-Glass world. But the import of these explorations is not restricted to the domain of abnormal cognition; CMT has demonstrated the fact that metaphors work as the basis of our ordinary thinking and understanding of the world, and that basic metaphorical concepts operate in automatic, unconscious ways. Novelists and poets utilise conventional conceptual metaphors, expanding them, enriching them, questioning them, and Carroll's creative inventions participate in this project.

Image schemas, which make up our cognitive models of reality, are combined in some standard, almost unconscious ways in order to guide our comprehension of the world, and this combination is often of a metaphorical nature (see Lakoff and Johnson 1980, 3–6). The use of metaphors by creative writers can generate new metaphorical spaces; novelists and poets (or artists in general) "appeal to the ordinary metaphors we live by in order to take us beyond them, to make us more insightful than we would be if we thought only in the standard ways" (Lakoff and Turner 1989, 215). The understanding of concepts, things, emotions, situations, events in terms of *something else* can be also called "image mapping" (the mapping of one image into another) and it is based on our personal practical experience of the world and on pre-existent cultural models. As Pettersson (2011) argues "Viewing metaphor as a kind of conceptual representation, as well as a figure of speech may make us more apt to recognise the dynamism inherent in the uses of metaphor, especially its extensions" (97). Such a view helps us see that creative writers can modify our standard cognitive mapping, introducing new, not pre-existent, metaphorical connections. In this way literature, and art, are able to shape our cognitive system in a deep and pervasive manner.

Carroll's "rabbit hole" offers the perfect example of this process. Before Carroll wrote *Alice's Adventures in Wonderland,* a rabbit hole was just a rabbit hole, the hidden place where a rabbit lives; but since the publication of the first of the *Alice* books until today the rabbit hole has gradually become a deeply rooted metaphor of our conceptual apparatus, used without need of further explanation. The rabbit hole leading to Wonderland in the *Alice* books is a passage towards the discovery of an alternative reality made of nonsense and madness, where unconscious meanings are explored, rules are inverted and the logic of dreams guides the events. Through the years Carroll's rabbit hole has developed into a general symbol of a journey into the unknown, leading to the revelation of hidden, often uncomfortable, truths.

As with all powerful metaphors, the rabbit hole has ramified into several different shades of meaning. It now has connotations of a descent into psychedelic experience produced by hallucinogens, as in the 1970s song "White Rabbit" by Jefferson Airplane; or of a psychological journey into the unconscious in order to process grief, as in the play and subsequent movie *Rabbit Hole*, written by Lindsay-Abaire and directed by John Cameron-Mitchell; or even of a parallel reality, as in *The Matrix* (directed by the Wachowskis), in which the protagonist, Neo, starts his journey into the Matrix by following a white rabbit tattoo, only subsequently discovering "how deep the rabbit hole goes". The popular general of "going down the rabbit hole" is now getting too absorbed in something to come out of it: another feature of the Carrollian rabbit hole is that, after the fall, Alice doesn't know how to get back to the surface of "normal reality": "in another moment down went Alice after it, never once considering how in the world she was to get out again" (*AAIW*, 12).

Starting from the basic spatial metaphors relying on the oppositions UP-DOWN and IN-OUT (Lakoff and Johnson 1980, 14–21) Carroll has given to the symbolic idea of a journey from up to down and from outside to inside an additional characteristic, the shape of a rabbit hole as a threshold between worlds. The whole experience of reading the *Alice* books, of immersing ourselves in Wonderland, can be described as a jump into the rabbit-hole. It is the passage to the discovery of the parallel, mad universe of Wonderland, and has therefore become a pervasive symbol of the transition from reality to fiction, from being awake to dreaming, from sanity to madness. If Oscar Wilde said that there was no fog in London before Turner, it is possible to add that a rabbit hole was just a rabbit hole before Carroll. In this sense the work of artists affects our minds at the deep level of our everyday conceptual metaphors, adding new connections and new image mappings to guide our cognitive grasp of reality.

The rabbit hole is the most famous of Carroll's metaphors, and probably the most powerful; it has become established in popular culture, and part of our cognitive cultural heritage. However, there are many other metaphors Carroll brought to life in the *Alice* books, and while none have had as strong an impact as the rabbit hole, some do still exert a certain cognitive power. Examples would include the association of feminine rage to the furious Queen of Hearts, or the popularity of the metaphorical figure of Humpty Dumpty among philosophers of language (see M. Gardner 2001, 224–227). The Red Queen's Race has evolved into a metaphor for scientific concepts such as the relativistic effect that nothing can ever reach the speed of light (Sartori 1996; Schmidt 1990); it has also been used in evolutionary biology ("the Red Queen hypothesis"), in environmental sociology, and as a symbol for science-fiction writers (Asimov 1992, Vinge 2006).

Carroll has also adopted some general metaphors already rooted in culture and made them more alive and significant; metaphors such as "life is a game" and "life is a dream", or the metaphorical implications related to mirrors, and going through them. "Life is a game" finds its narrative depiction in the two games dominating the "structure" (the slippery, dreamy, chaotic structure) of Wonderland and of the Looking-Glass world, respectively: cards and chess. However, Carroll's fictional versions of these games acquire bizarre, puzzling and nonsensical qualities: the cards play croquet (a game within a game) and have their heads cut off; and "the great huge game of chess played all over the world" (*TTLG*, 172) is populated by irreverent and absurd creatures, and ruled by the idea of going back to go forwards. If life is a game, then, for Carroll it is a game with incomprehensible, mad, changeable rules – and his fictional universe plays with extensions of the original conceptual metaphor to give a rich and complex idea of the elusive nature of reality.[5] For the idea of life as a

---

[5] The philosophical idea of life as a game was introduced by Plutarch in his *Lives*, where he compares life to a game of chess. Subsequently, the metaphor has been used in literary contexts by various writers such as Thomas Shadwell [1688], who wrote, in *The Squire of Alsatia*, that "Man's Life is like a Game at Tables. If at any time the cast you most shall need does not

dream, Carroll drew upon an extensive cultural and intellectual tradition including Shakespeare and Calderon de la Barca, Hume and Berkeley, and explored the potentialities of it by creating a dream-like narrative where the implications of the blurred boundaries between reality and dreams are made explicit. [6]

The mirror, as a passage into a virtual, reversed reality, plays a similar role to the rabbit hole for Carroll; but while the rabbit hole was a new metaphor, created by him *ex novo*, the mirror had a tradition, in fairy tales and superstitions, exploring its ambiguous power.[7] What Carroll did was to explicitly connect the mirror to the idea of a threshold between the possible and impossible, logic and illogic, straight and reversed. As with the rabbit hole before it, the mirror thus symbolises the mind accessing a new dimension, experimenting with new categories and multiplying its perspectives.

One of Carroll's most powerful narrative concepts is precisely this *magic door* onto new virtual possibilities: whether an abysmal hole or a dissolving mirror, the passage leads Alice to different microcosms with their own rules – though changing and absurd – in which space and time acquire new, challenging and mysterious features. T.S. Eliot recognised the effectiveness of Carroll's fictional passages into other worlds, and used the image of the door into the rose-garden as a reference to Alice's door to Wonderland (a redoubled passage; even after her fall into the rabbit hole Alice has to negotiate another small access to the prosecution of her adventures, *AAIW*, 15–16), and as "a metaphor for events that might have been, had one opened certain doors" (M. Gardner 2001, 16). In Eliot's hands (in his *Burnt Norton*) Carroll's metaphor assumes

---

come up, let that which comes instead of it be mended by your Play" (81); or George Herbert, who said "Man's life's a game at tables and he may / Mend his bad fortune, by his wiser play; / Death plays against us, each disease and sore / Are blotts" (quoted in Lepore 2012, xviii). Similarly, Thomas More [1551], in *Utopia*, compared life to a game "not much unlike the chess," in which "vices fyghte wyth vertues, as it were in battell" (1999, 78–79). English poet Nathaniel Cotton wrote, in 1794, "That life's a game, divines confess; / This says at cards, and that at chess; / But if our views be center'd here, / 'Tis all a losing game, I fear" (2010, 61). It is striking that the two games life has been mostly compared to are cards and chess, Carroll's own choices; and the nineteenth century witnessed a growing interest in games and game rules in general, and Carroll was particularly fond of inventing new games for his child friends. For a more complete account of the parallelism life/game, see Lepore 2012, xii–xv.

6 The Shakespearian context includes *A Midsummer Night's Dream*, *The Tempest*, *Hamlet*, *Romeo and Juliet*; for Calderon de la Barca, see *La Vida Es Sueño*. Hume and Berkeley address the phenomenological implications of the difficulty in distinguishing between the dreaming and waking mind (see Hume's *A Treatise of Human Nature* and Berkeley's *A Treatise Concerning the Principles of Human Knowledge*).

7 Some examples are the role played by the mirror in the Brothers Grimm's *Snow White*, or in Andersen's *The Snow Queen*, or in MacDonald's *Phantastes*.

more existentialist, intimist and psychological connotations: "the door we never opened into the rose-garden". There is also a pronounced atmosphere of loss and regret, which is however present in the *Alice* books themselves, already suffused with a sense of nostalgia and loss, of golden hours never to be experienced again, of never attained love.[8]

2.1.2 Wonderland and the Looking-Glass World as Blended Spaces

The figurative narrative worlds of the *Alice* books allow metaphors to become living characters, specific events, spatial configurations, and powerful new symbols. Up to this point, I have focused upon examples of single metaphors in specific passages of the books, but Carroll also creates much bigger metaphorical spaces, exploiting the features of more complex cognitive functions – in particular, the projection of story and conceptual blending. According to Turner (1996), the projection of a source story onto a target story is a fundamental cognitive function of metaphorical thoughts (12–25), while "the advanced ability to blend incompatible conceptual arrays is a basic part of what makes us cognitively modern" (2003, 121). Conceptual blending provides for greater complexity and richness of meaning in the metaphorical structure of thinking. As Fludernik (2011) argues, "double scope blendings and their alignment of metaphor, fictionality and, possibly, narrative, open wider ranges of application of these theoretical models for literature" (4). The idea of story projection combined with that of conceptual blending, in "double-scope stories", can provide for a fuller account of literary creativity.

In blending we use the projections of input stories to form a blended story, and in doing so we use the cognitive mechanisms of completion, elaboration and composition, adding expansion, ramification and extension to the basic model of metaphor. A blended story derives from different mental spaces and proposes a new one, often illuminating previously unseen connections; "a blend can produce knowledge [...] in the sense that it contains structure that is not calculable from the inputs and that can be developed, once constructed, on its own" (Turner 1996, 83). In this sense it can be connected with what Ramachandran (2003) defines as "the diffuse synaesthesia", the hyperconnectivity diffused throughout the entire brain, which provides for the inclination to create metaphors and connect apparently unrelated concepts (64–80). This faculty, although generally

---

[8] The complex emotional implications of the *Alice* books are the topic of my fourth chapter "Emotional Alice".

present at a basic level in our brains, can in some cases be much more extended, involving more far-reaching cross-activation of different brain regions. Ramachandran calls people with this characteristic "superior synaesthetics", and this mental feature has revealed itself to be correlated with the high level of creativity exhibited by artists, writers, scientists, and poets (Ramachandran and Hubbard 2003, 55–56).

In the *Alice* books, the prominent use of blending mechanisms is apparent from the beginning: the White Rabbit, repeating aloud that he is late, is an example of one of the most elemental and culturally established blends, namely talking animals,[9] "constructed in the blended space of animals with human characteristics" (Turner 1996, 59). However, the blended spaces Carroll elaborates in the *Alice* books are much more extensive, since their entire locations, in Wonderland and the Looking-Glass Land, are blends in themselves. These blends are complex, there are different ways of analysing the peculiar fictional realisation of the blend constituting each setting.

First, they are narrative worlds in which representations of the Victorian world are combined with the elements of a non-sensical fairy tale for children, resulting in places where we find both a parody of the Victorian Age and dreamy nonsense literature, neither of which can be reduced to the other. In both Wonderland and the Looking-Glass Land we recognise specific behaviours, institutions, and typical features of the Victorian period blended with elements coming from the unfettered imaginative space of children's literature and fantasy.

Second, the *Alice* books are blended stories in the sense that they amalgamate the story of Alice's journeys in Wonderland and through the Looking-Glass with the protagonist's private experience of growing up and making sense of the world around her, and the result is a complex structure in which imaginary landscapes, psychological meanings, dark implications and fantastical characters are mixed together. In the Looking-Glass world, for example, the two input stories, of Alice's progress towards maturity and of going through a glass and discovering a world of fantastic and imaginary creatures, are combined in ways that do not always align well with each other. On the one hand, Alice's desire to become a queen ("I don't want to be anybody's prisoner. I want to be a queen", *TTLG*, 247) matches with the idea of her growth as empowerment and conquest, but on the other hand it is represented as a senseless, ridiculous and in the end destructive achievement, in which she becomes a queen

---

[9] Talking animals, besides being simple mental blendings, are rooted in our culture thanks to children literature's tradition and to mystical narratives.

of *chess* – a rather bizarre version of the game of chess – namely a piece in a game which she cannot understand.

Moreover, her progress towards her goal takes place in a looking-glass world, where everything goes the other way: her journey entails a simultaneous going backwards and going forwards. This contradiction introduces a third element which further complicates the blend, which is Carroll's own personal feelings towards Alice.[10] It seems that Carroll intends to trap Alice in a backward universe, in a mirror which takes her back to her childhood, even as she proceeds towards her future – the ambivalently presented goal of becoming a queen. The blended space of the looking glass is thus a polyphonic construction, evoking multiple shades of meaning through the interplay of its different input spaces.

2.1.3 Cognitive Features of Carroll's Creative Inventions

Having outlined Carroll's elaborate and peculiar use of creative metaphors and blends in his construction of the virtual realities of the *Alice* books, in this authorial section I shall now situate those strategies in the context of Carroll's creative cognitive practices as an author. This reorientation involves a move from the outcomes of Carroll's creative mind (the powerful metaphors and images he invented in the *Alice* books) to a scrutiny of the mental processes characteristic of this highly creative imagination itself. Conceptual blending and metaphor are species of creative combination of different concepts, and "the fact that conceptual combination often results in new categories and emergent features implies that the process can be useful in making creative discoveries" (Finke et al. 1992, 96). If the capability of making "proximate associations" is a common function of the human mind, an aptitude for establishing "remote associations" distinguishes highly creative minds (Hogan 2003, 64–65). Highly creative associations often arise from prior expertise in discrete fields of knowledge and from the activation of a sort of "defocused attention" (64), which allows the mind to access a broad range of possible connections, and so reinvent or modify pre-existent schemas and prototypes.

---

10 This is obviously a huge topic, which I am going to address more extensively in the chapter about emotions. Many scholars dealt with the issue of Carroll's involvement with Alice Liddell, and references are to be found in Cohen's biography (1995) and Cohen's edition of Carroll's letters and diaries (1989), Clarke's biography (1979), Bakewell's biography (1996) and Douglas-Fairhust's *The Story of Alice* (2015) ... Karoline Leach in her *In the Shadow of the Dreamchild* (1999) addresses the topic from a different angle, while Roiphe's novel *Still She Haunts Me* offers a fictional account of Carroll and Alice's relationship.

According to Hogan, such "cross-domain borrowings" (70) are related to a neurological predisposition to synaesthesia,[11] which in turn encourages the production of analogies characteristic of complex abstract thoughts. This process can be viewed as the same one that Charles S. Peirce (1966) calls *abduction:* if one cannot find a law to explain a phenomenon within the field of that phenomenon, one can try "to borrow" a law belonging to another field, and apply it to the phenomenon of interest – the example Peirce uses is the one of the discovery of planets' elliptic paths by Kepler (230–232). How does all this apply to Carroll? His peculiar approach to literature was founded upon the vast range of his intellectual interests: the *Alice* books are so rich in possible meanings and ramifications, and so full of references to different fields of knowledge, thanks to Carroll's mental inclination for multidisciplinarity and cross-domain borrowings. The rabbit hole and the looking-glass are not only remarkably creative metaphors but also actual passages to other dimensions, where Alice experiences different conceptions of space and time. The fathomless hole and dissolving mirror, both leading to alternative worlds with different physical laws, are comparable to scientific speculations, and have affinities with later theoretical reflections on wormholes and Einstein-Rosen bridges (Rucker 2014, 120).

The narrative worlds of the *Alice* books include a huge number of playful speculations related to different scientific fields. We find conjectures on the nature of gravity, with Alice's fall into the rabbit hole and her taking the jar of orange marmalade, and with her fantasies about a trip to the centre of the earth, coming out on the opposite side of the world, where people walk "with their heads downwards" (*AAIW*, 13); logical conjectures on the ontological status of non-existent creatures, mathematical speculations on the null-class and negative numbers (see in particular "The Mock Turtle's Story"); and hypotheses on backward universes of anti-matter ("How would you like to live in a Looking-Glass house, Kitty? I wonder if they'd give you milk in there? Perhaps, Looking-Glass milk isn't good to drink", *TTLG*, 148). The looking-glass world anticipates theoretical conjectures about asymmetry that have appealed to some physicists: a magic mirror reversing atoms' charge, parity, and time, could hypothetically create a completely reversed world of anti-matter. According to Gardner, we can conceive of two galaxies that are mirror images of each other, in the sense that "intelligent beings in each galaxy would regard their own time as 'forward' and time in the other galaxy as 'backward'" (M. Gardner 2001, 38). Carroll was deeply interested in imaging backward universes: he was fond of playing tunes backward on music boxes; he wrote to his little friends

---

[11] See Ramachandran and Hubbard 2003.

letters in mirror writing, which had to be held to a mirror to be read; he drew pictures that reveal a different image when turned upside-down; he even invented a method of multiplication in which the multiplier is written backwards and above the multiplicand. In the same spirit, he invented the world on the other side of the mirror, where paths are corkscrews, the right foot goes in the left shoe, to go ahead you have to run backwards, and so on.

One of the main peculiarities of Carroll's literary creativity lies in this extraordinary capability for linking together different domains, fusing fairy tales and science, psychology and nonsense. The achievement of the *Alice* books is in part the equilibrium they sustain between these cross-domain significances, the balanced negotiation between different theoretical inputs being one of the discriminating factors of intense creativity (Hogan 2003, 68). Carroll does not allow any of these elements to prevail over or annihilate the others, and they all coexist in spite of their differences. This is one possible reason for the success of the *Alice* books, in contrast to the *Sylvie and Bruno* books, which are "largely unreadable and unread" (Haughton 2003, xxviii). In one sense *Sylvie and Bruno* is the definitive sum of Carroll's interests, treating in depth the topics already broached in the *Alices:* it is a *mélange* of little angelic girls, fairylands, religious topics, mathematical intuitions, inversions and paradoxes, melancholic reflections and scientific subjects. However, the way this *mélange* is achieved contrasts strikingly with the *Alice* books. *Sylvie and Bruno* lacks the balance between different elements so effectively realised in the *Alices:* the story is less cohesive, and hampered by redundancy, its narrative overburdened with melancholy and almost moralistic personal reflections ...

Hogan highlights another feature of creative thinking highly relevant to Carroll's artistic output, which is "the relation of genius – or more exactly the relation of radically innovative works of art – to childhood modes of thought and expression" (76). The form of narration found in the *Alice* books manifestly aims to realise not just a story about a child, but a story as *lived and experienced* by a child. Children were "three-fourths" of Carroll's life, as he himself asserted (see Woolf 2010, 127–128); and "at the heart of the *Alice* books is Dodgson's dream identification with his child heroine. The writer sees through Alice's eyes" (Haughton, xxv). It is generally acknowledged that Lewis Carroll was an eternal child in some sense, having much more in common with his hundreds of little girl friends than with other adults. [12]

---

[12] He also wrote in the prefatory poem of *Through the Looking-Glass:* "we are but older children, dear" (139).

> His child friend Isa Bowman called him 'the man who above all others has understood childhood' and Virginia Woolf thought that 'childhood remained in him entire' all his life, persisting as an 'impediment in the centre of his being' (...) and the cult of childhood was clearly central to his entire adult life. (Haughton 2003, xvi)

In this sense, Carroll's creativity is probably one of the most striking examples of the relationship between a childlike perspective and the highly creative mind.

The *Alices* literally follow the logic of narration proposed by Alice herself at the beginning of the first book. She thinks that a book is useless and uninteresting without pictures or conversations (*AAIW*, 11), so Carroll gives her the alternative to her sister's book: two stories made up of pictures and conversations, rather than of didacticism and moral sense. Howard Gardner (1984) says that for young children "the boundary between the fictional world and the real world is highly – excessively – permeable" (174) and Carroll was almost obsessed with blurring the boundary between real world and fantasy world, between actuality and dream (he develops this theme even further in the blurred worlds of *Sylvie and Bruno*). The nonsense, the confusion and the awkwardness of many narrative situations in the *Alice* books can be seen as caused by the childlike perspective Carroll adopts. A child is "simply happy to mix up frames and solution types" (Hogan 2003, 83), in spite of the possible loss of sense, coherence and linear story. It is also true, however, that Alice is not always *that* happy while dealing with the constant nonsense of Wonderland and of the Looking-Glass world, and the picture Carroll portrays of a child making sense of the world is more complex. On the one hand the stories exhibit disrupted narration, with mixed frames and meanings, and this accords with a childlike point of view; on the other hand, Alice's perspective upon the fantasy worlds around her is something *in between* being happily caught up in them and trying to impose her upper-world Victorian logic upon them. She can no longer speak good English, she recites poems distorting the original meaning, she is happy with children turning into pigs, but she also struggles to make sense of her experiences, and of the baffling speeches of the creatures she encounters. In this sense, the *Alice* books show a child's mind as a complex and mysterious environment, a mind still in formation and trying to find a balance between sense and nonsense.

Developmental psychologists (such as Piaget or Kohlberg) have argued that the moral behaviour of children until the age of ten is mainly based on fear of punishment, and their morality is at a "pre-conventional level" (Kohlberg 1984, 1). They "do not have a personal code of morality," but "instead, their moral code is shaped by the standards of adults and the consequences of following or breaking their rules" (McLeod 2013, 2). Carroll's imaginary worlds are not only senseless and a-logical, they are also amoral – it is as if he is leading his readers on a fictional journey into a child's mind. Indeed Gertrude Chataway, the girl to whom he dedicated *The Hunting of the Snark*, later recalled that Carroll has told her that for him it was the greatest pleasure to "feel the depths of a child's mind" (Collingwood 1898, 389).

The fact that Carroll is following a childlike model of narration is explicit in the prefatory poem of *Alice's Adventures in Wonderland*, where he writes that the tale was constructed according to the instructions of the three Liddell sisters (7–8), and Alice's own indication was "there will be nonsense in it!" (7). Gertrude Chataway comments that "one thing that made his stories particularly charming to a child was that he often took his cue from her remarks (…) so that one felt that one had somehow helped to make the story, and it seemed a personal possession" (Collingwood, 389). The contrast between childlike and adult perspectives is evident in the contrast between the content of the *Alice* books and the prefatory and conclusive poems that frame them. These poems present an almost idyllic description of the subsequent stories (which actually have so many sinister and nightmarish qualities), describing them as dreamy, childish innocent fairy tales: they seem almost unrelated. The poems present the books as faithful representations of the golden age of childhood, even as they are themselves intrusions of an adult point of view upon that world. Significantly, the tone in which Alice's sister briefly reconstructs the "dream of Wonderland" at the end of the first book clearly echoes that of the poems: Alice's sister is the representation of an adult perspective within the story. The poems are the words of an adult recollecting childhood from afar; the books themselves do indeed offer an experience in the realm of childhood, but not the characteristically Victorian remote, idealised vision of childhood the poems imagine. Rather, it is childhood as experienced by a childlike mind: amoral, illogical, ambiguous, confusing. A deeper exploration of child-centred experience in the *Alice* books will be the subject of the next section.

2.2 "He Was Part of My Dream of course – but then I was Part of His Dream, too!": The Character(s)

'If I wasn't real', Alice said – half-laughing through her tears,
it all seemed so ridiculous – 'I shouldn't be able to cry'
(*TTLG*, 198)

Alan Palmer (2005) has proposed the application of cognitive discourses on real minds to the study of fictional mental processes (87–169), and I argue that this approach can be crucial in realizing a more complete and complex account of

Fig. 4: Maggie Taylor, *These Strange Adventures*, 2013. Taylor's collage shows a floating Alice dreaming, surrounded by swirling cards: the world in the background is flat, while Alice and the cards seem almost three-dimensional, suggesting thus the possibility of dreams being more tangible and alive than actual reality.

the many phenomena that Alice experiences. In reading we experience the illusion of having access to a character's thoughts, of going into his or her mind, and discovering its hidden mechanisms. Although we are dealing with representations of virtual minds in action, not with real minds, the depiction of a character's mind is intelligible only with reference to how we understand real minds to work. It can be said that in a certain sense "characters in a fictitious world do exactly what our intelligence allows us to do in the real world" (Pinker 1997, 541), or at least that they are the creations of a real mind, and they are based on a real mind's experiences. In this respect, literature can be viewed as a journey into minds, and this is especially true of nineteenth-century literature, when

> as technology usurped romanticism, the essence of human nature was being questioned [...]. In the frantic search for new kinds of expression, artists came up with a new method: they looked in the mirror. (Lehrer 2008, viii)

As noted in the first chapter, Carroll was particularly interested in the working of the human mind, in its potentialities and its secrets, and the fictional representation of Alice's mind in action shows how detailed and deep were his observations. Alice's mind is a mirror revealing the working of several kinds of mental attitude and mechanism: Alice's virtual mental activities offer powerful insights into what real minds do. In this section I draw attention to some of the mental processes that the *Alice* books persuasively describe, through the cognitive vicissitudes of the main character's mind. More specifically, I shall examine the depiction of curiosity, the dreaming mind, and the child's mind.

2.2.1 A Curious Child

On the first page of the first *Alice* book, after having seen a white rabbit hurrying because he is late, consulting a watch and talking aloud, Alice follows him because she is "*burning with curiosity*" (11). Even in the second *Alice* book the heroine decides to go through the looking-glass because she wonders about the nature and the aspect of the Looking-Glass world and wants to see with her own eyes what it looks like. Later, Carroll describes Alice's character by saying that she is loving as a dog, gentle as a fawn, courteous, "and, lastly, curious – wildly curious" (Carroll 1887). What makes Alice drink strange potions, eat mushrooms and weird cakes, and follow the most bizarre creatures is always her irrepressible feeling of curiosity.

At the beginning of her first adventure, Alice exclaims, "what a curious feeling!" (17); when she comes back to the initial green summery lawn, she says to her sister, "Oh, I've had such a curious dream!" (130). More famously, Alice's first linguistic confusion (linguistic chaos being a peculiar characteristic of Wonderland) is her exclamation, "curiouser and curiouser!" (20). The occurrences of the word "curious" and its derivatives in the *Alice* books (especially in the first one) are quite significant: Alice uses it often as an exclamation to describe her feelings of wonder related to her experience, or as a word to describe what she encounters, as in "curious creatures" (*AAIW*, 28), "such a curious croquet-ground" (*AAIW*, 88), or (referring to the Cheshire Cat) "a curious appearance" (*AAIW*, 88).

The little Alice has become, over the years, a kind of symbol of curiosity, a successor of the unlucky female figures of myth, such as Eve and Pandora. The place discovered by the curious Alice contains in its name the main mental attitude of the heroine: Wonderland, the place capable of arousing wonder. It is well-known that curiosity is far from being a mere feminine flaw, and that it is actually a philosophical sentiment: Plato [369 BCE] wrote that "the feeling of wonder is the most philosophical feeling"[13] (1987, 55D) and the capability for wonder, itself made possible by intellectual curiosity, is closely related to the discovery of new realities and connections.

Recent neuroscientific experiments using functional magnetic resonance imaging (fMRI) have shown that the neural basis of curiosity is associated with the brain sites of dopamine (the nucleus in the ventral striatum, connected with the pleasure reward system), the activation of the opiates in the brain (linked to positive experiences) and the energisation of the hippocampus (where new knowledge and notions are collected to form long-term memories). An article in *Frontiers in Behavioral Neuroscience* concludes that "our results provide neurobiological support for a classic psychological theory of curiosity, which holds that curiosity is an aversive condition of increased arousal whose termination is rewarding and facilitates memory" (Jepma et al. 2012). It seems that the more uncertain or unknown the stimulus is, the more intense and mentally involving the feeling of curiosity; perceptual uncertainty strongly activates the brain. Alice is excited and animated when she is running after the white rabbit, all her sudden and irresponsible decisions prompted by her desire to know why a white rabbit has a watch with him, and where he is going – even though, when at last she catches up with him, these no longer seem relevant issues: actually, the white rabbit first ignores her, and then treats her like his maid, provoking Alice's irritation.

Recent research adopts the premise that curiosity "is a multifaceted construct, and several different types of curiosity can be distinguished. One important distinction is the difference between *perceptual* and *epistemic* curiosity" (Jepma et al. 2012) – the first being a more basic form of curiosity, common to animals and humans, and related to perceptual doubts and confusion, and the second connected to the desire for knowledge and theoretical information. Alice's curiosity is a complex phenomenon too, at first merely instinctive and perceptual (why is a white rabbit wearing a waistcoat pocket and a watch?) but developing in response to more elaborate stimuli raising issues of identity and intellectual dilemmas (doubts about herself, about gravity, about what hap-

---

13 θαυμαζέιν μάλα φιλοσοφικόν πάθος.

pens on the opposite side of the world, about how an anti-matter universe can be, about the power of dreams ...).

The consequences of our curiosity are highly positive for our intellectual configuration: the encounter with new realities and knowledge is the basis for the increase in shape, size and number of the neurons in our brain, and also for the establishing of new links between them. Thus, it can be said that Alice's frequent changes in size while she comes into contact with new, weird worlds, are a reflection of what normally, in the same conditions, happens in the brain as a result of intellectual and cognitive improvements. Alice is a child coming to terms with new experiences and situations, new words and new meanings: in the *Cognifit* website there is a section on neuroplasticity and cognition, where it is explained how "children acquire new knowledge in vast quantities and their brain changes significantly at these times of intensive new learning".

There are fundamental links between curiosity-driven learning and cognitive development (see Gottlieb et al. 2013). The modification of neurons and their connections in response to new experiences made possible by the stimulus of curiosity, while changing the conformation of our brain, obviously also influences our own identity and personality, especially during the process of maturation. In this sense, Alice's own identity is deeply affected by the new realities and experiences she encounters in consequence of the cognitive drive of curiosity, reflecting the often-puzzling experience of growing up. New discoveries change Alice's own attitude and character, and she keeps asking herself "who in the world am I? Ah, that's the great puzzle!" and "let me think: was I the same when I got up this morning? I almost think I can remember feeling a little different" (*AAAIW*, 22). Equally, she cannot answer the Caterpillar's insistent questions about her identity. The disintegration of Alice's univocal identity in Wonderland is something progressive and layered with different meanings, but it is surely in part a powerfully embodied representation of the mental process of growing up, in which her contact with what was previously unknown or indistinct to her has immediate impact in the form of dramatic swings of mood and changes of size.

It has been understood for centuries, before being studied scientifically, that in the architecture of the human mind curiosity has a crucial role in structuring our lives. What cognitive scientists now point out about the mental effects of curiosity is something literary tradition has already explored. Dante [1472] reminds us that without the impulse to know and to extend our experiences, to explore the unknown driven by curiosity, we, as human beings, are confined to the mere existence of "bruti" (2009, 26, v. 119). However, he makes Ulysses, the hero symbol of intellectual curiosity and of the desire to apprehend, being eternally punished. First sucked under the abyss by a whirlpool, and then burning in hell, his figure in Dante's hell shows an acute contrast between the pursuit of knowledge and the capability of acting morally. Another symbolic figuration of the importance of curiosity is Apuleius's character Psyche (in Apuleius's *Metamorphosis*), who, as her name makes clear, represents the human mind: incredibly beautiful, envied by the gods, clouded by Eros, and uncontrollably curious. Indeed, everything that happens to her is provoked by her curiosity: her emblematic journey of learning and growing is made possible only because she watches her lover Eros sleeping, curious to see his appearance. Nonetheless, this act of curiosity disregards a previous clear prohibition against watching her lover, thus Psyche breaks the rule, and again we face the moral problem. Similarly, Eve eats the apple driven by curiosity to acquire knowledge, and so commits a fatal sin; Pandora opens the box, and the consequences are irredeemable. It seems that the impulse of curiosity works hand in hand with moral darkening (and feminine behaviours).

Two features important for the arousal of curiosity are uncertainty and the unknown:

> the first thing the scientists found is that curiosity obeys an inverted U-shaped curve, so that we're most curious when we know a little about a subject (our curiosity has been piqued) but not too much (we're still uncertain about the answer) ... (Lehrer 2010a)

The gap between what we know and what we still do not know provokes the arousal of a kind of itch, which boosts our emotions, working as "a mosquito bite on the brain" (Lehrer 2010a). This itch can be so invasive in our mental scenario as to darken other brain activities, with potentially important consequences, such as the possible moral implications of acts driven by curiosity.

The neural bases of moral judgements are still largely unknown and, moreover, necessarily involve a great number of neurological processes. Nevertheless, neuroscientists underline that empathy, theory of mind, internalisation of rules and social conventions learnt during childhood, and experiences held in memory, all play a role in the elaboration of moral thoughts and behaviours.[14] Lehrer argues that what causes the lack of recognition of morality in psychopaths is an emotional deficit. Psychopaths' brains reveal, through brain imaging techniques, a broken amygdala: the amygdala is responsible for the arousal of aversive emotions, "(it) is activated when most people even think about committing a "moral transgression" (Lehrer 2010b). This discovery surprisingly shows that the rational

---

14 In the child's brain "des traces 'épigénétiques' d'apprentissage (par selection de synapses) se déposent dans le réseau nerveux en dévelopement" (Changeux 2008, 96). "traces epigenetic of apprehension (through synapses' selection) collocate themselves in the developing nervous system" (my translation).

activities of the brain do not play an essential role in building up our moral conduct. This does not mean that reasoning has no part to play in shaping moral concepts, but it does show that while acting immorally, our reason can be working perfectly.

But is Alice's curious behaviour actually immoral? Is she a psychopathic child? The study of pathologies (psychopathy in this case) can illuminate some interesting aspects of normal brain functioning: without reaching a psychopathic level of emotional deficiency, our amygdala can work less when the neural networks linked to the "itch of curiosity" are strongly activated. The impulse of curiosity is strong enough to cloud other stimuli, and, like some kinds of pleasure, curiosity is a totally absorbing act: "humans will expend resources to find out information they are curious about, much as rats will work for a food reward" (Kang et al. 2009, 964).

The connection between Alice's curiosity-driven actions and a certain kind of moral blindness raises the question of the implications of her behaviour. Carroll's description of his heroine, immediately after describing her as "wildly curious", adds "with the eager enjoyment of Life that comes only in the happy hours of childhood, when all is new and fair, and when Sin and Sorrow are but names – empty words signifying nothing!" (Carroll 1887).[15] Alice's curiosity is importantly that of a child. Carroll did not want to subject children, through his story, to some kind of moral message: while Victorian fairy-tales were often full of pious maxims and moral advice, Carroll's pervasively ironic attitude broke with this tradition. The two books of Alice's vicissitudes are filled with parodies of Victorian songs and poems for children, and all of Carroll's rewritings are macabre, caustic, and full of black humour. At the beginning of Alice's adventures, her curiosity makes her drink a potion with the famous, inviting message "drink me" on it; but before doing so, she recalls "several nice little stories" of Victorian origin that condemn curiosity, in which curious children "had got burnt, and eaten up by wild beasts, and other unpleasant things" (17). Alice's scepticism about such moral didacticism is wisely expressed in her later response to the Duchess, who is obsessed with the idea of finding a moral in everything, and is looking for one in a sentence: "perhaps it hasn't one," Alice suggests (*AAIW*, 94).

Three different but interconnected meanings underlie the link between Alice's curiosity and the absence of morality in her adventures. Firstly, curiosity is

---

[15] It is also true that Carroll wrote this description in 1887, many years later the publication of the first *Alice* book, in a period of his life where moral reflections were beginning to play a more relevant role in his thoughts.

such a potent mental stimulus that it abolishes other rational considerations; secondly, Alice is at an age still dominated by a "pre-conventional level" of morality, as discussed in the previous section, and so her actions, lacking the context of mature moral development, are not so much immoral as amoral. She follows her curiosity without further considerations, but this is normal for a child's mental disposition. The third connotation of Alice's amoral curiosity relates to her unawareness of "Sin and Sorrow". It is precisely through the exploration of the world motivated by her curious attitude that Alice's ingenuousness is destined to vanish, in the inevitable process of growing up. Her childish curiosity will drive her to become an adult, to discover that angelic innocent babies can actually be ugly pigs,[16] that it is possible to be drowned in tears and sorrow, that adult's rules are as nonsensical as children's lack of them, and that little girls can become snakes. Again there is an ironic association with myths related to curiosity: a curious girl, a snake, a garden – Alice is a little unpunished Eve. However, "the Wonderland garden is no childhood Eden, but a life-and-death croquet match presided over by a homicidal Queen" (Haughton 2003, xiii).

I am not arguing that Carroll pointedly inserted morality-related issues into the *Alice* books, but rather that his narratives explore the complexity of childhood and innocence, and challenge common representations of the purity of childhood. Consequently, "Sin and Sorrow", those "empty words", in spite of Carroll's own declarations, begin in Wonderland to actually signify something. The discovery of their meaning will eventually lead Alice to become a grown-up woman, no more the little girl of the golden fairy tale. Curiosity will in the end make Alice adult, and in Carroll's own eyes this amounted to the destruction of his Alice, her absolute loss. Accordingly, as she reaches the final stage of her journey, "Alice is beginning to sense the final danger inherent in Wonderland: her own destruction" (Rackin 1991, 58). It is at this point that Alice wakes up, and temporarily suspends the more complex implications of her descent into Wonderland. The frightful adventure she has just experienced is labelled under the reassuring category of "a *curious* dream". This retreat marks a significant difference with the second *Alice* book: if in *Alice in Wonderland* the heroine's discoveries are ultimately relegated to the realm of dreams and thus not completely realised, in *Through the Looking-Glass* she is far more conscious and far less ingenuous (when Carroll was writing the second book, Alice Liddell was nineteen, already of marriageable age). In the second book, after the initial

---

[16] "The pig-baby episode humorously dramatizes the arbitrary nature of conventional attitudes toward infants" (Rackin 1991,52). The metamorphosis discloses what the true nature of many children can actually be, despite their being often portrayed in Victorian songs and lullabies as angelic and pure creatures.

impulse of jumping through the glass, Alice pursues a precise goal (becoming a Queen); it is no longer just curiosity that drives her journey. This context gives poignancy to the Rose's remark to Alice in the garden of live flowers: "You're beginning to fade, you know" (169).

Fig. 5: Lewis Carroll, *Alice Liddell Asleep*, Spring 1860. Carroll's photograph of Alice Liddell shows his fascination with dreams, and in particular children's dreams (even better, Alice's dreams). Carroll took his inspiration for this picture from Tennyson's poem *The Sleeping Beauty* (see Douglas-Fairhurst 2015, 100–101).

2.2.2 The Dreamchild Dreaming

If Alice's curiosity enlightens some real and interesting aspects of our mental impulses, the same is true, even in a more complex and elaborate way, with respect to the representation of Alice's dreaming mind. As I have shown in the first chapter, Carroll's interest in the working of dreams was deep, and associated with his interest in the Society for Psychical Research. According to Douglas-Fairhurst (2015), "writing like a dream is exactly what Carroll attempted to do" (125). "The whole thing is a dream" (M. Cohen 1989, 29) Carroll declared about *Alice's Adventures in Wonderland*, although in that book the problematic aspects of dreams are not foregrounded as they are in *Through the Looking-Glass*, where an existential doubt about "which dreamed it?" is pervasive.

Carroll's dream-like writing tends to highlight the ephemeral nature of reality itself, often seen as like a long and confused dream, and the boundaries between waking and dreaming states are frequently blurred. In a much-quoted passage from his journal, Carroll observes, "we often dream without the least suspicion of unreality: 'Sleep hath its own world', and it is often as lifelike as the other" (Wakeling 1993, Vol II, 38). The neuroscientist William Domhoff (2010) bases his cognitive theory of dreams on the idea that there is no clear line of demarcation between waking thoughts and dreaming ones: the mental processes occurring during one's dreams are similar, even granted some obvious differences, to certain kinds of everyday thought; the structure of dreams is common to waking fantasies, daydreaming, wanderings of the mind, and drug-induced perceptions.

Neurocognitive inquires argue that our dream activity is "boosted" when we experience an adequate level of cortical activation, when there is a lack of external stimuli, and, finally, when a loss of conscious self-control occurs; and all of these phenomena can also happen in other mental contexts than sleep. In one sense, Alice receives stimuli only from herself: Wonderland and the Looking-Glass world are mirrors of her own mental world, full of characters from nursery rhymes, talking animals, pupil-teacher relationships, various kind of delicious foods – in short, everything that can have a place in a child's thoughts. Furthermore, Carroll wrote (and previously told) the story following the explicit instructions of the Liddell sisters (especially Alice, obviously). Thus, the story had to contain, as required elements: Alice herself as the main character; animals (particularly cats, Alice's best-loved animals); conversations, adventures, eating and drinking; the game of croquet (Alice's favourite outdoor game); and (Carroll underlines this in the prefatory poem of the first book) "there will be nonsense in it!" (*AAIW*, 7).[17] The Looking-Glass Land is also a reflection of Alice's own preferences and ideas: she supposes, at the beginning of the second *Alice* book, that

---

[17] This requirement is specified by Secunda (Alice was the second of the Liddell sisters in order of age).

through the mirror "the things go the other way" (147), and indeed they do; or again, all Alice's actions in the Looking-Glass world have the goal of becoming a queen, paralleling her own path towards growing up and marrying. Indeed, the adventures of Alice are a mirror of Alice's own identity and thoughts as Carroll sees them.

The necessary filter of the authorial perspective upon Alice's dreams complicates the picture. It is true that the real Alice Liddell instructed Carroll about how she would like her dream to be, but it is also true that she could have said what she thought Carroll wanted to hear from her: children are deeply influenced by adults' expectations, and often they like to please them. Such self-correction is analogous to the revision process necessarily involved in dream reports (Foulkes 1999, 17; Stoneham 2019). Different layers are merged together in the creation, recollection and writing of Alice's dreams. Firstly, there is the real Alice Liddell's mind, the most inaccessible of the layers, with her childish and mysterious dreams. Secondly, there is the real Alice telling her adult friend what her dream should be like. Thirdly, there is the adult writer obsessed with little girls and linguistic games who adds black humour and nonsense logic. And, finally, there is the virtual Alice, both the child who experiences the nightmarish atmosphere of Wonderland and tells her sister that it was all just "a curious dream" (130), and the Alice who subsequently goes through the looking-glass and begins to question the essence of dreams and mastery, and to realise that to be trapped in someone else's dream is not where she wants to be.[18] Carroll's narrative explorations of the dreaming child are able to offer a rich and complicated picture, exploring what a child's dream can be, but also recognising the complexities and possible contradictions of doing so, related to the child's own mediation of dream thoughts to an adult audience, and to the impositions of that adult perspective itself. The *Alice* books pursue Carroll's own conjectures about Alice's dreams, and his progressive realisation that the real Alice probably wants to escape from the eternal childhood created by his dream-writing trap.

One of the distinctive features of dreams, and children's dreams in particular, recreated by Carroll is the "loss of self-control" typical of dream experience. Alice changes size, she is not sure about her own name (in the Looking-Glass world she even *wants* to lose her name), and she is so surprised that she "quite forgot how to speak good English" (*AAIW*, 20). She makes spontaneous associations without any apparent immediate relevance (as very often happens in dreams): "do cats eat bats? Do cats eat bats? Do bats eat cats?" she repeats

---

[18] In this sense, *TTLG* continuously presents characters who want to be masters and dominate – but, as with Humpty Dumpty's fall, they all tend to fail.

obsessively while falling down the rabbit hole (*AAIW*, 14). The fact that dream-like states can occur even if one is *not* dreaming, under certain other mental conditions, raises doubts about what is really real, and this doubt is continuously present in the *Alice* books. The dream-within-a-dream motif confuses Alice and her sister, confuses us as readers, and perhaps confuses Carroll himself. When Alice wakes up from Wonderland, she runs in a hurry (exactly like the white rabbit of her dreams) and, also like two characters from her dreamy adventures, she goes to take her tea – "it's always tea-time," as the Mad Hatter remarks – (*AAIW*, 77). She is thus repeating the acts of her dream, even as her sister "sat on, with closed eyes, and half believed herself in Wonderland" (131), dreaming about Alice's dream. At the same time, as pointed out above, they both are also figments of Carroll's own dream: the White Knight, possibly a double for Carroll himself,[19] points this out continuously, saying "it's my own invention!" (*TTLG*, 245).

The similarity between the working of the human brain in the oneiric state and in the waking state, can also be shown by considering the narrative structure of dreams. The mind tends to work narratively, a process extremely useful in the construction of meaning, and this is equally true in dreams, even if our dream stories can seem more incoherent and the episodes disjointed. The human mind always tries to organise inputs, even, as in the case of dreams, internal inputs, into some kind of order: this is necessary to coping cognitively with a vast and polysemic reality. Domhoff (2010) reports that "the brain's goal is always to construct a reasonable image of the world based on the material it's receiving. If you're in a situation where it's not receiving any information from the outside, then it starts to invent". Alice, similarly, recollects her "rational" ideas, her everyday images of the world (cats, cards, chess, tea, candies …) and constructs a dream order, a fanciful story, from arbitrary stimuli, and that's Wonderland: as Nina Auerbach (1973) writes, "the dainty child carries the threatening kingdom of Wonderland within her" (32). It is true that Wonderland seems to exemplify the reign of chaos,[20] and there are two reasons for this. Firstly, Carroll's narrative presentation of the dream must not impose a too logical structure upon it, because that is not how dreams unfold: the improvised stories the mind creates while dreaming can't follow the same considered logic as the waking mind's narrations. Indeed, the waking mind's reconstruc-

---

19 I shall return to the association between Carroll and the White Knight in the third chapter.
20 Sewell (1952) writes that "if Nonsense is an art, it must have its own laws of construction" and be "a carefully limited world, controlled and directed by reason" (5–6). However, I am not here denying that Carroll's nonsense worlds have their own inner logic, but saying that this logic often appears as a dream-like one, with elements of chaos in it (even if a structured chaos).

tions of dream stories can only compound the difficulty, impaired by lack of memory or by distorted recollections, so that the narrative of a dream report is doubly unclear and equivocal.

Secondly, Alice is a child. The powerful insight of Carroll's non-conventional mind, and his affinity, though adult, with child-like mental states, enable him to recreate a child's dream. He could not know what cognitive studies have discovered in modern times (see Foulkes 1999, Domhoff 2010, Revonsuo 2000), but his fictional writings show a sort of awareness of it: children's dreams have a different neural conformation from adult's dreams. Alice is seven years old in Carroll's stories, and children do not possess adult-like dreaming skills until age ten (see Strauch 2005; Jepma et al. 2012). Her capability for dreaming would be still in formation, because she could not have yet developed a mature network of neurons capable of managing it as adults do. Mental imagery, a resource the mind only establishes gradually, is an important prerequisite for adult-like dreams, distinguished by their length, frequency, emotional tones, and connections with personality. Alice's Wonderland is thus an appropriately confused world, in which the cognitive grasp upon time, space, and meaning is still uncertain, and references to aspects of Alice's own personality are often obscure. When Alice goes through the looking-glass, on the other hand, she is more adult and has a more developed character, and so the Looking-Glass world is as appropriately characterised by its more logical configuration, its precise rules (those of chess), and Alice's own pursuit of the specific role of queen. The sexual and macabre elements of the Looking-Glass world are also more explicit, and Alice does not fail to notice them.[21]

The dream scenarios of Carroll's stories also have a bearing upon the question of moral impairment that I have discussed in relation to the stimulus of curiosity. The actions we perform in a dream have a complicated relation with morality, raising questions like: is there a direct correspondence between our waking self and our dreaming one? Do our dream-actions have moral implications in real life? Can we somehow control our behaviour in dreams? (see for instance Mullane 1965, Driver 2007). These are all open questions, and illustrate the difficulties involved in judging the moral status of dreams. In this sense, too, Alice is not her normal self in the parallel worlds of her dreams, and especially in her

---

21 I am here talking about the several ambiguous references scattered throughout the second Alice book. Such as, for instance: "shall summon to unwelcome bed" (prefatory poem, 139); the Rose telling Alice she is beginning to fade (169); the curious deaths of the Looking-Glass Insects (184–185); the almost cannibalism of the Walrus and the Carpenter (192–196); Humpty Dumpty saying to Alice she should have better "left off at seven" (222); the Red and White Knights fighting over the possession of Alice as a prisoner (245–247); the oyster riddle (277).

first dream of Wonderland she does not have a clear idea of what is happening, nor any real control of the situation. In the Looking-Glass world she is more aware of her actions and, when she wakes up, begins to question the nature of reality in consequence of the events of her dream. Thus, the amoral behaviour that characterises the *Alice* books is also connected to their dream-like qualities, and to Carroll's exploration of the elaborate and obscure nature of dreams.

One further quality of the *Alice* books related to dream-like structure is their predominantly negative tone. Antti Revonsuo observes that in dreams

> the various negative elements seem to be more prominent than the corresponding positive elements. Negative emotions are more common than positive emotions and aggressive interactions are more common than friendly interactions. (2000, 884)

This impression is borne out by the "nightmarish atmosphere of Alice's dreams" (M. Gardner 2001, xiv). Alice's vicissitudes have elements of the violence and horror typical of nightmares, and her numerous encounters are almost always marked by incomprehension and aversion (even when not accompanied by explicit violence). There is an obsessive recurrence of the theme of eating and being eaten; there is a caterpillar/worm who threatens the innocence of a child/rose; there is a dream-child who becomes a snake – "little girls eat eggs quite as much as serpents do, you know" says Alice to the Pigeon, and the Pigeon concludes "then they're a kind of serpent" (*AAIW*, 57); there is a lovely garden which turns absurd, and in which heads are cut off and cards are kings; there is a Duchess who tosses a baby violently up and down, and a baby that becomes a pig; there are poems in which "somebody killed something" (*TTLG*, 156); there is a garden of animate flowers who are rude and cynical; a gnat who always cries and deeply sighs, a bread-and-butter-fly who always dies; many fragile or tyrannical creatures, and an obsession with fish and dead fish that barely conceals a sexual meaning.

Carroll's fictional depiction of Alice's mind, of her curiosity and of her dreams, leads the reader on a convoluted journey into the mysteries of a child's inner self, and its relationship with an adult perspective: as Auerbach observes,

> other little girls travelling through fantastic countries, such as George MacDonald's Princess Irene and L. Frank Baum's Dorothy Gale, ask repeatedly '*where* am I?' rather than '*who* am I?' Only Alice turns her eyes inward from the beginning, sensing that the mystery of her surroundings is the mystery of her own identity. (1973, 33)

How readers' minds interact with these scenarios is the subject of the next section.

2.3 "The Magic Words Shall Hold Thee Fast: / Thou Shalt not Heed the Raving Blast": The Readers

> 'It's a great huge game of chess that's being played – all over the world – if this *is* the world at all, you know'
> (*TTLG*, 172)

What readers encounter when they engage with a narrative text is, in a figurative sense, a *world*, with its own specific rules, its inhabitants, its features and its landscapes. In order to better grasp the existential status and characteristics of these fictional worlds, literary theorists such as Ryan (1991), Ronen (1994), Doležel (1998) and Eco (1979) have adapted the philosophical model of possible worlds to the exigencies of narrative theory. Interdisciplinary exchange is always to be regarded as a fruitful possibility for literary studies, but the application of possible worlds, as developed in modal logic, to the analysis of literary worlds has often resulted in "a naïve adaptation or an inadvertent metaphorization of a concept whose original nonfigurative significance is far from self-evident" (Ronen 1994, 7). The use of the concept in fictional contexts requires theoretical adaptations and caveats: there are profound differences in theoretical orientation between the disciplines of literary theory and philosophical logic; and the logical and ontological status of possible worlds is an issue about which philosophers themselves are still debating.[22] Nevertheless, possible worlds theory does offer interesting insights for the analysis of literary texts, and touches upon several important issues regarding fiction: the ontological status of the fictional world; so called "trans-world relations"; the problem of accessibility between the "actual world" and the "textual world"; the different modes of existence of fictional beings; and the meaning of the categories of possibility and impossibility.

What fictional worlds reveal themselves to be, in contrast with the possible worlds of logic (mainly theoretical models concerned with logical and linguistic phenomena), are "pregnant" worlds (Eco 1979, 218), with a concrete ontological density of their own. In the literary context, "possible worlds are not theoretical terms but rather descriptive concepts that work within a descriptive poetics [...] they involve the ontology of concrete artistic worlds" (Ronen 1994, 74). In this sense, while possible worlds in philosophical terms need to respect certain log-

---

[22] "The diverging interpretations given to possible worlds within philosophy itself undermine any attempt to view a possible world as a clear, straightforward and unequivocal concept which the various disciplines can adopt for their own needs" (Ronen 1994, 72). For a summary of the different interpretations of possible worlds among philosophers see Ronen (especially 21–46), or Berto (2010, 105–120 and 207–228).

ical rules (such as the law of non-contradiction and the law of the excluded middle) in order actually to be possible, possible worlds of fiction incorporate violations of logical rules without becoming semantically empty: "for literary authors, impossibility is not a restriction, but rather a new domain for exercising creative powers" (Ronen 1994, 57).[23] This section adopts a perspective that takes advantage of the interpretative insights suggested by the application of possible worlds theory to fictions, but proposes a cognitive reorientation of the idea, highlighting the strong mutual dependence between cognitive interpretative processes and the creation of narrative worlds.

2.3.1 A Cognitive Approach to Fictional Worlds

Ryan, in her *Possible Worlds, Artificial Intelligence and Narrative Theory* (1991) offers a catalogue of the different universes of meaning embedded in a narrative world, elaborating on the internal system of that specific world (109–123). This includes, for instance, a "K-World," regarding the knowledge, ignorance or beliefs of the characters in a novel; or an "O-World," which concerns the social rules determining what is allowed and not allowed in a specific narrative scenario; there is then the "W-World," related to the wishes and desires of the characters; and, of particular significance in relation to the fictional worlds of the *Alice* books, there are the "F-Universes," which encompass the private spheres of fantasies, hallucinations, dreams, and fictions within fiction. Thus, characters can recreate themselves other fictional worlds, within the one they inhabit, by means of dreams and imagination. The "inherent recursivity of recentering" (Ryan 1991, 119) opens further possibilities within an F-universe, since dreamed characters can themselves dream, and the characters in a story told by Scheherazade may themselves tell further stories. This applies also to the recursive dreams of the *Alice* books: Alice's dream of Wonderland becomes a tale, which then becomes her sister's dream; and Alice's reality itself, in the end, becomes Wonderland (she wakes up and has to run because it's tea time, repeating again the "always tea time" of the Mad Hatter and the March Hare). "Alice's dream is not only introduced for its own sake, it even draws TAW [the "textual actual world"] into its own orbit" (119).[24]

---

[23] The extreme case of impossible fictional worlds, as related to the concept of the unnatural, is dealt with in the last chapter.
[24] This phenomenon is also explained by Ryan with the AI concept of the stack: in the standard form of the stack, the passages from one level to another are restricted to specific boundaries, and the only level which should be left at the end of the text is the ground level; but this order is

The potential recursivity of F-universes also offers a possible model of explanation for the famous scene in *Through the Looking-Glass* in which Alice finds the Red King dreaming, and Tweedledum and Tweedledee tell her that he is dreaming about her, and that if he left off doing so, she would be "nowhere", because she is only "a sort of thing in his dream" (*TTLG*, 198). As Martin Gardner (2001) writes, "an odd sort of infinite regress is involved here in the parallel dreams of Alice and the Red King. Alice dreams of the King, who is dreaming of Alice, who is dreaming of the King, and so on, like two mirrors facing each other" (198). Ryan (1991) calls this narrative device, quoting Hofstadter, "a strange loop" (191); that is, a vicious circle which prevents us from deciding which character is real or primary.

Fig. 6: Kenneth Rougeau, *The Red King Sleeping*, 2007. Rougeau's digital image perfectly portrays the "strange loop" involved in Alice's and the King's mutual dreaming.

---

subverted when an "unconditional" recursive act is performed, producing an "ever-expanding stack of environments from which no return is possible" (189).

The recursive logic of this passage, and the general sense of recursive representations to be found in the *Alices*, can also be viewed as an example of the circularity that characterises the relation between fictional worlds and the cognitive acts of their creation and re-creation. This is the perspective from which I am proposing to integrate the possible worlds' approach to fictions with a more cognitive orientation. From such a perspective Alice's dreams, as the cognitive acts of creation of her fictional adventures, themselves function as a narrative depiction of the reciprocity between creation and interpretation. Alice's cognitive acts serve to stage the idea that Wonderland and the Looking-Glass Land are narrative worlds *per se*, and at the same time they are the products of her dreaming activity. This dreaming activity itself is represented within those fictional worlds, enacting the sense in which the cognitive processes of creation and re-creation are deeply entangled with fictional worlds themselves.

A related problem in the application of possible worlds theory to fictional studies emerges when it comes to address the topic of *how* readers access these rich fantastical worlds with their various internal ramifications (including, as just said, specific internal rules, wishes, desires, fantasies, and recursive mechanisms). The fictional universe is a discursive universe for which the truth value of its statements is decided only *inside* that particular universe: "fictional texts are outside truth-valuation: their sentences are neither true nor false" (Doležel 1998, 24). The fictional operator (f) delimits the fictional world (Ronen 1994, 38), separating its ontology from that of the actual world. However, this poses the problem of what link readers can then establish between their own world and the world of the text; of what is entailed by the cognitive encounter with a fictional world. Ryan (1991, 31–47) addresses this problem by introducing a number of accessibility relations between textual actual worlds and the actual world of the readers. The characteristics of a fictional world are understood by readers through their various differences from and similarities with the readers' actual world; differences and similarities, for example, in physical properties, or in chronological markers, or even in logical relations. A key concept bearing upon accessibility relations is the principle of minimal departure (48–60), which states that the mind constructs a possible textual universe by making it as close as possible to our actual world, deviating only where there are specific indications in the text to do so. According to this theory, worlds like those of the *Alice* books on the contrary adhere to a "principle of *maximal* departure" (58) – they continuously challenge our prefabricated ideas of the actual world (be it Victorian or contemporary) and frustrate our attempts to apply actual world rules to Wonderland or the Looking-Glass world.

This way of conceiving the reader-text relationship, however, is based on a "relatively unproblematic view of the actual world as a stable reference world"

(Ronen 1994, 70), since the actual world is anything but a definite and universal cognitive certainty. The principle of minimal departure also highlights a tension between the idea that the readers need a previous reality-based experience in order to understand a narrative world and the cognitive-related view (see Turner 1996, *The Literary Mind*) of our mental processes as in part already narrative in their nature. As Stockwell (2002) writes, the possible worlds perspective on literary texts needs to be qualified by an approach that is "explicitly cognitive in its orientation" (96). Such an intervention would enable the approach to be adapted "so that we can speak of discourse worlds that can be understood as dynamic readerly interactions with possible worlds: possible worlds with a narratological and cognitive dimension" (93). Actually, the principle of minimal departure itself can be reinterpreted in a more cognitive fashion, helping in this way to balance the "worldiness" of fictional worlds with their cognitive reconstruction by readers. If the frame of reference of the principle of minimal departure is not taken as the actual external ontological world (which is too problematic a concept) but rather as readers' pre-existing cognitive parameters, it could be appropriated to a cognitive approach, helping to overcome the limitations of possible worlds theory.

In addition, several other cognitive concepts could be integrated into a modified possible worlds theory – concepts such as blending, conceptual metaphors and cognitive deixis. In spite of the "ontological density" of fictional worlds, which makes them existent *per se* even in the presence of logical contradictions, fictional worlds are nonetheless constructions of the imagination, and cannot be separated from the cognitive processes involved. In the author's section of this chapter I argue for the importance of conceptual metaphor theory and cognitive theories of creativity for a better understanding of the creation of the virtual narrative worlds; I am now claiming that these theories, combined with possible worlds theory, can help make sense of the re-creation of these worlds in readers' minds. What the world of the text realises is precisely this encounter between creating minds, the author's and the readers': the fictional world is a dynamic landscape across which imaginative processes are constantly at play. Yet possible worlds theory, as Freeman points out,

> has no adequate theory of metaphor, no theory that can successfully account for the conceptualising power of cognitive processes [...] it seems to have no way of describing [...] what role the imaginative processes have on 'real' world perception. (2000, 275)

One way to reduce this theoretical deficit would be to introduce the concept of cognitive deixis, which is the key mechanism of the cognitive recentering required by the mental act of accessing a fictional world. Following textual indicators, readers immerse themselves in different spatial, temporal, social, physical landscapes, adapting their own mental schemata and conceptual frames to the ones proposed by the fictional setting. This does not mean at all that readers immerse themselves in a somehow pre-existent and determinate fictional reality. The process is a dynamic and reciprocal negotiation between reader and text: there is no fixed, pre-existent narrative world, but neither do readers create a new reality ex novo. Rather, the act of cognitive deixis allows readers to create in their minds a mental model of a story world: a model in which events, persons and objects have the relations indicated by the text they are reading, a construction of the fictional world in mental space. This process does not result in the same construction for all readers: although cognitive deixis is a universal mental process, its working is shaped by the personal, historical and social environment of each reader. Immersion in a text involves some standard cognitive processes, the features of which are influenced by the individual characteristics and contexts of readers' minds. Such an account challenges Ryan's idea of a stable reference world in two ways: firstly, the historical and cultural settings of interpretation are relative and context-dependent, providing a variable background; and, secondly, this background is itself informed and shaped by the narrative encounter, so that the two realities are interconnected and interdependent. The concept of cognitive deixis as a means of recentering is also harmonious with the conceptual blending discussed in the previous section. The construction of a mental model of the possible world articulated by a fictional text is an instance of mental mapping between different frames (the text, and the reader's cognitive context). Extrapolating specific relationships between these spaces creates a new space, the blend. The fictional world is the result of such mapping.

Such an account of reading is worth testing in the specific context of the *Alice* books, because the cognitive efforts required by the Carrollian narrative worlds are challenging and peculiar. Cognitive deixis is informed by the specific nature and genre of the fictional indications: if the text reveals itself to be, for instance, a ghost story, our mental expectations would be shaped according to our knowledge of this particular genre, this particular *storyworld logic*, that "specifies what the possible properties of objects are and what relations can exist among them" (Segal 2005a, 72). Such genre knowledge is situated relative to mental predispositions like our own perception of ghost stories, our previous readerly experience with them, our taste, our cultural context. But the inner logic of narrative worlds is contingent because "textual genres are often characterised by distinctive configurations of deictic elements" (Hanks 2005, 100).

The first textual clues to genre in the *Alice* books are the introductory poems at the beginning of each, which direct us towards a kind of idyllic fairy tale for children. Our cognitive expectations are primed by the romantic idea of a "dream-child moving through a land of wonders" (*AAIW*, 7), and directed by the anticipatory description of "the love-gift of a fairy tale" (*TTLG*, 139). When we start following the white rabbit with Alice we may still be operating under that illusion. The first indications pointing towards a different kind of story are the nonsense dream-like words Alice starts to repeat while falling down the rabbit hole, such as "do cats eat bats? Do cats eat bats? Do bats eat cats?" (14), with their quite grotesque associations. Then we are directed back towards a fairy tale scenario when Alice finds the little golden key opening a secret door, and when she sees that this door leads to a passage to a wonderful flowery garden. However, this expectation is also short-lived, because Alice flouts the traditional laws of children's stories by drinking from the bottle labelled "drink me", despite all the "nice little stories about children who had got burnt, and eaten up by wild beasts, and other unpleasant things" (17) due to their irresponsible curiosity. This passage introduces one of the few constant features of the *Alice* books, their lack of morality and parodic attitude towards traditional Victorian stories for children. This feature, regularly reinforced by parodies of well-known moral poems, indeed functions as a deictic indication of genre, and in part guides our understanding of the text.

As Segal (2005b) argues with respect to fictions in general, "the deictic center does not remain static within the story, but shifts as the story unfolds" (16), but obviously the more cognitive shifts a text obliges readers to make, the more cognitively challenging and elusive the story will be. The complexity of the *Alice* books substantially concerns this difficulty in understanding what we are dealing with exactly: in following the two stories, we have to continuously change the framework of the mental model we are constructing as the cognitive space for these Carrollian worlds. We encounter pseudo-scientific speculations which lead us to think that Carroll is using fiction to probe new intriguing branches of exact sciences; and linguistic games that have prompted many philosophers to interpret the *Alice* books as logical playgrounds. Nonsense itself, while it is a constant feature of the two stories, is a difficult genre to grasp in a definite, univocal way. Multiple possible genres and types of story jostle with each other within the Carrollian fictional worlds; moreover, at the end of both texts we discover that Alice's experience has been a dream, revealing them to also be investigations into the mental processes of dreaming.

A cognitive version of the principle of minimal departure can help account for how we manage the perplexities of this situation. Alice's fictional worlds depart from our cognitive expectations in multiple ways, including their generic instability, and in doing so they put readers in a perpetual state of cognitive uncertainty. Our cognitive relation to the story world is a vexed one, confounded by the deceptive and contradictory indications of the texts. This confusion persists even to the conclusive poem at the end of *Through the Looking-Glass*, which takes us back to a romantic scenario of melancholic nostalgia, making us question once more the genre and the meaning of what we have just read.

Since readers use their previous knowledge to understand stories, the differences between a Victorian reader, a contemporary reader, an adult reader and a child reader are significant, and imply very different kinds of immersion in the textual worlds of the *Alice* books. Our own interest, age and historical context guide the cognitive representation we create of the *Alice* books, compounding the proliferation of possible interpretations they generate as literary works. As Douglas-Fairhurst points out, whether Carroll presents an imaginary land

> as borderless as Wonderland [...] or as strictly ordered as Looking-Glass Land [...] in either case, when we explore them in our heads no two readers will imagine exactly the same place; instead we are invited to construct our own mental maps as we move from page to page. (2015, 36)

Carroll plays with the range of possible cognitive expectations, destabilizing them and proposing new conceptual metaphors; the *Alice* books stage an encounter between different minds not only in their representations of various kinds of mental functioning, nor in the more general sense of the encounters between author, character and reader that provide the theoretical structure of my approach, but also in the juxtaposition of different types of cognitive representation they elicit from readers.

2.3.2 The Visual Aspects of Alice's Worlds

The cognitive and imaginative effort required by the *Alice* books is not limited to our recentering in different narrative spaces. The construction of these worlds also presents a distinctive challenge to our visual-related cognitive mechanisms. Elaine Scarry's enlightening *Dreaming by the Book* (1999) declares the goal of analysing and explaining the mental processes books elicit, in order to understand how "in the verbal arts images somehow *do* acquire the vivacity of perceptual objects" (5). Some of the concepts she introduces are helpful in considering the types of imaginative construction we activate in order to grasp certain specific passages by Carroll. Scarry's concepts are evocative rather than scientifically rigorous, but their deep aesthetic intuitions offer "a truly revealing phenomenology of imagination" (Baker 1999), and will help us to better fathom the imaginative tissue of Alice's worlds.

To begin at the end, with the final feast from the last chapters of *Through the Looking-Glass*, we find an example of what Scarry calls "radiant ignition"

Fig. 7: John Tenniel, illustration for *Through the Looking-Glass*, 1871. Tenniel's picture perfectly captures the initiating power of movement of the sparkling candles/fireworks.

(77–88). One of the effects writers can achieve through description is to evoke moving pictures in our minds, and among the means by which they do so is the evocation of shimmering lights, which Scarry shows to be a class of images frequently exploited by poets and writers in the creation of moving scenes (79–85). A sense of motion is created in readers' minds by the description of flashing lights, the idea of something moving in the space being compared to the movements of a point of light. The final scene of *Through the Looking-Glass* is one of the most vivid in the *Alice* books, and infused with movement. The motion is first initiated, in the book as well as in our re-creative imagination, by the candles, which "all grew up to the ceiling, looking something like a bed of rushes with fireworks at the top" (278): this idea of a group of brilliant things shooting upwards is a catalyst that makes all the creatures and objects in the scene begin to move crazily around Alice. So the bottles, with plates as wings and forks as legs, turn into bird-like creatures fluttering around, and all the characters present at the feast start to undergo similar metamorphoses. This highly dynamic situation terminates with a final movement, Alice shaking the Red Queen, who has turned into a doll, which leads to the end of the dream: Alice wakes up to find herself shaking the black kitten.

In this way, Carroll employs two different devices at the same time to stimulate readers' imagination of the characters' movements: not only "radiant ignition" but also the device of addition and subtraction (Scarry 1999, 100–110). If the feast gains dynamic power from the flashing candles moving towards the ceiling, the scene's active, chaotic vitality is sustained by the continuous substitution of one thing for another: we are invited to imagine a certain object or character (the Red Queen, the pudding, the White Queen) and then replace it with something else as it metamorphosises, creating in this way a constant sense of movement. This practice of subtraction and addition linked to the metamorphosis of creatures is a device Carroll frequently uses, especially in the Looking-Glass world, to generate a constant flow of movement from one creature to another, and from one scene or situation to another. Examples would include the White Queen turning into the Sheep, or the transformation of the needles the Sheep is using into oars, or the egg Alice buys at the Sheep's shop turning into Humpty-Dumpty.

The same chapter ("Wool and Water") furnishes an example of what Scarry calls "rarity", the evocation of movement by imagining airy, tissue-like objects. Scarry states, "filmy objects – hair, paper, light cloth, flower petals, butterflies (petals in motion) – continually move about in the mind almost without effort" (91). Indeed, the main feature of this chapter from the second of the *Alice* books is precisely such airy, almost insubstantial motion: "things flow about so here!" (211), exclaims a puzzled Alice. All the things on the shop's shelves elude Alice's efforts to grasp them: the stability of the shelves contrasts with the ephemerality of the objects on them, anchoring this idea of a slippery movement in readers' minds. The same thing happens with the beautiful rushes Alice tries to catch: as soon as she reaches some of them, other, more beautiful rushes appear further away. Moreover, the ones she manages to collect, "being dream-rushes, melted away almost like snow, as they lay in heaps at her feet" (215). Scarry notes, "we have seen that objects with rarity easily float or drift" (98), and by comparing the rushes to melting snow, Carroll gives to solid things the ethereal and elusive quality of a dream fading away.

Carroll's prominent depiction of floating and ephemeral elements is linked to the goal of representing the slippery and unformed nature of memories. The chapter's title, "Wool and Water", refers to two amorphous, shapeless materials, evoking the peculiar essence of memory. The White Queen, who explains to Alice the advantages of living backwards (206–207), becomes the Sheep, wearing a pair of big spectacles, so as to see better through the mist of time, and working with countless needles in an effort to give shape to the wool, as if trying to mould nebulous remembrances. When Alice and the Sheep find themselves in another shapeless element, water, Alice notices that there is "something queer about the water" (212), in which her oars are continually getting caught, like the mind indulging obsessively in distant memories. Alice picks the dream rushes, but the most beautiful ones are always out of reach, like nostalgic memories of a distant past; and the ones she does pick immediately begin "to fade, and to lose all their scent and beauty" (215). However, Alice does not give too much attention to the fading of (we assume) her childhood memories, or to the fact that what her memory does catch ceases to be interesting or beautiful, because she is already too absorbed in seeing what will happen to her next: "Alice hardly noticed this, there were so many other curious things to think about" (215). The topic of losing childhood, of growing up, of Carroll and Alice being "half a life asunder" (139) and of Alice forgetting about her former friend, is an obsessive motif in *Through the Looking-Glass*, but it is Carroll's obsession, not Alice's.[25] Carroll's use of rarefied, airy objects in this chapter not only functions to evoke mental images of movement, but reciprocally becomes a thematic representation of the poignant and peculiar nature of memory.

Scarry points out also how mental images evoked by books can be additionally manipulated by "stretching, folding, tilting" (111); she describes the process of

---

[25] The same division of attention recurs with the White Knight, who tries to keep Alice with him for a little more time, even as she has already "turned with an eager look" (*TTLG*, 259) in another direction.

stretching the picture, as though the image itself were a small piece of cloth or transparent tissue with a picture imprinted on it that we can elongate by holding it firm at the bottom and tugging gently at the top, or widen by pulling at the lateral edges. (1999, 111)

It is apparent how this description is particularly apt in relation to *Alice in Wonderland:* Alice's changes of size oblige us to visualise her stretching and enlarging, and then shrinking and folding in relation to her surroundings. Following the textual cues, we do in our minds what Tenniel makes Alice do in his illustrations, and Scarry's concept highlights once again that Alice is a papery creation, whom writer and readers can manipulate at their own will: "we can flutter or shake [mental images] even more easily than we can opera scenery, if we can only remind ourselves of their papery two-dimensionality and not be misled by the solidity of their real-world equivalents" (137). Alice Liddell might be out of Carroll's effective reach, but the literary Alice is a cloth-like, easily moulded creature, whom both author and reader can model in their minds.[26]

The last hint I would like to draw from Scarry's book is what she calls the "floral supposition" (158). She explains in detail that imagining flowers is one of the easiest creative processes (40–71), and therefore that many writers use flowers in their descriptions, as actual elements in the scene, or as comparative figures or metaphors. Carroll uses flowers in the chapter "The Garden of Live Flowers" (which is also a parody of the speaking flowers in Tennyson's *Maud*). The flowers here use their own cognitive frame of reference to understand what Alice is, picturing her as also a flower. According to Scarry this is also the easiest way the mind has to create and compose images (158–192), that "flowers are a rehearsal for perception" (179). As such, they are not only an effective element of a composition, they also represent an aspect of the compositional process itself. On the one hand, the living flowers in the Looking-Glass garden picture Alice as a flower because cognition involves bringing objects into relation with our own frame of reference; on the other hand they do so as a symbol of the act of imagining itself and its focus upon the heroine of the book. Alice's petals are "tumbled about", because she's "beginning to fade, you know – and then one can't help one's petals getting a little untidy" (169). Alice's true nature, in Carroll's image of her, is thus revealed: she is a fading flower that even imagination begins to find difficult to keep fresh.

The virtual realities with which readers engage in the *Alice* books, then, can be understood on several levels. The application of possible worlds theory to fictions has a particular kind of purchase upon the worlds Alice discovers in Won-

---

[26] It is Carroll's own imagination that makes even the papery Alice elude his own control, ever eager to go ahead, to end the story, and escape from its pages.

Fig. 8: Lewis Carroll, Illustration for *Alice's Adventures Underground*, 1864. This is one of the original illustrations made by Carroll himself for the first manuscript of *Alice's Adventures Underground*. This Alice has the same dark and intense eyes as Alice Liddell, the same charming and somehow disturbing expression. Carroll draws her as she is growing in size, expanding to the limits of the page, trying to escape the uncomfortable status of a paper doll.

derland and through the looking-glass. But a more cognitively oriented perspective on literary worlds can better account for the relationship between readers' minds and the texts of the *Alice* books, especially with respect to concepts of recursivity, their challenge to the principle of minimal departure and cognitive deixis. Finally, prompted by Scarry's suggestions in *Dreaming by the Book*, we can give some specificity to the work our imagination has to do in order to recreate the visual aspects of Carroll's fictional worlds.

Fig. 9: Kenneth Rougeau, *In the Garden of Live Flowers*, digital collage, 2007. This image is a particularly appropriate representation of human and flowery frames of reference. Alice and the flowers share the same facial features and the same colour patterns.

Chapter 3
Mirrored Alice

> For this curious child was very fond
> of pretending to be two people.
> (*AAIW*, 18)

George MacDonald, who was Carroll's friend and who populated his novels with mirrors too, gives this famous definition of mirrors' mysterious power:

> what a strange thing a mirror is! And what a wondrous affinity exists between it and a man's imagination! For this room of mine, as I behold it in the glass, is the same, and yet not the same. It is not the mere representation of the room I live in, but it looks just as if I were reading about it in a story I like. [...] The mirror has lifted it out of the region of fact into the realm of art. (MacDonald [1858] 2008, 125)

MacDonald's description of the fascinating features of the mirror, features which makes it a symbol of the re-creative acts of writing and imagining, is particularly significant in relation to the perspective I adopt in this second chapter. I explore here the mirror-related mechanisms represented and implied in the *Alice* books and invoke the conceptual metaphor of the mirror to explain and illuminate some of their narrative aspects. The *fil rouge* of the chapter consists of the various symbolic implications of the concept of the mirror, as related to the mind and the image of the mind. The powerful symbol of the mirror features in the *Alices* in a number of different ways, including the books' narrative construction, their overarching metaphors and the kinds of mental reaction they stimulate in their readers. The complex interconnection between reading and re-imagining is explored in the readers section using the mirror metaphor in the way MacDonald's quote suggests. Carroll's own obsession with mirrors and reversals offers a point of departure from which to develop the conceptual ramifications of the mirror motif, among which are the *mise en abyme*, the cognitive significance of duplication-related processes, double-embedded narratives, mirror neurons, Theory of Mind (ToM) and meta-representational capabilities.

3.1 "The More Head-Downwards I Am, the More I Keep Inventing New Things": The Author

In this section focused upon the author I want to foreground some peculiar uses Carroll made of mirror-related narrative devices, as well as the high degree of

3.1 "The More Head-Downwards I Am, the More I Keep Inventing New Things" —— **69**

Fig. 10: John Tenniel, illustration for *Through the Looking-Glass*, 1871. The White Knight, one of the possible alter-egos Carroll inserted in the *Alices*, is the clumsy, slightly mad inventor, who spends more time turned upside down than standing. This image also shows another reversal: the conceptual inversion of the typical Pre-Raphaelite painting of the knight saving the damsel in distress: here is the little Alice who is helping the knight to get out of a ditch.

symbolic importance he attached to mirror figures in his construction of the *Alice* books. The section follows an expanding theoretical path, starting with Carroll's first introduction of the conceptual function of the mirror, i.e. his use of the *mise en abyme* in *Alice's Adventures in Wonderland* and then going on to show the pervading role it has in relation to Carroll's nonsense writing from a broader perspective.

Carroll's interest in mirrors should be situated in the cultural context of the Victorian Age, that critic Isobel Armstrong defines as "a glass culture" (see *Victorian Glassworlds: Glass Culture and the Imagination 1830–1880*, 2008) and which was characterised by the exploitation of mirror and glass-related motifs in all the diverse fields of culture, with the glass fountain in the Crystal Palace epitomizing this pervasive importance. Armstrong gives a compelling list of cultural elements influenced by this "many-faceted poetics of glass" (16), ranging from the new enthusiasm in the study of optical instruments to the proliferation of glass and crystal objects, decorated mirrors, chandeliers … it is art though the area where the semantic of glass expresses all its complexity. Pre-Raphaelite painters obsessively depict reflecting surfaces, women in front of mirrors, liquid and glassy images; and in Victorian literature (especially Victorian fairy-tales) all the cognitive, philosophical and existential symbolism connected to glass surfaces and mirrors is repeatedly represented and investigated. Carroll's peculiar perspective on mirrors can be analysed following different theoretical ramifications: hence, the re-interpretation of fairy tales' typical motifs, the extensive use of *mise en abyme* to highlight specific meanings, the connection between mirrors and revealing powers (in different senses: spiritual, psychological, satirical ...), are all topics which Carroll explores in the *Alices*. Mirrors are "crystal labyrinths" (Armstrong 2008, 151) in Carroll's novels, a powerful medium through which he gives his readers a kaleidoscope of conceptual extensions.

I begin this section with the topic of mirrors in fairy tales, especially in Victorian ones, and introduce Carroll's own special interest in inversions and duplications. I then show how Carroll makes use of the *mise an abyme* technique in *Alice's Adventures in Wonderland* and explain its specific cognitive importance. I go on to trace the evolution of mirror concepts and experiences in Carroll's narrative worlds, the ultimate realisation of which is the construction of the Looking-Glass Land in the second of the *Alice* book. Here the *mise en abyme* first explored in *Alice in Wonderland* becomes a pervasive narrative element; I elaborate upon the special features of the Looking-Glass world's architecture and the cognitive meaning behind them. I then move from the characteristics of Carroll's storyworlds (or "glassworlds"?) to analysis of the symbolic role of mirror concepts in relation to Carroll's own literary identity. I examine Carroll's representation of himself in the *Alice* books, focusing on his literary doubles as mental projections realised in the literary space. The author section concludes by considering mirrors and language, illustrating the ambivalent role the theoretical conception of language-as-mirror has in Carroll's nonsense poetics.

3.1.1 Magic Mirrors and Lewis Carroll

Throughout his life Charles Dodgson was "obsessed with inversions and reversals in words, mirrors, mirrors-writing, photography, logic, and life itself" (Rackin 1991, 73). He enjoyed playing tunes backwards in musical boxes, he had a vast knowledge of stage-illusions involving mirrors, performed by "magicians" of his time (Fisher 1973, 16–17) and his nom de plume Lewis Carroll was "simply a backwards mirror image of his adult name above the ground and on the outer

3.1 "The More Head-Downwards I Am, the More I Keep Inventing New Things" — 71

Fig. 11: Charles Dodgson, Annie Rogers and Mary Jackson as Queen Eleanor and Fair Rosamund, July 3, 1863.

72 — Chapter 3. Mirrored Alice

Fig. 12: Charles Dodgson, Reflection, 1862. In both these pictures Carroll expresses his fascination with mirrors through the art of photography, which can itself also be considered a sort of mirror-play.

side of the looking-glass" (Rackin 1991, 73).[1] Also his passion for photography has something to reveal about mirrors, since "negatives depicted a world of opposites: left was right and right was left; white was black and black was white" (Douglas-Fairhurst 2015, 187). His interest in reversals and mirrors played a significant part in his life: other examples of this interest are the letters he used to write to his child friends, which had to be held in front of a mirror to be read, or had to be read backwards from the end. He also drew pictures which revealed a different image if turned upside down; and he "invented a new method of multiplication in which the multiplier is written backward and above the multiplicand" (M. Gardner 2001, 149).

The neuroscientist Ramachandran named the neural syndrome that causes the inability to distinguish a real object from a mirrored one "the looking-glass syndrome," after Carroll's book. He wrote

> indeed, Lewis Carroll is known to have suffered from migraine attacks caused by arterial spasms. If they affected his right parietal lobe, he may have suffered momentary confusion with mirrors that might not only have inspired him to write *Through the Looking Glass* but may help explain his general obsession with mirrors, mirror writing and left-right reversal. (1998, 124)

Even if this claim might be inaccurate regarding Carroll's own biographical records, it is nevertheless useful to underline how Carroll's depiction of mirrored realities presents a complex view of the mind's relation with mirrors, even offering insights into possible mental pathologies, and of interest in this respect from the perspective of a neuroscientist like Ramachandran.

Eco in his *Sugli Specchi ed altri Saggi* enumerates a number of possible mirror constructions, or *catoptric theatres*, in which mirrors are used to create illusory effects. Mirrors that multiply themselves and alter virtual images of objects, curved mirrors, plane mirrors superimposed, inclined mirrors, deforming mirrors: in all these cases mirrors function revealingly as signs. They are emblems of artistic creation, in the sense that, as artworks do, they take one's mind beyond a direct link with the referent and establish the possibility of amplifying the content (Eco 1985, 27). This is also what Carroll's mirrors do; they display an additional meaning, disclosing what someone *really* is, or what he or she *could* be. Art is the instrument *par excellence* for creating possible realities or alternative, amplified, distorted visions of actual reality. In other words, art is a

---

[1] The name "Lewis Carroll" was created by Charles Dodgson by translating his first two names "Charles Lutwidge" into Latin as "Carolus Lodovicus", then anglicizing them and reversing their order (Rackin 1991, 72–73).

maker of mirrors; it is accordingly a means to manifest hidden truths and to reveal identities. In this sense, the mirror is set up as a threshold phenomenon, which "marca i confini tra immaginario e simbolico (Eco 1985, 10)."[2] The mirror is also a problematic tool that shows and hides changes. The reflection is identical to what it mirrors, but at the same time is different, exemplifying in this way the paradox of identity: the fact that it often consists in multiple possible coexistent identities, as what Chiara Cappelletto (2009) calls "una nozione caleidoscopica dell'identità (135)."[3]

In a similar way, in fairy tales and myths mirrors often have a magical and revealing function: they show the true nature of the person that they mirror, or they distort it, or they show something different. The mirror has a semiotic function, the specular image always producing a revelation: Narcissus discovers in a reflection the sterile reflexivity of an impossible love withdrawn into self-obsession; the queen of *Snow White* sees in her mirror the beauty of someone else, awakening her own negative side, consumed by anger and envy; the mirror in *The Beauty and the Beast* can show distant and beloved realities, inaccessible in the present moment; in Andersen's *The Snow Queen* the mirror shatters and in doing so also fractures and distorts the identity of the mirrored one; while Cinderella's meaningful glass slipper is nothing but a mirror transformed into a fashionable item. "All mirrors are magic mirrors" (2008, 73), writes MacDonald [1858] in *Phantastes* (published just a few years before *Alice's Adventures in Wonderland*), a book in which "the centrality of the mirror is an intellectual and a material structural component" (Soto 2004, 4). [4]

A more historically situated context, however, would be the prominence of mirrors and glass in Victorian culture, a presence so significant that it leads Armstrong (2008) to claim that the Victorian Age was characterised by "a dazzling semantics of glass" (1). Armstrong in her *Victorian Glassworlds* explores in detail how glass symbolically and practically holds together different aspects of Victorian culture, one she sees as permeated by "the poetics of transparency" (1). In

---

[2] Which "marks the boundaries between the imaginary world and the symbolic one." Eco is here referring to the Lacanian distinction between imaginary and symbolic, where the imaginary mastery of one's mirrored image is preliminary to the symbolic stage, where the recognition develops into linguistic expression. I am quoting this particular sentence in order to show how the mirror works as a means of constructing one's identity, highlighting its powerful role in the formation and understanding of the self.
[3] "A kaleidoscopic notion of identity." (My translation)
[4] Carroll owned a first edition version of *Phantastes* (Lovett 2005, 200), and Shaberman (1982) lists several passages where it is possible to find influences from *Phantastes* in the *Alice* books (17–18).

this sense, Victorian glass can in fact be re-interpreted as being in significant relation to the fantastic and to fairy tales. Victorian interest in fairy tales was extensively mediated by glass-related elements such as magic mirrors, conservatories, newly invented optical lenses and related visual tools (magic lanterns, telescopes, kaleidoscopes, spectroscopes); and infused by the substance of glass itself, characterised by its metamorphic essence. If, as Armstrong points out, the different Victorian adaptations of *Cinderella* produced "a mythography of glass and its transformations" that explores the boundaries "between animate life and human being and human beings and things" (204), other fantastical narratives of the time also elaborated on the poetics of glass, as a symbolic technology, in between science and fairy tale. Apart from the already mentioned magical mirror he invokes in *Phantastes*, MacDonald uses a mirror in *Lilith* to symbolise access to the mystical timeless dimension of the afterlife. Tennyson explores the mysterious power of refraction and reflection in *The Lady of Shallot*, as does Christina Rossetti's *Passing and Glassing*; Prince Dolor in Dinah Mulock Craik's *The Little Lame Prince* uses magic magnifying glasses to watch the world around him; the glacier described by Ruskin in *The King of the Golden River* has the mysterious quality of a hybrid substance, partly ice, partly mirror, partly human-like creature; in Lucy Clifford's dark story *The New Mother* it is the breaking of a looking-glass which causes tragic consequences (while the evil new mother is depicted as having glass eyes); and Kingsley's *The Water Babies*, as Douglas-Fairhurst (2015) remarks, "had entertained readers with an aquatic version of the same [mirror-related] fantasy" (186).

Lewis Carroll thus inserts himself in a rich literary tradition of fairy tales and stories populated by magical mirrors and was sensitive to the intuition that "a mirror resembled a story in other ways: both offered the viewer a neatly framed simulacrum of life; both flattened reality into two dimensions while giving the illusion of depth" (186). However, Carroll's contribution to the interlaced mythography of mirrors and stories represents a particularly complex interpretation of both the traditional fairy tale component and the specifically Victorian cultural device. He offers an original and deep exploration of the intriguing possibilities that mirrors offer for fairy tales, as well as for philosophical meditations and existentialist questioning and merges these different approaches in a rich and inspiring elaboration of the different symbolic implications suggested by the mirror as figure. In this sense, his *Alice* books constantly play with the idea of duplication and reflection, showing the numberless possible ramifications of meaning that these processes entail and highlighting their cognitive potentialities.

Fig. 13: John Tenniel, illustration for *Through the Looking-Glass*, 1871. The illustration of Alice reappearing on the other side of the looking-glass was originally positioned on the next page of the book, playing with mirror-images and efficaciously engaging with the leading concepts of the narration: inversions, *mise en abyme*, duplications.

3.1.2 The Cognitive Significance of Carroll's *Mise en Abymes*

Carroll was playing with logical contradictions and inversions already in *Alice's Adventures in Wonderland* (M. Gardner 2001, 148–149), but it is with *Through the Looking-Glass and What Alice Found There* that the mirror-theme becomes pervasive. Before exploring the multiple, sometimes conflicting, meanings the Looking-Glass Land has for Carroll, however, I would like to examine a mirror-related narrative technique Carroll exploits in both the *Alice* books, the so-called *mise en abyme*.[5] The *mise en abyme*, an artistic technique used in both literature and painting, exemplifies the revealing power of mirror-related devices, since it functions within an artwork as a mirror reflecting and explaining in some way the artwork itself. As Lucien Dällenbach (1977) puts it "est mise en abyme tout miroir interne réfléchissant l'ensemble du récit par réduplication." (48).[6] Famous examples of literary *mises en abyme* are the *One Thousand and One Nights*; the players' play in *Hamlet*, which represents the precipitating events of the drama itself; Narcissus's story in Ovid's *Metamorphoses*; the conversation in the library about *Hamlet*'s plot in Joyce's *Ulysses*; the episode of Demodocus in the *Odyssey*; Cervantes's *Don Quixote*; Poe's *The Fall of the House of Usher*; the play of *Pyramus and Thisbe* in *A Midsummer Night's Dream*. The mirroring effect of the *mise en abyme* can expand the meaning and conceptual apparatus of the story in which it is inserted, enabling it to "rendre l'invisible visible" (100). Following McHale's (2006) statement that *mise en abyme* has "cognitive potential" (178), I would like to show how the specular mechanism used by Carroll enriches the reader's cognitive grasp of the story.

Carroll puts several short stories inside the two main *Alice* stories, and these short narratives work as little mirrors of the main narrations. Due to the nonsensical tissue of the *Alice* books, however, the *mise en abyme* also has a more elaborate and intricate role. I shall consider the Dormouse's story in *Alice's Adventures in Wonderland* as a prominent example. This short narration is about three little sisters, who live in a treacle-well, eat only treacle and spend their time drawing things which begin with the letter "M", "such as mouse-traps, and the moon and memory and muchness" (80). The three little sisters are obviously the Liddell sisters: their names, says the Dormouse, are "Elsie, Lacie,

---

[5] Carroll's mise en abymes do not meet the specifications of a "purist criterion", but they do accord with the "middling definition" he proposes: they maintain a demonstrable relation with the overall story within which they are inserted, and they are ontologically subordinate to the primary world of the story (McHale 2006, 176–177).

[6] "Mise en abyme is every internal mirror reflecting by means of duplication the whole of the story". (my translation)

Fig. 14: Kenneth Rougeau, *Alice Through the Looking-Glass*, 2007. This digital collage which looks like a vintage postcard is the perfect image to illustrate the infinite recursive power of mirrors and of the related *mise en abyme*.

and Tillie" (78), where Elsie is Lorina Charlotte, Lacie is an anagram of Alice and Tillie refers to Edith's nickname Matilda (M. Gardner 2001, 80). At a first glance the Dormouse's story seems as nonsensical as its surroundings, without any specific relation to them, and the reference to "muchness" as "any sort of all-pervading sameness in a situation" (M. Gardner 2001, 82) does not appear to apply to the things the Dormouse is listing. Nevertheless, it is precisely their "muchness" that is the key to the *mise en abyme* role of the story. Looking more closely at the things the little sisters (themselves a mirror of the three Liddells) are drawing inside the treacle-well, it is possible to link each of them with Alice's experiences in Wonderland. Thus "mouse-traps" refer to Alice's first encounter in Wonderland, with the Mouse, and her constant latent predatory attitude towards it (26–28); "the moon" (which is a general figure for the nonsense genre)[7] evokes the Cheshire Cat's grin and its vanishing like "the waning of the moon" (M. Gardner 2001, 63); "memory" is the most problematic mental faculty in Wonderland, emphasised by Alice's persistent forgetfulness (she does not remember how to speak good English, she cannot recall the poems she used to know by heart, and she forgets even her own name and identity). In this sense the three sisters are drawing three main themes of the book, all related to specific features of the mind: latent aggression, lunacy and loss of memory and identity. The *mise en abyme* therefore highlights key topics of the book, serving as a cognitive cue to the narrative's larger meanings.

Additionally, Elsie, Lacie and Tillie live in a treacle-well, and precisely at the bottom of it, which recalls Alice's fall into a deep hole and her finding, during her fall, orange marmalade on the hole's shelves. Treacle and marmalade are sweet and delicious, but here they are associated with a deep and dark well or hole. Wonderland is a place marked by ambivalence, by the first promise of marvellous and pleasant experiences ("the loveliest garden," 16) and the subsequent revelation of madness and confusion ("we're all mad here," 68). The fact that the sisters in the Dormouse's story are drawing things which represent the experience of Wonderland using treacle, is itself another reflexive mechanism, a duplication inside a duplication. The story is a *mise en abyme*, and within it the treacle-drawing act of the three sisters is a further *mise en abyme*.

This single example illustrates in detail the practical use Carroll makes of mirror-related narrative techniques in his *Alice* books, but there are a lot of other possible illustrative cases, including all the parodies Alice and the other characters recite, which are microcosms of the prevailing mocking perspective of the overall narration. The concept of parody itself can be interpreted as a mirror-related form: parodies give us back a modified version of their targets, working as distorting mirrors. Even when the poems or songs are not created by Carroll as explicit parodies, they typically contain elements which function as

---

[7] As M. Gardner (2001) remarks, the moon "has long been associated with lunacy" (63).

mirrors of the general sense, structure and atmosphere of the stories: see for instance the White Knight's song (*TTLG*, 256–259); or the *Jabberwocky* itself, (*TTLG*, 155–156), which in fact has to be held in front of a mirror to be read.

The *Jabberwocky* is a remarkable and significant example, which incorporates several of the peculiar aspects of the Looking-Glass Land. *Jabberwocky* is written in mirror-writing; it is a parody of ancient poetry (it presents itself as "a quasi-heroic narrative poem in which, as in *Beowulf*, a fabulous monster is slain," Haughton 2003, 329); it fragments and deconstructs language and meanings; and, in Tenniel's drawing,[8] it depicts a reversal of the Pre-Raphaelite motif of the knight killing a dangerous dragon, putting little Alice[9] in the place of the armoured knight. Hence, *Jabberwocky* functions as another *mise en abyme*, incorporating features of the whole of *Through the Looking-Glass:* reverse logic, linguistic and semantic deconstruction, parodist attitude, nostalgic outlook towards ancient forms of narration. In conclusion, as these examples emphasise, the *mise en abyme* in the nonsense narrative context of the *Alices* not only has the cognitive function of aiding comprehension of the framing texts, but also contributes further to their complexity and to their multiplication and reshaping of perspectives.

3.1.3 The Looking-Glass Land: A Multi-Faceted Narrative Dimension

It is with the second of the *Alice* books that the mirror topic becomes more and more explicit, being the essence of the story itself and of its represented world. The *mise en abyme* here is no longer simply a narrative technique, but instead is embedded in the content of the whole story, in which everything exists as a duplication with a surplus of meaning. The frequent use of the *mise en abyme* in *Alice's Adventures in Wonderland* introduced Carroll's exploitation of mirror-related techniques of narration; here, in the Looking-Glass Land, mirror motifs provide the essential structure of the entire narration. To recapitulate the major topics briefly: Alice goes through a looking-glass, and this physical and symbolic act marks the beginning of her adventure. The world she finds on the other side is located on a huge chessboard, itself a configuration marked

---

[8] A drawing that Carroll, significantly, at first wanted to be the frontispiece of the book, although he subsequently changed his mind, worried that the image could be frightening for young children (Haughton 2003, 333).
[9] Even though in the poem Carroll mentions a "beamish boy" as the hero fighting the Jabberwocky, in the illustration Tenniel depicts a young person who looks a lot like Alice (see Haughton 2003, 333).

3.1 "The More Head-Downwards I Am, the More I Keep Inventing New Things" — 81

Fig. 15: John Tenniel, Illustration for *Through the Looking-Glass*, 1871. In this colourful version of the original illustration, the elements of parody and reversal, mixed with a sort of nostalgic patina, as discussed above, are plainly visible.

by a contrast of opposites, foreshadowed by the black and the white kittens of the opening scene. It is a world where everything is back to front and upside down: Alice has to run to remain still in the same place, she has to walk in the opposite direction to where she intends to go, she quenches her thirst with dry biscuits, she discovers that looking-glass cakes have to be handed round first and then cut and that memory there refers to future events. The mirror structure works at many different narrative levels, from the architectural aspects of the fictional world to the writing methods used to construct it, from the philosophical reflections the story provokes to the personal psychological connotations it had for Carroll himself.

Philosophical considerations related to the figure of the mirror are pervasive in *Through the Looking-Glass*. Jonathan Holt (2001) mentions Baudrillard's concept of simulacra as a possible analogue for the deconstruction, reconstruction and alteration of reality (leading to the creation of a "hyperreality") realised in the Carrollian world on the other side of the mirror. Alice has to navigate this new dimension, which presents her with different ways of thinking, new possibilities for perceiving and conceptualising space and time, altered languages and nameless identities.

> In the Looking Glass World, the logic of knowledge, of identity, of language, and of reason are broken down to their most basic parts and projected into a construct that is at once the same as and different than our own reality. By the time she wakes from her nap in front of the fire, Alice has been forced to hold every aspect of herself up before a mirror, and learned to question everything. (Holt 2001)

The conceivability of unnatural worlds is another aspect of Alice's encounter with the Looking-Glass Land, where even the categories of the possible and impossible experience a reversal.[10] A further philosophical nuance of the world on the other side of the mirror has been teased out by Ackerman in *Behind the Looking-Glass* (2008), which emphasises the mystical qualities attributed to the mirror in Neoplatonist, Theosophical and spiritualist beliefs, all currents of mystical thought in which Carroll was interested. Going through the mirror, according to this perspective, means leaving material illusions behind and gaining access to the knowledge of Forms (23–24). Alice's journey through the looking-glass thus acquires additional meaning as a symbolic mental pilgrimage through the privileged means of dreaming, in order

---

10 Experiencing the unnatural in the *Alices* is one of the main topics of the fifth chapter, "Unnatural Alice".

> to explore the mysteries of interiority, of moods and motives, inner conflicts and contradictions, memories and dreams, to bring the unconscious into consciousness, to experience extreme and ineffable states of consciousness, and to know the infinite. (33)

Another quality of the land Alice finds through the mirror has more existential features, as well as stylistic reverberations. Embedded in the narrative world of the second *Alice* book there is a nostalgia for a lost past, articulated in different, and even self-contradictory ways. On the one hand, in the Looking-Glass world, "things go the other way," everything seems to be going backwards. "*Looking-Glass* is haunted by the past," with its stylistic reminiscences of "Spenserean romance and German fairy tales" (Haughton 2003, xlviii), along with the presence of Medieval characters and creatures from nursery-rhymes and explicit moments of almost lyrical melancholy. Equally directed towards the past is the essential idea upon which the book is founded, that of making Alice, who by that time was nineteen, into a seven-year-old child again, in order to go back to the summery golden days of childhood and Wonderland. On the other hand, the reversal also reverses itself: in the world where things go back, Alice manages to go ahead. She proceeds across the chessboard, following her goal of becoming a queen, although in the end, as before in the lovely garden in Wonderland, it turns out to be a dissatisfying and absurd experience. While Carroll tries to defeat the cold winter days of the other side of the Looking-Glass (where Alice sees "the snow against the windowpanes," 146) by recreating the first Alice, moving through a summery land of wonders, in the event his story rebels against itself. As Douglas-Fairhurst concludes,

> it is as if Carroll needed to include a private story within the public one, even if the sight of Alice leaving these bumbling and grumbling figures behind was a way of tapping one of the most common plots in the world. Children grow up. They move on. (2015, 193)

Therefore, the mirror-like architecture of the second *Alice* book permeates the conceptual tissue of the story at different levels, philosophical, existentialist and psychological, and also offers a meta-reflection on the essence of narrative itself. The story is a dream, as was Wonderland, but with a difference: in Wonderland the dream was Alice's, and afterwards became Alice's sister's, suggesting the idea of a continuity of re-dreaming and re-telling. In the Looking-Glass Land the dreamer of the dream is not known for sure and the idea of an interconnection of two dreams is introduced. Tweedledum and Tweedledee point out to Alice that she is just "a sort of thing" in the Red King's dream (198), while Alice is dreaming her adventures in the looking-glass, dreaming of herself and of the Red King dreaming about her. As already quoted in chapter two, Martin Gardner (2001) says about this passage: "an odd sort of infinite regress is involved here in the parallel dreams of Alice and the Red King. Alice dreams of the King, who is dreaming of Alice, who is dreaming of the King, and so on, like two mirrors facing each other" (198).

What I would like to add here is that the metaphor of the mirror and its pervasive presence in the book, is a particularly useful conception of this recursive process, established not only between the fictional world and character's minds, but also with respect to the reader's mind. Alice jumps through the mirror and finds a parallel world that functions as a revelation and a parodic mirror of the "real" one, while this framework mirrors readers' immersion in the book itself and the revealing mirror it holds up to their own world and its complexities. The double dream logic running through the story shows how the creative process is entangled with the re-creative process of reading, and at the same time mirrors the complicated relationship between the author and his main character.

3.1.4 Carroll's Own Literary Doubles

The representation through the mirror metaphor of the complex relationship between Carroll and Alice also entails that Carroll uses it in order to present literary doubles of his own self. The Red King dreaming of Alice can be interpreted as a conceptual metaphor of the author dreaming of the story and determining the life and vicissitudes of the characters, while at the same time being influenced by the characters themselves. Carroll had already inserted characters mirroring his role as author and as Alice's friend, in *Alice's Adventures in Wonderland:* he appears at the beginning, during the Caucus-Race, disguised as the Dodo,[11] one of the first encounters Alice has in Wonderland. His self-representation as a Dodo was motivated by his stammer, which made him pronounce his surname as "Do-Do-Dodgson" (M. Gardner 2001, 28). The Dodo is a funny looking bird with a terrible story behind it (Dodos were extinct because they were exterminated by humans, M. Gardner2001, 28); it is a tragicomic figure that anticipates somehow the other literary doubles who would appear in the second of the *Alice* books.

Nevertheless, in *Alice's Adventures in Wonderland* the separation between the author and his main character is much less pronounced than in *Through the Looking-Glass:* in Wonderland Carroll actually often identifies himself with

---

[11] Among the Caucus-Race's participants Carroll inserts the actual members of the boat expedition where he first told the Wonderland story: the Duck is the Reverend Duckworth, the Lory is Lorina Liddell, the Eaglet is Edith Liddell and the Dodo, Carroll himself (Haughton 2003, 304).

his heroine. His actual proximity with the real Alice, his being still a young man, his book being his first children's book, all contribute to make the fictional Alice not only a surrogate of Alice Liddell, but of the author himself. Morton Cohen (1995) argues that "Alice and her adventures would not have materialised had the boy Charles Dodgson not earlier lived through those trials and adventures" (145). The experience of the little girl trying to understand a world of weird and aggressive creatures, using her sense of humour and her survival skills, matches Carroll's own personal history, the history of a delicate little boy who had always been more similar to (and more at ease with) little girls than athletic and bullying boys (18–22) and who had used his wit and cleverness to find his path in the world. Morton Cohen writes that the heroine of Wonderland "is really Charles himself in disguise" (215), and in this sense the first Alice can be considered as a mirror of him; the formula *Alice c'est moi* can properly define Carroll's relationship to his character. The author's own mind produces a projection of itself in Alice's wandering in a land of bizarre beings, confronting the (pre-) Freudian lapsus, madness, dreams and memory-related issues: "no novelist has identified more intimately with the point of view of his heroine" (Levin 1974, 221).

In the Looking-Glass world the situation is quite different: "Charles plays several roles in this book" (M. Cohen 1995, 215). The mirror multiplies his identity into several distinct, but in the end similar, figures. Apart from the already mentioned Red King dreaming of Alice, it is highly plausible that Carroll depicted himself as the White Knight, and probably also as his counterpart, the Red Knight. Morton Cohen states that Carroll *is* the White Knight, because of the several resemblances between the two (215–216); Martin Gardner (2001) observes that "many Carrollian scholars have surmised, and with good reason, that Carroll intended the White Knight to be a caricature of himself," and goes on to enumerate the many characteristics Carroll shares with this character (249–250); and Taylor named his biography of Carroll *The White Knight*. The comparison with the Red Knight is less popular, though Morton Cohen mentions it (215), but I argue that if we accept Carroll's identification with the White Knight, we are led to admit that then he is also the Red Knight, because the latter is the manifest counterpart, the "dark side," of the former. The duplication mechanism becomes almost obsessive: Carroll, who is already Charles Dodgson's double, creates the White Knight as his literary double, who has in turn his own double in the Red Knight, as well as in the Wasp of the suppressed chapter "The Wasp in a Wig" (chapter to be found in *The Annotated Alice* 2001, 293–315).

We are thus left with the impression of a never-ending duplication process, a perpetual projection and re-projection of the self, as if desperately trying to catch an ultimate meaning, which is always further displaced. The human mind can be drawn deep into its own twists and turns just by attempting a self-observation from above; that is, by trying to duplicate and study itself from a transcendent perspective, which is the defining paradox of the mind that tries to analyse itself. The problematic of objectivity in any kind of auto-analysis is well highlighted by Carroll: he represents himself as the gentle, caring White Knight, but he is also the Red Knight, who wants to make Alice his prisoner (*TTLG*, 245–246). In the just-mentioned suppressed episode he is also the Wasp, an old and whining individual, and it is probably no accident that he tries to keep Alice behind the brook, preventing her from becoming a Queen, immediately after she has taken leave, too hastily, from the White Knight. Several similarities between the Wasp and the Knight are identified and listed by Martin Gardner (2001): Alice "waves good-bye to the White Knight with a handkerchief; the Wasp has a handkerchief around his face. The White Knight talks about bees and honey; the Wasp thinks Alice is a bee and asks her if she has any honey" (301). If the White Knight sings a melancholy song about "an aged aged man", the Wasp *is* an aged aged man. In a "somewhat terrifying scene" (314) the Wasp reaches out a claw to remove Alice's hair; similarly, the White Knight grabs hold of Alice's hair to save himself from falling for the umpteenth time from his horse. Their pathetic attachment to Alice (which can be read as a mirror of Carroll's own) seems to be related to some kind of violent instinct; the same kind of violent instinct that makes the Red Knight willing to fight to keep Alice imprisoned with him in his chessboard square. The mirror of literature reflects back to Carroll his own identity, but even this last one is doubled, divided between what he would like to be and in part is,

and in what he would not like to be but in part is. "Alice's encounter with all three of these pitiful characters is a transparent exaggeration of what had happened in real life to Charles and his favourite child friend" (M. Cohen 1995, 217).

3.1.5 Language Is Not a Mirror: Looking-Glass Insects

The problematic essence of the Looking-Glass Land seems comparable to the complexity of the role of language itself. Both language and the magic mirror reflect outside reality, and, in reflecting it, they forcefully re-elaborate it; nonetheless, reality cannot be expressed without such re-elaboration. The Carrollian language of nonsense, however, manages to depict this representational conflict, within the means of representation itself. Nonsense portrays the lack of a perfect correspondence, using language to highlight the limits of language.

Carroll makes these theoretical considerations explicit in the chapter "Looking-Glass Insects" (177–188). Alice's encounter with these absurd creatures is accompanied by continuous linguistic games, paradoxes and meta-linguistic references, with the Gnat making silly jokes playing on a supposed similarity between words and "real things". The insects themselves "are not insects at all but compounds of words" (Sewell 1952, 128–129). In this chapter Carroll "sets real and unreal names side by side, and creates imaginary insects by adding a second adjective or substantive to a name that is already compounded of a substantive and an adjective (or substantive)" (Haughton 2003, 337). The melancholy Gnat enumerates to Alice several insects' names, showing how their weird physical appearance mimics the paradoxical features expressed in their names. So, the Rocking-horse-fly is a wooden insect which looks like a miniature of a rocking-horse, "swinging itself from branch to branch" (182); the Snap-dragon-fly[12] is made of plum-pudding, lives in a Christmas-box and has a raisin burning in brandy as its head; the Bread-and-butter-fly has thin slices of bread and butter as wings, "its body is a crust and its head is a lump of sugar" (184).

Alice says to the Gnat that she knows some insects' names herself (182–183), but the Gnat observes "what's the use of their having names, if they won't answer to them?" (182). Alice explains "no use to *them*, but it's useful to the people that name them, I suppose. If not, why do things have names at all?" (182). The Gnat and Alice are here expressing two different notions of language: language as answerable to its referents and language as a pragmatic tool of its users, independent of any resemblance between name and thing. Alice assumes that names are conceived for a purpose, that they are (arbitrarily) chosen for practical use (this conception will be taken to its extremes in Humpty Dumpty's tyrannical and solipsistic naming practice). The Gnat points out to Alice the existing connection between the names of the Looking-Glass insects and their actual appearance, to underline how there must be a direct correspondence between names and things. The Gnat keeps making obsessive jokes about this supposed correspondence, but their effect is to make the insect "so unhappy" (185): firstly, because jokes in the Looking-Glass world have the opposite effect to the one they would "normally" have, making people sad instead of provoking laughter; secondly, because it is precisely in this mirrored world on the other side of the Looking-Glass that words are shown *not* to be mirrors. In fact, the fragile lives of the insects show the precariousness of a theoretical conception of language as the mirror of the external world. The Snap-dragon-fly has a head burning in flames, while the Bread-and-butter-fly can eat only "weak tea with cream in it" (184), and, since this is very difficult to find, its final destiny is to starve to death ("it always happens", remarks the Gnat to Alice, 184).

---

[12] Snapdragon was a game which Victorian children used to play during the Christmas season: for a longer explanation, see M. Gardner 2001, 184.

It is worth noticing that the Gnat, so eager to prove the link between words and things, is the only insect without a name revealing its nature. The main characteristic of the Gnat is its continuous deeply melancholic sighing: as Eco writes,

> il sogno semiotico di nomi propri che siano immediatamente legati al loro referente (così come il sogno semiotico di un'immagine che abbia tutte le proprietà dell'oggetto a cui è riferita) nasce proprio da una sorta di *nostalgia catrottica*. (Eco 1985, 21) [13]

This nostalgia is consuming the Gnat, which, while yearning for a world of specular correspondences, "sighed itself away" (185), just as Echo, obsessively mirroring the words Narcissus *does not* speak to her, dissolves in the air, consuming herself with an impossible desire.[14]

In creating this Looking-Glass world of repetitions, reversions and distortions, Carroll keeps running after an ultimate sense, whilst showing how this is unreachable: identities are duplicated and never univocal; roads go back and forth at the same time; places (like the location of the Mad Tea Party and Tweedledum and Tweedledee's house) are bidirectional;[15] the author's own self is fragmented into different self-projections; language is slippery and ineffable. The mind cannot see itself perfectly reflected in the mirror, because the mirror gives back more meaning, or less, or a distorted one. The ultimate meaning, like Alice's dream-rushes (*TTLG*, 214–215), remains out of reach, ephemeral and inconsistent. As Anna Rosa Scrittori affirms

> il divario tra segno linguistico e referente si manifesta in una sorta di paradigma della non coincidenza – tra significato e significante, tra il soggetto e la sua memoria, tra il desiderio e la realtà – che chiamiamo appunto nonsense. (2003, 290) [16]

Carroll's nonsense writing, with its emblematic and melancholic Looking-Glass insects, represents this ineffability and this discrepancy.

---

[13] "The semiotic dream of proper names immediately linked to their referents (as well as the semiotic dream of an image holding all the proprieties of its referred object) has its roots in a sort of *catoptric nostalgia*" (my translation).

[14] Echo, condemned by the Goddess Hera to be unable to speak except to repeat someone else's last words, keeps repeating Narcissus's words, words meant to reject her. See Ovid [8 AD], *Metamorphoses* 2015, bk. 3, vv. 402–510.

[15] A more detailed explanation of this concept in the next section.

[16] "The separation between the linguistic sign and the referred object shows itself in a sort of paradigm of non-correspondence – between signified and signifier, between the subject and his memory, between desire and reality – a paradigm which we call nonsense." (my translation)

Fig. 16: Illustration for *Episodes of Insect Life*, Acheta Domestica (pseudonym of Louise Budgen). This book is one of the several examples showing the Victorians' fascination with entomology and the way they often mixed up fairy tale creatures with insects: "fairies made frequent appearances in Victorian entomology, as fanciful works played on the supposed similarities between insects and fairies, from size to wings to movement to ephemerality" (Keene 2015, 55). Carroll's Looking-Glass insects, imaginary creatures made out of wordplay, are possibly a parody of this attitude.

3.2 "So You Are Another Alice": The Character(s)

> To the Looking-Glass world it was Alice that said
> 'I've a sceptre in my hand I've a crown on my head.
> Let the Looking-Glass creatures, whatever they be
> Come and dine with the Red Queen, the White
> Queen, and me!'
> (*TTLG*, 273)

In this section I show how the mirror mechanisms of duplication and inversion function as essential elements in shaping the *Alice* books' characters and their

Fig. 17: Screenshot from Walt Disney's *Alice in Wonderland*, 1951. Despite the numerous changes the Disney movie forces upon the Carrollian books, a particularly visually interesting representation, and one which the original book lacks, is the one of the bread-and-butterflies.

minds. The argument of this section moves from analysis of the multiple double identities of the central character (Alice), to a general claim about the doubleness inherent in *all* of Carroll's characters. The last part turns to investigation of the characters' interactions with each other, focusing on the mirror-related mechanisms of the mind reading process in Wonderland and in the Looking-Glass world. Accordingly, I first present the different transformations Alice has to deal with, in her real and fictional life, examining the different identities the mirror of literature gives back to her and their complex significance. Secondly, I expand the perspective to include the ubiquitous duplication of characters in the Carrollian worlds, especially in the Looking-Glass one and the reflections on identity and alterity that this duplication inspires. Thirdly, I further extend the topic of doubleness in Carroll's narrative scenarios by focusing on the interactions between characters and on the role the concept of "doubly embedded narratives" (Palmer 2005, 230) has in this interplay, that is, how fictional minds are reflected (or not reflected, in this case) in other fictional minds and the peculiarity of the *Alice* books in this respect.

3.2.1 Queen Alice

When Humpty Dumpty points out to Alice that the best thing for her would be to "leave off at seven", since seven years old is a kind of perfect irreplaceable age, and she replies "one can't help growing any older", he retorts "one can't, perhaps ... but two can" (*TTLG*, 222). Douglas-Fairhurst (2015) highlights the importance of this dialogue in order to grasp the relationship between Alice and her creator: fictional girls, he observes, have the power of remaining forever young (185). This is why it is impossible for us to disentangle Alice from 'Alice', the real girl from the literary character: they merged in Carroll's fantasy and they will be forever merged in our own imagination, even though Alice Hargreaves (Alice Liddell's married name) was herself moved to remark, "I am tired of being Alice in Wonderland!" (Douglas-Fairhurst 2015, 5). The dialogue with Humpty Dumpty seems to barely conceal a kind of murderous purpose, but Carroll's solution is a little less violent: the duplication of Alice, the creation of an eternal papery heroine, is the other possible way to keep the little girl in a perennial youth.

Therefore, the first, basic duplication, and the foundation of the *Alice* books' construction, is the projection of Alice into 'Alice'. The literary mirror gives back an image of the immortal little Alice. It is not the first time this kind of literary transformation has happened: Borges (2001) emphasises how Dante, because he could not have Beatrice, closed her up in the infinite literary dream of the *Divina Commedia*, trapping her in the sublimity of the Pure White Rose, repeating in his literary dream his unfulfilled love. In a similar sense, Alice becomes 'Alice', a little Beatrice forever young in the impossible lands of Wonderland and of the Looking-Glass world. Carroll wrote about Alice, after meeting her as a grown-up woman,

> it was not so easy to link in one's mind the new face with the older memory, the stranger with the so intimately known and loved 'Alice', whom I shall always remember as an entirely fascinating seven-year-old maiden. (Wakeling 1993, 465)

If the first mirrored Alice is the fictional Alice, the same fictional girl experiences several other duplications within the storyworlds. The mirror mechanism becomes more subtle and complex, and is connected to Alice's different mental attitudes, which themselves represent different fragments of her identity. My claim is that in *Alice in Wonderland* Alice's identity ultimately merges with that of the Queen of Hearts, finding in her a secret counterpart (whereas in the Looking-Glass Land the process of becoming a Queen will be explicit, and stated from the beginning as Alice's goal). This is not to encapsulate the multiple and inexhaustible meanings of *Alice in Wonderland* in a progressive identification between Alice and the Queen of Hearts; as it is well known, and as my analysis aims to reaffirm, any attempt to attribute an ultimate, definitive significance to the *Alice* books is destined to fail. However, it is worth pointing out that Alice's journey in Wonderland is also a demystification process, in which she gradually loses all the ingrained habits and restrictions of her normal life and manifests more and more instinctive impulses and aggressive, predatory behaviours. This transformation is mirrored in the different characters she meets (Milli Graffi, 2000, notes how "ogni personaggio che si oppone ad Alice è anche una parte di sé stessa", xvi);[17] and she finds her final and most comprehensive reflection in the figure of the Queen of Hearts. As Jenny Karlsson (2009) states, "Alice's adventures in Wonderland reflect the child-adult conflict of Alice on her inner quest for identity" (11).

The Queen of Hearts is created by Carroll "as a sort of embodiment of ungovernable passion – a blind and aimless Fury" (Carroll, "Alice on the Stage") and in her Alice finds her own alter-ego: her whole dream-journey down the rabbit-hole is a crescendo of allusions to death and violence, showing Alice's aggressive side and culminating in the Queen of Hearts' uncontrollable rage. References to eating and being eaten and to creatures killing each other, start to appear immediately, even while Alice is still falling, with her "do cats eat bats? Do cats eat bats? Do bats eat cats?" (14). Immediately afterwards, she approaches the Mouse and continuously talks about her cat Dinah and her habit of catching mice, unable to stop herself from touching upon the topic (26–28). As the story unfolds the incidents of violence turn more and more explicit: Alice kicking the little lizard (44); the crocodile's jaws (23); the Duchess tossing the baby "violently up and down" (64); the Cheshire cat's "*very* long claws" and "great many teeth" (66); the macabre story of the Mock Turtle (94–103); the suppression of the guinea pigs in canvas bags (119). This escalating violence reaches its climax with the trial and Alice's evidence, when Alice herself reacts violently against her own dream.

Alice's habit of virtually doubling herself is stated at the beginning of both the *Alice* books. Immediately after her fall into the rabbit hole Carroll says of her that she is "very fond of pretending to be two people" (18), while just before going through the mirror we learn how she enjoys the "let's pretend" game, imagining being someone else. In particular, she had recently pretended to be "a hungry hyaena," asking her nurse to be a bone, really frightening the poor nurse (147). There is from the beginning a hinted connection between the dou-

---

[17] "Each character that confronts Alice is also a part of her own identity". (my translation)

bled Alice and the revelation of a predatory and aggressive self. In Wonderland Alice's identification with the Queen is just a subtle suggestion, whereas in the Looking-Glass world she will actually become a Queen. Thus, both journeys can be viewed as long and bizarre dreamy paths which finally lead Alice towards a Queen: in Wonderland to her secret double, the Queen of Hearts, in the Looking-Glass world to herself becoming a Queen, alongside the Red Queen and the White Queen. Considering both of Alice's experiences, it seems that being a Queen in the *Alices* is somehow metaphorically connected to something dangerous, with negative connotations; to the loss of someone (the White Knight in *Through the Looking-Glass*) and to the unstoppable explosion of passions.

The "loveliest garden" (16) that Alice has aimed to reach since the beginning of her adventures in Wonderland and which reveals itself to be the triumph of Chaos, first welcomes her with the awkward scene of the gardener-cards painting white roses red (83). They are violating the delicate and ethereal nature of the white roses, which in the language of flowers symbolise purity. In the Victorian period the language of flowers was common knowledge; Carroll himself plays with it in his parody of Tennyson's *Maud* in the chapter "The Garden of Live Flowers" (165–176). Here in the Queen's garden the pure white roses are forced to become red, the colour of violence and passion. The white innocent Victorian Alice becomes the red and wild Queen of Hearts. My interpretation is that, faced with this antithetical mirror image, Alice rebels against the Card Queen, becoming as aggressive and violent as her (*AAIW*, 129–130).

Alice's waking identity finds its final deconstruction in the last confrontation with her dream-counterpart. Tiresias, in the Greek myth of Narcissus, had predicted that Narcissus could have survived only "si se non noverit"[18] (Ovid [8 AD] 2015, bk. 3, vv. 344–348), so when Narcissus looks in the water and sees his mirrored image, he is condemned to death. Alice destroys her own dream, and with it the identity the mirror of dreams has given back to her, in the moment when she fully realises it by taking the Queen of Hearts' role in guiding the final trial (129). She aggressively reacts against Wonderland, screaming "you're nothing but a pack of cards!" (129), whereas the King of Hearts had previously said to the Queen "she is only a child!" (86). At the end of her hallucinatory journey of initiation she has learnt the other half of her identity and, to forget this unpleasant discovery, "such difficult self-knowledge" (Marcus 1984, 184), she has to wake up. The Gryphon has previously said to Alice, about the Queen, "it's all her fancy, that: they never execute nobody, you know" (99): *it's all her fancy* can as well be used to explain all Alice's vicissitudes in Wonderland; or

---

[18] "If he had not known himself". (my translation)

at least it is the necessary explanation Alice gives to herself to cope with the alarming realities she has discovered in her "curious dream" (130).

There is one last duplication Alice experiences, in the Looking-Glass dimension, but this one is a biographical one: a cousin of Carroll, Alice Raikes, claimed that an incident between her and Carroll when she was a child was at the origin of his ideas about the Looking-Glass land. Apparently, he addressed her saying "So you are another Alice. I'm fond of Alices" and then he led her in front of a mirror with an orange in her right hand, asking her in which hand the girl in the mirror was holding the orange. This other Alice said "if I was on the other side of the glass, wouldn't the orange still be in my right hand?". [19] Even if this episode was clearly not the only inspiration behind the second of the *Alice* books, it is nonetheless significant, in the sense that it introduces a further complication to the several duplications Alice experiences, a further step away from any single and stable identity for one distinct Alice. I would like to conclude by showing how the turmoil and violence latent in Alice's experience of doubled identity is well expressed in these lines from Allen Tate:

> "Turned absent-minded by infinity
> She cannot move unless her double move,
> The All-Alice of the world's entity
> Smashed in the anger of her hopeless love,
> Love for herself who, as an earthly twain,
> Pouted to join her two in a sweet one;
> No more the second lips to kiss in vain
> The first she broke, plunged through the glass alone." (1973, vv. 13–20)

3.2.2 Two Sides of the Same Coin? Mirrored Characters

If Alice discovers, through her doubles the Queen of Cards and the Queen of Chess, that she can be a tyrannical monarch and at the same time a piece in a manipulated and nonsensical game, the surplus of meaning made possible by the artistic device of duplication works with other characters as well. The kind of disclosure Alice experiences through duplication is a general effect for the characters in Carroll's worlds. The doubling of worlds, senses and identities is first alluded to in Wonderland, where the characters are constructed according to a pervasive mechanism of doubling which functions as a complex enlargement of cognitive frameworks. This happens first with Alice herself, then also with the other creatures she meets in her adventures. Sewell (1952) highlights

---

19 Episode recounted by Haughton 2003, xxxviii and M.N. Cohen 1989b, 196–197.

that "nonsense is a game which requires opposition between two forces, not the reconciliation of the two nor the complete suppression of one or other" (163). In the *Alices* this existence of two opposites (different pairs of opposites, as we shall see) permeates the stories, dictating the construction of the characters themselves and functioning as the main criterion in defining their personal traits.

In accordance with this logic, the Cheshire Cat tells Alice that if she goes on walking in one direction she will find a Hatter, while in the *other* direction there will be a March Hare. Actually, Alice finds both of them in the direction she chooses, which, indeed, is not an unequivocal choice (*AAIW*, 69–72). Carroll's paradoxical narrative worlds are characterised by the coexistence of the two senses (or sense and non-sense) simultaneously, the two directions at the same time (Deleuze 1969, 76). The Mad Hatter and the March Hare, with their similar names, are each the mirror of the other, trapped in a bidirectional place and in a timeless tea party. If the Looking-Glass world *in itself* can be conceived as a duplication of Wonderland, where "Alice I would become Alice II by passing through a mirror into Looking-Glass Land" (Douglas-Fairhurst 2015, 185) and where other characters from the first book reappear (189), all the characters presented in the second of the *Alice* books have a counterpart. The book begins with a black kitten and a white one; the chess pieces Alice meets obviously are always two (the Red Queen and the White one, the White Knight and the Red Knight …); and then there are Tweedledum and Tweedledee, Haigha and Hatta and the Lion and the Unicorn.

The topic of bidirectional places, introduced with the Mad Hatter and the March Hare in Wonderland, is taken up again in the Looking-Glass world with Tweedledum and Tweedledee's house. Alice finds two signs, "TO TWEEDLE-DUM'S HOUSE" and "TO THE HOUSE OF TWEEDLEDEE," and she assumes that they point to different destinations, but then finds out that they lead to the same house *(TTLG*, 188). The two inscriptions are left-right inversions, "in keeping with the fact that Carroll intended the two brothers to be mirror images of each other" (M. Gardner 2001, 188). Rackin (1991) underlines how Alice's reflection upon discovering that there is just one house – "I wonder I never thought of that before" (188) – shows that Alice now begins to understand how the different sides of herself are ascribable to the doubleness inherent in one single person (79). Tweedledum and Tweedledee are twins, and "twins are a special case of looking-glass doubling […] their penchant for 'Contrariwise' conversation represents a different kind of mirror effect, inversion" (Haughton 2003, 339). The two twins would like to be two different persons, and they fight against each other, but actually they are only two diverse aspects of one individual not conciliated with himself: "they are deluded like the self-enamoured Narcissus of ancient myth" (Rackin 1991, 80). While Narcissus would like to duplicate himself in order to be able to love himself, Tweedledum and Tweedledee represent a narcissistic stage of growing-up, a splitting in two of the self for autocontemplation. The mirror effects created by Carroll in this case are helpful to enlighten the complex psychological aspects of the possible (or impossible) conciliation between the different sides of one personality.

Other characters who embody the figure of the double are Hatta and Haigha, a "double double", who are at the same time two parallel creatures and the mirrored version of the Mad Hatter and the March Hare. Then there are the Lion and the Unicorn, perennially together and perennially fighting. At the same time the Unicorn's thoughts about Alice are a reversal of Alice's own opinions about him ("one of the most beautiful of the looking-glass's inversions", Haughton 2003, 347): when the Unicorn first sees her, he "stood for some time looking at her with an air of the deepest disgust" (241), hardly believing she is real and alive. He says that he has always thought children were fabulous monsters;[20] after Alice replies that she has always had the same idea about unicorns, he tells her "if you'll believe in me, I'll believe in you" (241). Nevertheless, a short while after this agreement between Alice and the Unicorn, the absurd existence of one reciprocated by the absurd existence of the other, the Unicorn describes her again as a legendary monster (244); and Alice's first thought after they part is "that she must have been dreaming about the Lion and the Unicorn" (245). Alice and the Unicorn are each other's mirror image, showing the fragility and ephemerality of each other's existence. Which one is more unreal? The non-existent entity par excellence or the forever young little girl lost in nonsense dreams?

This powerful looking-glass inversion leads to further reflections on the mystery of similarity and dissimilarity involved in the multiform relationship of identity and alterity. In the Looking-Glass Land the boundaries between appearance and reality, alterity and identity, dreamed and dreamer are constantly blurred and interchangeable. The ill-defined dividing line between the two opposites in each pair does not provide for either a rigid opposition or a complete conciliation (see the above quote by Sewell); but also, the nature of the opposition between these pairs is itself unstable. By this I mean that the set of oppositions Carroll presents, whether embodied in two different characters or within the same one, themselves have overlapping traits. The dreamer can be identified with oneself, while the dreamed one is the other, or the other way around. The dream can be the appearance, but also the dream can actually coincide with reality. Using the mirror as a conceptual device to create complex opposi-

---

[20] A similar device is Swift's depiction of the Houyhnhnms in *Gulliver's Travels*.

tions and problematic doubles, Carroll is able to explore the heterogeneous meanings and ramifications of his characters' doubleness.

3.2.3 "Impenetrability! That's What *I* Say!": *Here* Minds Are Not Mirrors

Palmer's (2005) approach of applying discourses on real minds to the understanding of fictional ones (86–170) implies also what he defines as "the doubly embedded narrative" (230), which involves the duplication of "a character's mind as contained within another character's mind" (231). Palmer emphasises that "*all* fiction is read by means of doubly embedded narratives" (231) and subsequently outlines different ways in which these doubly embedded narratives may work: as an individual's representation of another individual, or as an individual's thoughts about a group, or as a group's ideas about an individual (233). On the other hand, Uri Margolin (1996) proposes a fundamental distinction between presentations of a character's mind, contrasting ontological and epistemic versions (114–115). The former refers to a character's mind as presented in the storyworld of a third person narrative, while the latter consists in the ideas another character has of it. Palmer questions Margolin's distinction in the sense that, although it might be applicable to many novels, in others "the ontologically real character is less real than the epistemological versions" (233). Palmer's approach is thus more flexible and open to "how the various embedded and doubly embedded narratives interweave, merge, conflict, become reconciled, and so on. Rich and complex patterns result" (233).

In relation to the *Alice* books, Margolin's distinction is not really applicable, since our main frame of reference is only Alice's mind: as readers we are dealing with the narrative mechanism of internal focalisation. Consequently, most of our constructions about the other characters are related to Alice's own impressions, the ontological and the epistemic coinciding. Moreover, these impressions are rather subjective, since "she discovers that she has entered a world in which she has no access to anyone else's thoughts" (Douglas-Fairhurst 2015, 149).[21] If sometimes we cannot access Alice's thoughts, "it is because she has the opacity of a real person", whereas "every character we encounter in Wonderland (and in the Looking-Glass Land) is flat" (Douglas-Fairhurst, 149). In consequence, Alice cannot read the other characters' minds; all the creatures she encounters are

---

21 As I explain in the next paragraph, the minds of Wonderland and Looking-Glass creatures are not even partly readable. Real-life minds and realistic characters have behaviours, speeches and attitudes that suggest what they are thinking; Carroll's creatures, however, do not follow any recognizable logic of behaving or talking.

completely indecipherable. With characters modelled on real minds "the reader infers the working of fictional minds and sees these minds in action from observation of characters' behaviour and actions" (Palmer 2005, 246), and this is how readers grasp Alice's mind. But the other characters in the *Alices* do not have any form of comprehensible behaviour which can help Alice (and with her the readers) to understand what is going on in their minds, or if they have minds at all.

As Douglas-Fairhurst (2015) highlights, in the worlds of the *Alice* books "believable psychology is replaced by obscure or absent motivation, and conversations are always on the verge of disintegrating into catchphrases" (149). We cannot find the minds of the characters mirrored in other characters' minds: on the one hand, the Wonderland and Looking-Glass creatures are inaccessible by any means, and the only thing Alice can often detect is their aggressive attitude towards her (although the reason behind it is not clear).[22] Alice cannot really know what they think about her, or if they have any internal representation of her own mind. On the other hand, Alice's own mental constructions about other characters' minds are blank, because she has no comprehensible clues on which to build. For instance, why is the Duchess throwing the baby around the kitchen? Why is the Queen of Hearts so mad at everyone? Is the Mock Turtle really saddened by his soup destiny? What are the Red Queen and the White Queen thinking? All of these questions have the same answer as the famous "why is a raven like a writing desk?" (*AAIW*, 73). In Carroll's worlds conversations are dominant, but they don't follow any cooperative principle of conversation (see Lecercle 1994, 69–114), and don't give any substance to the speakers, whose purposes and personalities remain flat and non-existent. "The result is that nonsense, not a mimetic genre, does not construct characters, but rather presents eccentricities, more often than not quirks of language" (71).

There is, though, one exception to the impossibility of reflecting each other's mind in the *Alice* books, even if in a unilateral direction. There is one character who has direct access to Alice's mind, who can read her thoughts as if they were his own: I am referring to the Blue Caterpillar, a strange and enigmatic creature who gives Alice some good advice (although obviously in a rude manner). Alice first tries to communicate with him by reading his mind, but she utterly fails: in order to encourage his understanding of her constantly changing situation, she argues that he too would feel a little queer, in the process of changing from a caterpillar to a butterfly. However, the Blue Caterpillar looks at her coldly and just replies "not a bit" (*AAIW*, 49). Contrariwise, the Caterpillar is able to answer

---

[22] For further reflections on impoliteness in the *Alices*, see Schneebeli 2013.

to Alice's unexpressed doubts "as if she had asked aloud" (55), apparently having a mysterious access to her thoughts.

Thus, in the nonsense worlds where totally opaque unnatural minds are represented, and with them the constant impossibility of mirroring each other's minds and thus understanding each other, Carroll also introduces a character with psychic mind-reading powers. As already mentioned in the first chapter, Carroll believed in psychic phenomena, ESP and psychokinesis. Martin Gardner (2001), regarding this specific passage in *Alice's Adventures in Wonderland*, quotes a letter Carroll wrote in 1882, where he said "all seems to point to the existence of a natural force, allied to electricity and nerve-force, by which brain can act on brain" (55). His Blue Caterpillar is the embodiment of these theoretical speculations: in Wonderland, the world where minds are unreadable, Carroll portrays also the utopian possibility of direct mental communication and absolute transparency, symbolised by the enigmatic figure of the Caterpillar, a creature whose life is in itself a mysterious metamorphosis from a grounded existence to the ethereal, almost immaterial nature of the butterfly.

3.3 "Which Do You Think It Was?": The Readers

> And the moral of that is – 'Be what you would seem to be' – or, if you'd like it put more simply – 'Never imagine yourself not to be otherwise than what it might appear to others that what you were or might have been was not otherwise than what you had been would have appeared to them to be otherwise.
> (*AAIW*, 96–97)

In this section I address the concept of the mirror as connected with mirror neurons and mind-reading skills. The metaphor of the mirror is particularly useful to describe the way we deal with literary texts. However, this metaphor is not taken here as signifying a passive mirroring, but rather an active reflection, where the reflection is not possible without the minds which reflect it, and, in reflecting, in part create. This metaphor is illustrated by the move Alice makes in *Through the Looking-Glass*; by jumping through the mirror, she takes an active role in creating the mirrored reality. Such a conceptual perspective orients this section, from the way I propose to utilise the notion of mirror neurons in narrative studies, to the way I depict the reader's interaction with the text. I introduce mirror-neurons and related theories with the necessary caveats that literary theorists should keep in mind, whilst emphasizing the usefulness that a metaphorical meaning of this notion can have for the field of narratology. Then I develop this concep-

Fig. 18: David Delamare, illustration for *Alice's Adventures in Wonderland*, 2015. Delamare intriguingly suggests the Caterpillar's ability of seeing into Alice's mind. The telescope is also significant as an extremely popular optical instrument in Victorian times, and one already used by Carroll as a metaphor at the beginning of *Alice in Wonderland* (16).

tual approach by applying it to the *Alices* in progressively more complex ways: I start by showing the different ways in which readers reflect the minds they encounter in the *Alice* books, and their own experience of these minds, using their ToM capabilities; and I conclude by describing the peculiar ways in which the *Alice* books deconstruct the mirror-illusion of many of our representations, revealing their origin as meta-representations.

3.3.1 Mirror Neurons: Caveats and Carroll's "Bright Silvery Mist"

I would like here to introduce the problematic topic of mirror neurons, and to clarify my theoretical perspective in relation to it. In alignment with the other sections of this chapter, the concept of mirror is used in mainly a *metaphorical* way. Mirror neurons have a real, scientific existence, but the scientific evidence about them is still discussed and controversial, and the possible use of this discovery in narrative contexts is even more debatable, as Ryan points out in her article "Narratology and Cognitive Science: A Problematic Relation" (2010).

Mirror neurons are neurons which are activated when we just witness someone performing an action, without the need of any personal practical involvement. They are in this sense significantly interrelated with the conceptual scenarios of virtuality, imitation, empathy, mind-reading, imagination. If neuroscientists like Ramachandran (1998, 2003) and Gallese and Goldman (1998) and Rizzolati and Sinigaglia (2006) have highlighted the possible implications of this neurological finding for the understanding of the behavioural processes of imitation and mind-reading, narrative theorists like Luca Berta (2010) have made a further step linking the work of mirror neurons with the mental construction of virtual realities. Berta emphasises how important the discovery of mirror neurons could be for narrative studies, stressing the fact that these neurons "fire" even in the presence of only a written description of a situation, scientifically "proving" in this way how mentally intense and realistic is the immersion in a literary world (428). He continues:

> come to think of it, it is not even necessary that the episode actually occurred in order to unleash my emotional (mirror?) reaction. Linguistic evocations rally the firing of mirror neurons, which turns to the shared space of motor acts and emotions in order to achieve a first-person intuition of the pain felt by the other. But then, where is this shared space located and with whom is it shared, if the real presence of the other's emotions is not necessarily required in order to set it off? It looks as though it might not take root in facticity. (428)

Nevertheless, cognitive concepts like mirror neurons should not be appropriated to the field of narratology without theoretical precautions and without the introduction of a conceptual metaphorical level.

Ryan's "Narratology and Cognitive Science: A Problematic Relation" (2010) can help to clarify some points. She observes that the discoveries of cognitive science, such as mirror neurons, have so far just "verified commonsensical ideas," since for narratologists interested in possible worlds the relevance of notions such as virtual reality, or the creation of mental models based on the storyworld's instructions, is "self-evident" (2). Ryan distinguishes between two approaches cognitive narratology can take, one related to the theoretical dialogue with neurological research (what she calls the "hard cognitive science," 3), and the other connected to the more speculative branches of cognitive studies, such as philosophy of mind. She dismisses the first approach because the scientific methods of neurological research, such as brain scans, are not yet sophisticated enough to give really interesting insights from a narratological perspective; and while she distinguishes two methods related to the second one, a top-down approach and a convergence method (4–6), she considers both of them to lack a consistent and valid methodology. Ryan argues that for cognitive narratology to be a significant discipline it must wait for scientific methods to progress and give narratology a "genuine feedback loop" of its ideas; in the meantime, narratologists should develop a set of "right questions" for an understanding of "the nexus of narrative and mind" (10).

Embracing Ryan's perspective, I agree that there clearly has been too much theoretical enthusiasm for mirror neurons or other "hard" cognitive science concepts, while the "soft" cognitive science-related approach has lacked systematicity. However, scientific findings such as mirror neurons can still be conceptually interesting from a narrative view point, if approached cautiously: they can still give substance and a new source of inspiration to narratological research, providing an interdisciplinary link. The lack of a rigorous method and of tangible results in the second type of approach certainly needs to be addressed, but many interesting theoretical suggestions have been made (as Ryan herself acknowledges, mentioning the works of Suzanne Keen and Herman, for instance), and these suggestions can also be correlated to the set of questions Ryan suggests, waiting for further advancements in practical research.

In my theoretical position, I would like to adopt the "soft" approach, but in a *more* metaphorical sense. The use of cognitive science concepts like mirror neurons can inspire several types of narrative reflection, dealing with topics from the construction of storyworlds to the interactions among characters themselves. However, such reflections concern our ideas and theories about the working of the human mind, not a methodical scientific empiricism about it – what a narratological outlook can do is to offer reflections upon *how we think* about the mind and its intricacies. Using again the mirror metaphor, cognitive narratology can reflect upon reflection about the human mind, through the interaction between cognitive science concepts and narrative scenarios. It can offer insights, speculations, and even questions (as Ryan highlights) about how the human mind constructs the human mind itself.

With these caveats in mind, I would like now to proceed to show how, from a metaphorical perspective, concepts such as mirror neurons and the related ideas of ToM and meta-representational skills can be useful in understanding of readers' experiences with the *Alice* books. Regarding mirror neurons, Richard Walsh (2016) stresses that, while many narratologists tend "to understand the metaphor in terms of the virtual image in the mirror [...] the metaphor was originally used to characterise the *action* of these neurons" (10). In this sense, the focus of the metaphor as adopted in narratological contexts would shift from the written representation to the reflective representational act of the part of readers: "a reflection, indeed, is *not* a representation in the artefactual sense in which that term is commonly understood, but the effect of a situated process of observation; there is no image in the mirror independent of the act of viewing it" (10).

Through the Looking-Glass and What Alice Found There may work as an exemplification of this way of conceptualising mirror neurons: the reality of the Looking-Glass land, with all its revealing cognitive meanings related to processes of duplication and inversion, is not a mere visual reflection. Alice *goes* through the mirror, the idea of action that the exploration of the mirrored reality entails is made clear already in the title, with its emphasis upon "through" and the action verb attributed to Alice. The metaphor of the mirror proposed by the second of the *Alice* books thus conveys both the idea that mirror mechanisms are revealing and powerful and the fact that these mechanisms are deeply entangled with actual interpretative action. Alice's jump through the mirror and her active interaction with the Looking-Glass world is what makes it possible for that world to project any meaning at all. Alice's going through the "bright silvery mist" (149) of the mirror can symbolise readers' interplay with the textual reality, which does not exist without their interpretative acts.

3.3.2 Mind Games and ToM in Alice's Worlds

In chapter one I outlined the concepts of ToM and of meta-representational capabilities, as well as the existence of different approaches to it (simulation theory and theory-theory) and what Lisa Zunshine points out about their relevance to the narratological study of readers' interactions with literary texts. I would like here to focus on the specific implications these concepts may have in relation to the *Alice* books as reading experiences. The mirror metaphor of Alice jumping through the looking-glass is a conceptual framework for readers' experiences with the text, functioning as another kind of *mise en abyme*, an interpretative one this time, metaphorically picturing how readers approach the narrative.

There are several levels on which readers' ToM-related skills are challenged and on which they are reflecting[23] the minds they encounter in Carroll's stories. First, it is worth considering readers' alignment with Alice's mind. The minds of the characters Alice meets in the bizarre worlds of her two dreams are completely inaccessible and opaque, and their actions illogical and incomprehensible: Alice's ToM-related capabilities prove to be totally useless there, and the same happens for readers, since they share Alice's perspective. Readers directly follow her thoughts, questioning and doubts, because "the sole medium of the stories is her pellucid consciousness" (De La Mare 1932, 55). If Carroll has identified with his heroine, he has also managed to make his readers do the same: Alice's mind, and the products of her dreaming mind, constitute the pervasive point of view of the stories.

Secondly, Alice's mind can become itself the object of readers' reflections. On the one hand, the Wonderland and Looking-Glass Land creatures' minds have been created by Carroll in a non-mimetic way that leaves us, like Alice, in a constant state of mental puzzlement (the applicability of real-minds discourse on them not being a viable option). On the other hand, readers' identification with Alice's perspective means that we are looking at the world with a child's mind. Karlsson (2009) mentions that Alice's cognitive abilities are not as developed as an adult's: in particular, at the age of seven she does not have a fully developed capacity for hypothetical thinking, and "the lack of advanced hypothetical thinking affects the child's ability to view something from the perspective of others" (4). This might itself be why Alice constantly fails to understand the characters she encounters. Therefore, readers may identify two different reasons for their difficulty in grasping what is happening in the minds of the Carrollian creatures. Maybe we are facing the depiction of unnatural and unpredictable minds, or maybe we are constrained by a little girl's mind, and presented only with her own mental scenario. In this way Alice's mental frame becomes an object of reflection and doubt: in other words, is the Alice who encounters these creatures a reliable focaliser? We are able to question Alice's reliability since our relation to her viewpoint is not one of complete and

---

[23] "Reflection" intended here in the active way outlined above, with readers' minds matching Alice's dynamic interaction with the mirrored world.

blind alignment: the internal focalisation presupposes a conceptual distinction between the character Alice and the dreaming Alice. It makes us follow her frame of reference, but at the same time we still retain a kind of detachment, which allows us to doubt her, or the extent to which she knows her own mind, and so to make her an object of our attention.

Thirdly, our own correspondence with Alice itself becomes the object of our mental focus, when we are forced to step back from her perspective. There are two moments in which the narration explicitly makes readers disentangle from Alice's way of looking at the world around her: the two endings of the books. In *Alice's Adventures in Wonderland* our standpoint shifts from Alice to her sister, and the dream begins again: a dream about Alice and the strange creatures of her Wonderland dream. At first our detachment from Alice's viewpoint is just illusory: her sister's perspective is immediately reabsorbed by the strength of Alice's dream, as an inescapable frame of reference. Then, in the last paragraph of the text, the vision of Alice's sister acquires the tones of the book's prefatory poem: dreaming, melancholy, making the whole text shimmer away as an only half-remembered mirage. The almost romantic tones of the conclusion are in total contrast with the atmosphere that Alice's dream has just conveyed: readers' object of attention shifts to Alice's sister's dream and viewpoint, prompting them to pay attention to their own alignment with the characters' perspectives, and consequently question *both* sisters' dreams.

The second book's conclusion is different but not less puzzling: Alice comes back to the initial scenario, the living room and her cats' company, but this time she does not dismiss the "curious dream" in a melancholy absent-minded repetition of it (both in her own actions, hurrying to tea-time like the Mad Hatter and the March Hare, and in her sister's mind); instead she rationally questions it, trying first to figure out the roles her kittens play in it, and then posing a metaphysical question about the essence of dreaming itself. The shifting of perspective comes more abruptly this time, with a sudden and unexpected question to the readers themselves "which do *you* think it was?" with the "you" marked by the use of italics. We suddenly lose our mental identification with Alice, and the brusque change to the second person makes us all at once clearly aware of this previous identification, and of the fact that there is *someone else* there, apart from Alice. Throughout the whole story we read (or actually do not read) other minds, and interpret situations, only through Alice's eyes, not always noticing it; but at the end Carroll troubles this almost unconscious mental attitude with that abrupt question. The author's presence is suddenly made more prominent, and we are also led to question our own identity as readers. What does it mean to be "you"? Who are we supposed to be? Having read through the chapters of *Through the Looking-Glass* trapped in "a dream of a pawn's-eye view of a looking-glass game of chess" (Haughton 2003, 325), we finally realise it was "only" the main character's dream; and then we are induced to consider whether this dream might be contained within another dream, and even that our own reading perspective might be included. In addition, Alice is talking to her kittens while questioning the nature of her own, or someone else's, dream, and pointing out that, firstly, the cats themselves were an important part of the dream; secondly, in the dream there was a strange recurrence of fishy references. Another question might be: are the readers supposed to be *cats*? Have we just been led unconsciously into a cat-perspective, continuously oriented towards food, and fish in particular, and not at all interested in mind-reading? Our ToM-related capabilities having been repeatedly challenged in our active interaction with the mirror of the text, "we are left with a feeling of a mental vertigo" (Zunshine 2006, 104).

3.3.3 Worlds Upside Down and Meta-Representations in Trouble

The *Alice* books also challenge readers' source-monitoring mental devices (see Zunshine 2006, 60–65) through the continuous failure of the heroine's (and readers') meta-representations of reality. Meta-representational capabilities are closely linked to ToM-related skills: they are those mental tools that allow us to discern the sources of opinions, sentences, thoughts. The representations that Alice has internalised about other people's thoughts, beliefs and habits have come to form her version of how the world should be. In Wonderland, Carroll makes her and his readers (again, our mental expectations are entangled with hers, as above) begin to understand how many representations of the reality around us are in fact meta-representations, only we have forgotten the "source tag" (50). In other words, many meta-representations have actually become "semantic memories," which are "representations that are stored without the source tag" (Zunshine 2006, 51); but we can nonetheless come to recognise them once again as meta-representations.[24] The mirror metaphor in this case emphasises the instability of meta-representations: when we forget their "meta-" status we unthinkingly assume that our thoughts are mirroring the world around us, when we are actually dealing with how *other minds* have mirrored it. In the Looking-Glass world the exposure of such errors is especially pervasive, as the

---

[24] Zunshine (2006) gives as an example the past belief that the Earth was at the centre of the universe, which had acquired the status of semantic memory, as incontrovertible knowledge; subsequently, however, it became a meta-representation with the source tag "people used to think that" … (51).

mirror element in the narrative functions to turn the world back to front, highlighting the relativity of our world-image representations.

In *Alice's Adventures in Wonderland*, Alice decides to follow the White Rabbit because he is a curious and funny creature, with unexpected attitudes; we anticipate he will be a nice little speaking pet – what else can a little cute white bunny be? – so, when Alice actually talks to him, we are quite disconcerted to discover that with the powerful he is "nervously shilly-shallying" and "feeble" (Carroll 1887), but he is irascible and angry with lower status characters – including Alice, whom he takes for his housemaid. Indeed, the confrontation with the White Rabbit is a disappointing one for Alice, marking from the beginning the disillusioning nature of her discoveries in Wonderland. Similarly, she drinks potions in order to enter the little door into Wonderland because she thinks it is "the loveliest garden you ever saw" and "she longed to get out of that dark hall and wander about among those beds of bright flowers and those cool fountains" (16). But this wonderful and enchanted place, at which she will arrive only after countless vicissitudes, finally reveals itself to be the triumph of absurdity, the culmination of all the nonsense we have encountered along with her on her complex journey.

In the course of this journey all her Victorian constructions of the world, her meta-representations, are questioned. The Duchess is represented as anything but a typical Duchess, or what a Duchess is generally *supposed to be:* she is "*very* ugly", she is very rude, and, moreover, nurses a horrible child by tossing him violently up and down, and singing him this lullaby: "I speak severely to my boy, / I beat him when he sneezes; / For he can thoroughly enjoy / The pepper when he pleases!" (*AAIW*, 64). Meanwhile the cook contaminates the air with pepper, and throws dishes, pots and plates at everyone. The cosy idea of a serene and decorous Victorian interior is overturned by this disturbing picture. Carroll reveals the unstable essence of social constructions, taking what is normally *represented* by the social-constructed mind as sublime and noble, and showing its hidden impulses of violence and selfishness. Meta-representations, it seems, are *not* reliable mirrors of an objective reality. The Duchess's baby begins to grunt as Alice nurses it and quickly turns into a pig; Alice takes note of the fact, reflecting that she would enjoy, like another Circe, turning other children she knows into pigs. The metamorphosis unveils the real nature of many children, so celebrated and exalted in Victorian songs and lullabies: "the pig-baby episode humorously dramatizes the arbitrary nature of conventional attitudes toward infants" (Rackin 1991, 52). Alice humorously adapts herself to these puzzling new circumstances, and wisely concludes: "if it had grown up it would have made a dreadfully ugly child: but it makes rather a handsome pig, I think" (*AAIW,* 66).

Fig. 19: Arthur Rackham, *Pig and Pepper*, illustration for *Alice's Adventures in Wonderland*, 1907. This image vividly and dynamically shows the reversal of the normal expectations of a typical Victorian interior.

On her Wonderland trip, Alice finds that familiar things are continually being transformed and parodied: cats, her favourite animals, have as their representative the "animale totemico del nonsense" (Scrittori 2003, 45),[25] the king of paradoxes whose ineffable grin is the subversion of sense. The Cheshire Cat's smile twinkles alone like an erratic half-moon, in the sky of non-sense, persisting even when all the rest of the animal's body has disappeared, to Alice's perplexity: "I've often seen a cat without a grin, but a grin without a cat! It's the most curious thing I ever saw in all my life!" (*AAIW*, 69). The Cheshire Cat is the incarnation of non-sense, enacting the insubstantialities of language and logic: Rackin (1991) points out the supreme danger that the grin without the cat represents, by breaking "the seemingly indestructible bond between subject and attribute, a crucial element in the logic by which we live our rational lives" (53). Alice's favourite pet becomes the embodiment of common logic's collapse, a perverse symbol of the arbitrariness of language and logic. Even tea-time, an occasion that Victorian readers in particular, and English readers in general, recognise as a cultural ritual, is transformed in Wonderland in an absurd event, in one of the best-known comic episodes of the book: the mad tea party. Here, in the setting of the usual Victorian ceremony of 6 o'clock tea, "practically all pattern save the consistency of chaos, is annihilated" by the absurd dialogues with the Mad Hatter and the March Hare (Rackin 1991, 36).

After this encounter, Alice arrives at last in the lovely garden that had aroused her curiosity and desire from the beginning, sustaining her through the absurdity and non-sense of her progress towards it. Yet even this garden demolishes common ideas about enchanted fairy tale gardens: the wonderful garden with "bright flower-beds and cool fountains" is actually the Queen of Hearts's croquet-ground, where the roses are fake and where Alice experiences the definitive collapse of her mental categories. Representations are thus shown in Wonderland for what they often are: *meta*-representations (representations about others' representations, frequently fallacious), structures of the mind built up to deal with the world's confusion. In the Queen's croquet-ground even the basic distinction between animate beings and inanimate objects, something which Alice was sure she could rely upon as a solid objective truth, is under discussion: the subjects, the soldiers, the sovereigns, are cards (objects, in the "real" world), whereas flamingos and porcupines, living animals in normal usage, are treated here as inanimate objects (croquet bats and balls). In Wonderland Alice herself, whom we picture as a little girl, has already become a snake, a cruel animal, in the episode with the Pigeon, where "the golden child herself be-

---

25 "The totemic animal of nonsense." (my translation)

comes the serpent in childhood's Eden" (Auerbach 1973, 41); at the climax she discovers her alter-ego, the Queen of Hearts, who is no more than a playing card. What Rackin (1991) calls the destruction of Alice's self in Wonderland (58) is also the destruction of our own representational categories.

We likewise discover that the objective world can be completely reversed in *Through the Looking-Glass and What Alice Found There*, but in an even more decisive way (since here the act of turning everything back to front is the narrative cipher of the story). The reversals made possible by the mirror reveal that our representations do not simply mirror an objective world. The mirror itself is a means of inverting and modifying: a perfectly correspondent reflection does not exist. Common beliefs about reality turn out to be almost unconsciously acquired meta-representations, the sources of which (parents or social environments perhaps) are no longer identifiable; as Zunshine (2006) puts it, "although the distinction between semantic and episodic memories (or between representations and meta-representations) is useful [...], this distinction is always context-dependent and potentially fluid" (52).

In *Through the Looking-Glass*, we find that things can go "the other way" from the one we are accustomed to. As in Alice's previous adventures, the first place she sees and the one she longs to reach is a beautiful garden (including "a large flower-bed, with a border of daisies, and a willow-tree growing in the middle," 166), but again it proves quite hard to get there. Basic conceptions of spatial reality are totally overturned: she walks straight ahead, towards the garden, and she finds herself at her point of departure, in the house. Alice is upset until, by trying to move in the *opposite* direction from the place she wants to reach, she actually finds herself moving *towards* it. However, the garden is another disappointment: the flowers can talk, but rather than being gentle and pleasant, as our mental associations tell us flowers should be, they prove very rude and annoying. They talk to and about Alice very impolitely, commenting that her face is "not a clever one," that her petals (i.e., her hair) should be "curled up a little more," that she "never thinks at all," that she is fading, and, finally, from the Violet, "I never saw anybody that looked stupider" (166–169). Flowers, whose secret language was regarded as metaphorically resonant and poetical in Victorian times, speak here aggressively and impertinently; the picture of flowers as kind creatures is foregrounded as another meta-representation, in the product of a specific cultural context.

Going "forwards" in the Looking-glass world, we come to realise that the known world can be completely upended; what is considered as common knowledge turns out to be only *one* possible perspective. By crossing to the other side of the looking-glass, Alice discovers that growing-up is an illusion of happiness; that is, becoming a Queen, which is Alice's goal from the beginning, turns out to be another disappointment. She finds herself with a golden crown, but trapped between two old silly creatures (the other two Queens) in a dimension of nonsensical riddles and chaos (where bottles become birds, candles turn into fireworks, the White Queen drowns in a soup and the Red one turns into a little doll). In general, normal convictions about how our world works are revealed to be meta-representations and thus apt to be relativised. On the other side of the mirror it is possible to stay still in the same place even while running at speed; thirst can be quenched by eating dry biscuits; Nobody turns out often to be Somebody; proper names can have a meaning while common names can be meaningless; memory concerns expectations and projections of the future ... In this sense, the *Alice* books show the fragility of our mental representations, helping us to question the world and its meanings, to reshape common notions and to challenge accepted beliefs. The mirror metaphor, which has helped already highlighting Carroll's own writing approach to nonsense, the representation of the characters' minds and their interactions, and the way the readers' minds *reflect* upon the text, finally reveals to be useful also in this demystification process and relativizing of perspective.

Chapter 4
Emotional Alice

Fig. 20: Trevor Brown, *The Pool of Tears*, from *Alice*, 2010. The emotional impact of this image strongly contrasts with Tenniel's original depiction of the same scene. Even if nonsense never explicitly shows intense emotions, I argue in this chapter that emotions are there indeed. Moreover, the act of crying in the *Alices* is quite an important, recurrent one, which I would like to emphasise through this initial illustration.

> 'She's in that state of mind,' said the White Queen, 'that she
> wants to deny *something* – only she doesn't know what to deny!'
> 'A nasty, vicious temper,' the Red Queen remarked.
> (*TTLG*, 265)

A shift in cognitive studies has begun to give more and more attention to the role that emotions play in our cognitive system. Already theorists such as Damasio (who writes that "feelings are just as cognitive as any other perceptual image", 1994, 158, and who explores the connection between emotion and the body with consciousness, 1999), Sacks (1985) and Ramachandran (2003) have contributed to the idea of the centrality of the emotional mental apparatus. The focus on emotions is also connected to the idea of the "embodied mind", instead of a conception of a purely cognitive mind, understood on the basis of a "computer metaphor" (Wojciehowski and Gallese 2011, 1): emotions offer a good ground for establishing the deep interrelation of bodily reactions, perceptual sensations and physical feelings with the mind's functioning, emotions being more directly "embodied" than abstract cognitive processes. Literary scholars like Hogan (2010), Zunshine (2006), Young (2010), Herman (2007), Stockwell (2002) and Keen (2007, 2011, 2013) have followed this theoretical lead, pointing out how a vision of the mind where cognitive processes are inextricably merged with emotional responses, where intersubjectivity, empathy and bodily sensations play an essential role, can be helpful in the field of literary studies, expanding and enriching our understanding of how narratives are created and perceived. Hogan goes even further, by saying:

> Given recent advances in research on emotion, it seems clear that any theory of narrative would benefit from a more fully elaborated treatment of emotion based on this research. Indeed, I would go further, and argue that narrative is fundamentally shaped and oriented by our emotion systems. (2010, 65)

The concept of mirror neurons actually has its roots in an embodied, action-based conception of the mind: "mirror neurons allow a direct form of action understanding through a mechanism of embodied simulation", writes Gallese (2009, 532). Theory of Mind-related narrative studies have thus been recently combined with what Wojciehowski and Gallese (2011) call Feeling of Body (FoB), making it possible to develop an understanding of literary texts, cognitive creative processes and reader-responses that encompasses actions, affections, and bodily feelings. As Andy Clark (1998) underlines, this "requires us to abandon the idea (common since Descartes) of the mental as a realm distinct from the realm of the b ody; to abandon the idea of neat dividing lines between perception, cognition, and action" (xiii–xiv). In this chapter I address the implications of both theory of empathy and so-called "affective narratology" for the understanding of Carroll's *Alice* books, and Carroll's own exploration of the embodiment of emotions.

4.1 "Is This an Extempore Romance of Yours, Dodgson?": The Author

> And, though the shadow of a sigh / May tremble through the story, / For 'happy summer days' gone by, / And vanish'd summer glory – / It shall not touch, with breath of bale / The pleasance of our fairy-tale.
> (*TTLG*, 140)

How does an approach through feeling inform our comprehension of the author's work? As Keen (2013) points out, "authors' empathy bears on fictional worldmaking and character creation" (9), and in this authorial section of the chapter I describe the emotional components behind the creation of the Alice books. First, I consider Carroll's work and its address to issues of emotion and bodily sensation in the broader context of Victorian literature. As a second step, I explore the peculiar rhetorical contrast between nonsense and emotions that Carroll manages to create in his Alice books, and examine their complicated relationship. Finally, relying upon Marjorie Taylor et al.'s (2003) suggestion that "the adult activity most closely aligned with having imaginary friends is the creation of fictional characters by novelists" (362), I touch upon the controversial and huge topic of Carroll's own involvement with his main character, Alice. My theoretical path in this section goes from the more general cultural context of Victorian literature, referring to texts such as William Cohen's Embodied: Victorian Literature and the Senses (2009) and Dames's The Physiology of the Novel: Reading, Neural Science and the Form of Victorian Fiction (2007), to the peculiarity of nonsense and especially Carroll's special use of nonsense words, leading into a focus upon authorial feeling, especially concerning Carroll's relationship with Alice, one of the most-explored and interesting relationships between an author and his main character.

4.1.1 The "Discovery" of Emotions in Victorian Literature and the Rhetoric of Nonsense Vs Victorian Sentimentality

Rachel Ablow highlights in a 2008 issue of *Victorian Studies* focused on "Victorian Emotions", that "emotions continued to function as a central epistemological tool throughout the era – a way of defining not just male and female, public and private, but also subject and object, human and nonhuman, determined and free" (375). Victorian writers deeply explored the emotional world, building an idea of subjecthood where feelings and sensations were a dominant element in the construction of the characters and the plot. Among scholars pursuing em-

4.1 "Is This an Extempore Romance of Yours, Dodgson?": The Author — 115

Fig. 21: Lewis Carroll, "Open your mouth and shut your eyes", July 1860. This is one of the many photographs of the three Liddell sisters that Carroll took. Alice is captured at the point of trying to reach something pleasant, which she has not yet attained: she is permanently fixed in a suspended moment, "reaching for something that will remain forever out of reach" (Douglas-Fairhurst, 139).

bodied approaches to literature, William Cohen (2009) shows the use of sensory experiences in the building of characters in Dickens and Charlotte Bronte, as well as the understanding of the body in the poetry of Hopkins as a recipient of perceptions interconnected with the world. Young (2010) analyses George Eliot's representations of sounds as essential boosters of emotional connections between minds; Hardy's Tess as "an embodiment of embodiment", with "the drama of Tess's mouth" (163) as a starting point for the converging emotions of the male characters; and Sue Bridehead from *Jude The Obscure* as "an embodiment of feeling", where emotions constitute "the core of her consciousness" (141). The strong connection between Victorian novels and the depiction of feelings has also been addressed by Dames's *The Physiology of the Novel* (2007), which claims that "the Victorian neural sciences" established "a collaboration with literary criticism, for which a range of cognitive and physiological activities involved in the reading act seemed suddenly capable of study and definition" (7). In this sense, studies of emotions and attention were incorporated into the writing of many popular novels of the time, Dames argues, using examples taken from Thackeray, Eliot, Meredith and Gissing.

If emotions and their analysis played such a relevant role in Victorian literature, what about nonsense literature, which was itself a mainly Victorian phenomenon (its most important representatives being Lear and Carroll)? One consequence of the Victorian focus on emotions is the cultural phenomenon of "Victorian sentimentality," which might appear to be subject to mockery in nonsense representations of emotion. I would argue, however, that nonsense literature can actually be an expression of the same complex concern with the emotional side of our minds.

Having once been labelled a kitsch phenomenon, a sign of unrefined tastes and generally an aesthetic failure, Victorian sentimentality has recently started to be re-evaluated both as a meaningful expression of the Victorian imagination, and as a rhetoric encouraging an affective and empathetic reaction in readers (see for instance the special issue of the journal *19* called "Rethinking Victorian Sentimentality", edited by Nicola Bown, 2007). As Marie Banfield (2007) argues, sentiments in Victorian culture (in literature, poetry and visual arts alike) were associated with the idea of "a monism directed by discoveries in physiology and psychology, which in the nineteenth century increasingly saw body and mind, thought, feeling and sensation as inextricably linked" (4) – a theoretical approach which is surprisingly modern and in line with contemporary cognitive research. Nonsense, on the other hand, is a genre from which emotions seem banned and sentimentality ridiculed: according to Sewell (1952), nonsense "is a game, to which emotion is alien" (129). She regards as artistic failures those of Carroll's nonsense works into which emotions intrude, like *Sylvie and Bruno* with its "insipidity and sentimentality" (154), and *The Hunting of the Snark*, in which "dream, delirium, madness" (169) are allowed to manifest themselves without the formal constraints of the Nonsense game which characterise the *Alices* (163–182). Wim Tigges, in *An Anatomy of Literary Nonsense* (2013) reinforces this idea: listing the "four essential elements of literary nonsense", he presents as second necessary feature "a lack of emotional involvement" (55). Yet Victorian sentimentality is always somehow present in Carroll's nonsense, even in the *Alices*, as Sewell herself admits (181); this is not a case of poetical failure, but both another way of exploring a cultural product of his time's imagination, and a problematic personal issue.

Victorian nonsense, especially Carroll's nonsense, [1] does not define itself in opposition to the Victorian exploration of emotions, as a caricature of Victorian sentimentality; instead it represents another contribution to the new deep interest in the emotional components of the mind, a different way of engaging with sentiments, often involving parodies and awkward juxtapositions (such as the rather sentimental prefatory poems of the *Alices* versus the humorous and caustic narrative content), but with a complexity comparable to the tonal shifts in Dickens's novels.

4.1.2 "The Poignant Love Song Beneath the Invented Nonsense Words"

The numberless parodies Carroll inserted in the *Alices* are often directly addressed to Victorian morality and sentimentality. Parodies are widespread in the *Alice* books, especially in the first one, covering well-known and revered didactic poems ("How doth the little bee", 23–24; "You are Old, Father William", 51–54; "The Spider and the Fly", 106; "The Sluggard", 110; "Summer Days", 228); mocking versions of lullabies and songs ("Speak Gently", 64; "Twinkle Twinkle Little Star", 76; "Star of the Evening", *AAIW*, 112); and works written by eminent Victorian authors, like Tennyson's *Maud*, of which Carroll gives an hilarious parodic version in "The Garden of Live Flowers" (*TTLG*, 165–176). Carroll's humorous attitude towards works highly considered among the Victorians should not, however, be regarded as just an irreverent critique. It is true that the programmatic exclusion of moral messages from the *Alice* books was extremely innovative and a radical alternative to Victorian instructive children stories, a veritable literary revolution; but nonsense was still a poetical product of Victorian times, not an anomaly, and Carroll was, at his core, deeply Victorian.

---

1 I'm here obviously focusing on Carroll's nonsense, although Lear also dealt with Victorian sentimentality in his own complex way (see Sewell 1952, 149–162).

The peculiarity of nonsense is not its opposition to sense, but its ability to retain different instances of meaning all together, offering a kaleidoscopic glimpse of the paradoxical coexistence of opposites. As Lecercle (1994) points out, "nonsense texts are the locus for a polyphony of discourses" (169), a breeding-ground for the concurrence of different, even contrasting, significances. In this sense, Carroll's *Alice* books can be *both* a parody of Victorian sentimentality and an expression of it. Carroll himself "was fond of saying that one parodied the best poems, or anyway that parody showed no lack of admiration" (Empson 1974, 263). Therefore, Carroll's moral concerns in daily life, his religious belief, and his later sentimental works, are not to be viewed as incompatible with the *Alices*. Only, in the *Alices* he managed to achieve a delicate and complex balance of different antithetical components. If nonsense is a sort of pastiche (Lecercle, 171), it is a pastiche in which the different constituents "are also echoes of the various discourses that made up Victorian culture" (Lecercle, 195), and reflect upon the meaning and role of these discourses. If in the *Alice* books we can find traces of logic, science, occultism, psychology and social critique, we can also discern in them a place for reflection upon emotions and sentimentality.

The main body of the texts, especially *Alice's Adventures in Wonderland*, seems almost deprived of authorial emotional involvement, but the prefatory and concluding poems tell a different story. Here we find melancholy recollections of "a golden afternoon" with "such dreamy weather", a place where "Childhood's dreams are twined in Memory's mystic band" and where "the dream-child" (*AAIW*, 7), the "child of the pure unclouded brow" (*TTLG*, 139) "moves through a land of wonders" (*AAIW*, 8) and is always capable of haunting the author, of making him obsessively remember those "other days, when summer suns were glowing" (139), even later, when "Autumn frosts have slain July" (287) and he and his dream-child "are half a life asunder" (*TTLG*, 139). In *Alice's Adventures in Wonderland* these explicit sentimental tones are almost limited to the beginning and the conclusion of the book (with the melancholy atmosphere of Alice's sister dreaming Alice's dream and thinking about a grown-up Alice), but in *Through the Looking-Glass* the irruption of emotions is much more pervasive in the rhetorical tissue of the text. Apart from the introductory and concluding poems, it is worth recalling the melancholic Gnat who always sighs (185), the almost enchanting tender encounter between Alice and the Fawn (186–187),[2] the romantic description of the dream-rushes in the "Wool and Water" chapter

---

[2] This encounter is reminiscent of the encounter with the puppy in the first *Alice* book: in both cases the rhetorical atmosphere is different from the nonsensical comedy of the surroundings, and both scenes involve animals whose tenderness and graciousness Carroll (1887) later compared to Alice herself: "she was loving as a dog … gentle as a fawn".

(204–217), which has a "Pre-Raphaelite pictorial taste shaping the narrative" (Haughton 2003, 343), the widespread troubling question about who is dreaming the dream of the story (with poetical references to Shakespeare, Shelley, Tennyson, and Wordsworth – see Haughton 2003, 355) and the chapter on the White Knight (245–262).

This last example in particular (the chapter "It's my Own Invention!"), is the most explicitly sentimental chapter in the *Alice* books. Carroll more or less explicitly identifies himself with the White Knight (see also Stern 1990): indications of this identification are, for instance, his "old age" in comparison to Alice's, his creativity (the White Knight is an inventor of the strangest devices, 248–255) and his clumsy and sweet attachment to Alice. As Martin Gardner (2001) says, "it is noteworthy that, of all the characters Alice meets on her two dream adventures, only the White Knight seems to be genuinely fond of her and to offer her special assistance" (250). Consequently, the narration of this chapter contains some passages which are almost elegiac and very different from Carroll's usual style in the *Alices*. The most tonally striking scene depicts Alice listening to the White Knight reciting a long poem of his own invention (based on a poem Carroll himself wrote some years before, "Upon the Lonely Moor", see M. Gardner 2001, 257).[3] It is worth quoting the entire passage:

> Of all the strange things that Alice saw in her journey through the Looking-Glass, this was the one that she always remembered most clearly. Years afterwards she could bring the whole scene back again, as if it had been only yesterday – the mild blue eyes and kindly smile of the Knight – the setting sun gleaming through his hair, and shining on his armour in a blaze of light that quite dazzled her – the horse quietly moving about, with the reins hanging loose on his neck, cropping the grass at her feet – and the black shadows of the forest behind – all this she took in like a picture, as, with one hand shading her eyes, she leant against a tree, watching the strange pair, and listening, in a half-dream, to the melancholy music of the song. (256)

The slow rhythm of the description and the poetical tones offer a strong contrast with the nonsense surroundings. As Haughton remarks

> this sudden time-shift to a mood of anticipated retrospection indicates that this incident has an exceptional status in the text [...] the tonality is close to that of the introductory poem and the 'picture' is an instance of Victorian, even Pre-Raphaelite, medievalism. (2003, 349)

---

[3] The White Knight's ballad is also a parody of different Wordsworth poems: see M. Gardner (2001), 256–261, and Gregory (1974), 170.

What such examples clearly show is that Carroll's nonsense texts are not a literary manifestation alien to the Victorian culture of emotions within which they were produced. Carroll's representational style struggles with the insurgence of sentiments, it plays with it and ridicules it, but also sometimes succumbs to it, allowing sentimental tones to invade the stories. I would say further that sentimentality is *always* present, even when Carroll does not directly indulge in sentimental descriptions, in that his parodic attitude is just another way of dealing with what was a pervasive literary interest in Victorian times. As Walsh (2007) points out, literary discourse is "an integral part of a culture's discursive exploration of itself. Fictionality is the inaugurating move of a specific rhetoric, which enables a process of imaginative exploration of values" (168), and Carroll's specific way of expressing this process of imaginative exploration of values was mainly through the rhetorical means of parody, but also through the occasional insurgence of emotional landscapes in his nonsense writings.

4.1.3 "Still She Haunts Me"

The character of Alice was, notoriously, modelled on the real person of Alice Liddell, one of the daughters of the Dean of Christ Church, Oxford.[4] Whatever the much-speculated upon actual relationship between Carroll and Alice Liddell had been, there seems to emerge in his writings a certain difficulty in distinguishing his character from the real Alice, which leads to the creation of a blurred female figure, in between symbolism, idealisation and reality. In a letter he wrote to Alice Liddell when she was a woman he revealed how she had always been "his ideal child-friend" and he wrote in his diary, after having seen her as a grown-up woman,

> it was not easy to link in one's mind the new face with the olden memory – the stranger with the once-so-intimately known and loved 'Alice' whom I shall always remember best as an entirely fascinating little 7-year-old maiden. (Wakeling 1993, 465)

This creature, half real and half fictional, half idealised and half frozen in distant memories, continued to haunt Carroll's writings for his entire life. He kept coming back to the *Alices*, creating new versions of them (like the *Nursery Alice* for young children, or *Alice on the Stage*, a theatrical adaptation of *Alice's Adven-*

---

[4] There are many historical accounts about the "real" Alice: see for instance Cohen, 1995, especially chapter three "The Don, the Dean and His Daughter" and Douglas-Fairhurst, 2015. A somewhat different perspective is offered by Karoline Leach, 1999.

tures in Wonderland) and searching for Alice in all the innumerable little girls he was friends with, but who, as he wrote himself to Alice, "have been quite a different thing" (465). "Alice. Alice and another Alice. In front of flame-coloured roses. Great conjurer, master creator, lonely landscapist, Dodgson was making more Alices and might never stop" (Roiphe 2001, 143) writes Katie Roiphe in her novel about Carroll and Alice, significantly entitled *Still She Haunts Me*.

Taylor et al., in "The Illusion of Independent Agency: Do Adult Fiction Writers Experience their Characters as Having Minds of Their Own?" (2003) argue that writers often go through the same sort of mental processes that allow children to believe in imaginary companions; in particular, the illusion of independent agency (IIA). The authors of this article first drew upon written accounts by famous writers (such as Alice Walker, J.K. Rowling, Philip Pullman, Marcel Proust, Henry James) who describe their peculiar relationship with their own characters, who very often seem to have a mind of their own and their own independent will; subsequently, Taylor et al. conducted an experimental study based on fifty different contemporary writers, to discover to what extent fictional writers experience their characters as independent agents. The results show that all the writers scored much higher than the average population in all the mental processes connected with IIA (such as fantasy, empathetic concern, personal distress, perspective taking: see Taylor et al. 2003, 369–376). [5]

I would like here to take up this peculiar relationship between authors and characters in consideration of Carroll and Alice. As Taylor et al. (2003) underline, "the essence of this conceptual illusion (i.e. IIA) is the sense that the characters are independent agents not directly under the author's control" (366). Often seeming to decide their own destiny, or to annoy the author with their own personality, they *haunt* the author even when he is not writing (363–365). It is worth focusing on this specific verb, *to haunt*, because of the significance it has in English literature in general and in relation to Carroll in particular. There is an interesting reflection in Javier Marìas's novel *Tomorrow in the Battle Think on Me* (1996), in which he highlights how there is no equivalent in Spanish or Italian for the English verb "to haunt". He writes about the complex meanings of this verb, which can

> ... describe what ghosts do to the places and people they frequent or watch over or revisit; [...] it can also mean 'to bewitch', in the magical sense of the word, in the sense of 'enchant-

---

[5] Walsh (2007) deals with this topic with a different approach in chapter seven, "Narrative Creativity: The Novelist as Medium" of his *The Rhetoric of Fictionality*, where he focuses more on the interrelation between the narrative act and the novelist's "control" on it, rather than specifically on the relationship between author and characters.

ment', the etymology is uncertain, but it seems that both come from other verbs in Anglo-Saxon and Old French meaning 'to dwell', 'to inhabit', 'to live in' permanently [...] a kind of enchantment or haunting, which, when you think about it, is just another name for the curse of memory. (59)

In this sense, if being haunted is a peculiar English literary feeling, Carroll was not excluded from it: he uses the verb to haunt in the final poem at the end of *Through the Looking-Glass,* and its implications for his relationship with Alice are significant: he famously writes "Still she haunts me, phantomwise / Alice moving under skies / Never seen by waking eyes" (287).

Alice had a host of different intertwined connotations in Carroll's eyes. As Douglas-Fairhurst repeatedly points out in *The Story of Alice* (2015) "the precise nature of the triangular relationship between Carroll, the real Alice and the fictional Alice has always been notoriously hard to pin down" (18). What further complicates the picture in thinking about Carroll's relationship with the main character of his nonsense stories is precisely the fact that Alice was also a real person. Hence the phenomenon of IIA just described should have been felt by him as even more tangible and pervasive, being appropriated to the fictional Alice from the living person Alice Liddell. As Roiphe says in her compelling novel:

> *Who are you?* Asks the caterpillar in the story he was writing [...] all kinds of creatures are constantly asking Alice who she is and she is constantly demurring. And that was how Dodgson felt as he sat in the library: the constant nagging question, the absence of answer. (2001, 155)

Alice's "true essence" is nowhere to be found, her elusiveness is part of her never-ending literary charm. Other possible explanations and connections related to her enigmatic identity and to the emotional link between her and her writer are to be explored in the following section.

4.1.4 "Lolita Has Been Safely Solipsized"

Returning to the White Knight's episode, it is hard not to perceive in it what Rackin (1982) describes as "the fleeting love that whispers through this scene [...] a love between a child all potential, freedom, flux and growing up and a man all impotence, imprisonment, stasis, and falling down" (37). Nevertheless, some critics have recently questioned Carroll's affection for Alice and for little girls (critics such as Karoline Leach, 1999), claiming that "the mythic image of child-centeredness was already the assumed reality of 'Carroll' " in the Victorian

4.1 "Is This an Extempore Romance of Yours, Dodgson?": The Author

Fig. 22: Lewis Carroll, *Alice Liddell As a Beggar Maid*, private collection, 1858. The most famous, and yet the most elusive, of Carroll's visual portraits of Alice.

era, when his audience began to construct a distorted image of him, and that this image influenced all subsequent biographers in such a way that they pursued the construction of this mythological figure "in a curious quasi-religious realm of faith and intuition" (K. Leach 2000).

The fact that I am using, as the title of this section, a quote taken from Nabokov's *Lolita*, does not mean I am defending an opposite view or suggesting sexual implications in Carroll's relationship with Alice – however Carroll and Alice *did* inspire Nabokov, who chose to build his portrait of Humbert Humbert by expanding and distorting the myth of Lewis Carroll (he explicitly says that he calls Carroll "Carroll Carroll" because of the similarities he perceives in the two figures – 2000, 377). Something *was* there to offer a source of inspiration; if not the historical facts (which have never been proven to have actually happened), then the *Alice* books themselves contain nuances and allusions which can be interpreted in different ways and which can lead to the exploration of the emotional undertones contained in the books.

If it is unquestionable that the portrait of Carroll as a socially awkward man with an infamous obsessive passion for little girls is a biographical inaccuracy and exaggeration, it has nonetheless been recognised by many Carroll scholars (including Morton Cohen 1995, Douglas-Fairhurst 2015, Haughton 2003, Beer 2016, Guiliano 2019 and Rackin 1982) that his relationship with Alice was a peculiar, complex and special one. Even Wakeling, who insistently highlights Carroll's connections with the artistic and academic milieu of his times and resists the aura of myth that tends to distance him from his cultural context admits that

> there can be no doubt that Dodgson had a great affection for Alice. The outcome of the relationship was a token of love and admiration: a small notebook [...] which became the foundation of one of the most popular children's books that has ever been written. (2015, 251–252)

Alice's Adventures in Wonderland itself, it seems, was born out of an emotional attachment, a gift for a beloved little girl.

Whatever we might think of the "Carroll myth", just a look at the famous picture *Alice Liddell As a Beggar Maid* might suffice to give us the idea that Alice was something more than a simple little girl for him. As many have pointed out before, this is a fascinating and haunting picture: Alice's gestures and expression in the picture are "simultaneously innocent and knowing" (Douglas-Fairhurst 2015, 98), and there is something enigmatic, provocative, mysterious and almost threatening in the way she is looking directly at the camera (and at the man behind it). As Roiphe (2001) puts it, the picture has "a strange beauty of contrasts, so childlike and knowing, so elusive it offers a man a hide-and-seek with himself [...] the exact truth cannot be pinned down because the truth is not there. The truth is somewhere in between" (202–203). The *Alices* continue this hide-and-seek of the man and the artist, both inside and outside the narration, his emotions effaced through most of the development of the story, but expressed and explored in some melancholy passages (as seen in the two previous sections); his presence neutralised behind Alice's dominant viewpoint but then emerging, concealed in the guise of a Dodo, a Wasp and a White Knight obsessively and pathetically repeating the formula "it's my own invention!".

Catherine Robson in her book *Men in Wonderland: The Lost Girlhood of the Victorian Gentleman* (2001) explores how the symbol of the "perfect little girl" (8) worked in Victorian times as "not only the true essence of childhood, but an adult male's best opportunity of reconnecting with his own lost self" (3). She explains how a male Victorian's early childhood was highly feminised and how the sudden separation from the feminine home environment, happening with "trousers and school" (4), provoked in many Victorian writers a sort of nostalgia for "a man's lost girlhood" (5). What further complicated the picture was the contradictory vision of children in the Victorian period, on the one hand infused by an idea of childhood as a golden age of purity and on the other hand influenced by Evangelical reflections on human corruption, embodied by the child as soon as he appears into the world (6–7).

Robson deals with various Victorian writers, among them Ruskin and Carroll, the most significantly and complexly related to little girls. On Carroll in particular, Robson offers a conjunct study of his pictures of little girls and his narrative texts (129–153), claiming that in Carroll's artistic expressions "the little girl is made mesmerizingly enigmatic by her ability to be both a thing and its opposite" (144). In this sense, Carroll's texts play with these two opposite views of childhood, seen either as a pure idealised mythical time (influenced also by Romantic poets such as Wordsworth, Blake and Coleridge – see Morton Cohen 1995, 105–112) or as an age menaced by corruption, depicted in a more cynic way (as many passages in the *Alices*, including the parodies, well show).

Carroll's personal involvement with Alice is thus charged with many different influences and features, both personal and cultural. We cannot look for a definitive resolution of Carroll's feelings and attitude, because the *Alices* are constitutively an enigmatic puzzle with more questions than answers. In "Alice on the Stage" Carroll recollects the lost summery days with Alice like this:

> Stand forth, then, from the shadowy past, 'Alice', the child of my dreams. Full many a year has slipped away, since that 'golden afternoon' that gave thee birth, but I can call it up almost as clearly as if it were yesterday – the cloudless blue above, the watery mirror below,

the boat drifting idly on its way, the tinkle of the drops that fell from the oars, as they waved so sleepily to and fro […] … (1887)

It seems from this passage that *his* Alice was born the 4 July 1862, when Alice Liddell was already 10 years old. "Alice Liddell was his passport to Wonderland" (xxv), writes Haughton (2003), and as such she has remained – comparisons with famous literary muses like Dante's Beatrice and Petrarca's Laura press upon our minds, and, last but not least, although just a fictional muse, the controversial and somehow dangerous parallel with Humbert Humbert's Lolita.[6] Alice moves through the fictional pages, imposing her own will on her writer, expressing her firm desire of being "not anybody's prisoner", but "a queen" (*TTLG*, 247) – she departs from Carroll's fictional double, the White Knight, towards her golden crown, crossing the brook and finding herself on a soft lawn covered with flower-beds (260), just as Beatrice bids goodbye to Dante's [1472] fictional self-portrait, turning towards the splendour of the her throne in the Empyrean White Rose (1999b, Canto XXI, 1–65).

However Carroll returns once more to his memories of her, in the last poem of the second of the *Alice* books, haunted by her presence "Moving under skies / Never seen by waking eyes" (287, 11–12) and trying to enclose her again in the immortal fictional space, making the poem an acrostic of her name. As Nabokov's Humbert Humbert beautifully puts it in *Lolita*'s last lines: "I am thinking of aurochs and angels, the secret of durable pigments, prophetic sonnets, the refuge of art. And this is the only immortality you and I may share, my Lolita" (2000, 309). Alfred Appel points out how Humbert Humbert, in his weekly game of chess with Gaston Godin, connects Lolita with the role of the Queen, and, at the same time, how Nabokov constructs *Lolita* following the idea of the "novel-as-gameboard" (2000, lxv). This is what happens with Alice and with the *Alice* books: Alice is a Queen, but a Queen of chess, and the two books about her are constructed as playgrounds enclosing her. Alice, as Lolita, is "safely solipsized" inside the pages of the book.

---

[6] For an extensive comparison and a detailed account of Carrollian influences in Nabokov's writings, see for instance Hetényi Zsuzsa 2018, or Elizabeth Prioleau 1975.

4.2 "What Are Little Girls Made of? Sugar and Spice and All That's Nice": The Character(s)

'I hope so,' the Knight said doubtfully: 'but you
didn't cry as much as I thought you would.'
(*TTLG*, 259)

This section examines what "affective narratology" can offer if applied specifically to the analysis of character construction. Characterisation is here considered in the least dualistic way possible: Alice's mind should not be thought of as a hypostatised entity which narrative clues can help us to picture. In fact, those narrative clues *themselves* form Alice's character, and this important remark should help in pointing out two aspects of the idea of characterisation here presented: first, its rhetorical quality and second, its relation to a more general idea of the mind as expanded and embodied (more on this and on the correspondence between fictional and real minds, in the readers' section). Through Alice's case I show how the identifying qualities of a character are not only made of the report of his/her thoughts, but that representations of emotions, through thoughts, actions and bodily indications, form those qualities as well. I first deal with the role Alice's emotions have in defining her, their differences between the two books and their repercussions on the structure of the stories themselves – which are modelled, after all, on Alice's mind, being representations of *her* dreams. I focus on Alice's interactions with other characters and on their embodiment of specific emotions; I connect Alice's own emotions with her actions and purposes, both in Wonderland and in the Looking-Glass Land. The section concludes by articulating the representation of Alice's body, the interconnections between mind, emotions and body, and the peculiar narrative devices Carroll uses to depict this complex interrelation.

4.2.1 Alice's Emotions

Palmer (2005) highlights "the importance of the emotions in any analysis of the whole of the fictional mind" (112), listing the different ways in which emotions deeply contribute to fictional texts, from being related to descriptions of behaviours and external physical signs, to being "inextricably linked with cognition" (113), so influencing actions and interpretations. As Herman states in "Cognition, Emotion and Consciousness"(2007) , the ways to understand fictional minds have been recently expanded, from a narrow "speech-category approach" to a wider perspective including different cognitive influences – from cognitive linguistics, to theory of mind, to the new importance given, in a general sense, to the understanding of cognitive emotional value. Herman stresses the importance of "emotionology" (255) for fictional scenarios, both in the sense of emotions as representations of a specific emotional cultural context and in the sense of "how stories have the power of reshaping emotionology itself" (255). Herman (2007) explains that "stories do not just emanate from cultural understandings of emotion, but also constitute a primary instrument for adjusting those systems of emotion, terms and concepts to lived experience." (255–256). I would like here to show how emotional states are an essential part of Alice's character, and how the depiction of Alice's emotions essentially contributes to the shaping of the stories' own structure and to the development of events.

At the very beginning of *Alice's Adventures in Wonderland* the first words used are a description of Alice's state of boredom; and all her subsequent actions are determined by her "burning with curiosity" (*AAIW*, 11). Emotions initiate Alice's adventures and they play a fundamental role in what happens next. Alice's emotions are not conveyed to the readers only by third-person descriptions or reports of inner speech, they appear instead as events throughout the narration, manifesting themselves in sudden resolutions, pools of tears, Freudian *lapsus*, violent actions (like kicking the poor Lizard Bill out of the chimney, *AAIW*, 44), physical transformations.

Alice is dreaming, and in dreams emotions run freely with the relaxation of the constraints of waking consciousness – the nature of Alice's dreams is itself an insightful recognition of the role of the emotions in shaping our minds. Alice is by turns curious, aggressive, frightened, puzzled, sad and angry, these emotional states leading on her actions and decisions. Moreover, as Palmer (2005) writes, there are short-term emotions, which are better called moods, and long-term ones, which are closer to dispositions (114), and it is from witnessing the sort of emotions Alice experiences more frequently and more intensely that we can picture in our mind an idea about her character's personality traits. For instance, we can think about her as being a clever child, because curiosity is a symptom of cleverness, but also as an irresponsible one, because her curiosity leads her not to think about consequences. She appears instinctive, in the way she suddenly cries and then stops and then cries again; and she has a problematic latent aggressiveness, which erupts extremely often in the *Alices*.

Auerbach (1973) argues that each human character Alice encounters is a reflection of a part of her personality: the Duchess obsessed by morals reflects Alice's own constant search for rules; the Cook's hostility towards the baby reflects Alice's own dislike of it; the hungry Knave of Hearts reflects Alice's own continuous thoughts of food; and "when the Duchess' Cook abruptly barks out "Pig!" Alice thinks the word is meant for her, though it is the baby, another fragment of

Alice's own nature, who dissolves into a pig" (36). As I have argued in the previous chapter the Queen of Hearts herself (whom Carroll described "as a sort of embodiment of ungovernable passion" in "Alice on the Stage", 1887) is the final projection of Alice's inner nature, an explosion of violence and fury.

In this sense, emotions play a crucial role in the building up of Alice's character, they are a vital force behind the story's vicissitudes and even come to be *characters* themselves. The dream narrative makes possible the realisation of a recursive logic in the process of characterisation: the dream-characters of Wonderland and of the Looking-Glass Land can be thought of also as embodiments of the dreamer's emotions. Being expressions of emotions, they can be considered, as Auerbach does consider them, projections of Alice's personality, since persistent emotions form dispositions, which are manifestations of one's character. I do not mean to represent this as a sort of multi-stage development; these different aspects form a part of the same narrative operation of characterisation and they go on together at the same time. Representations of Alice's emotions *are* her character, there is no real distinction between qualities and personality.

Besides considering some characters as living emotions, we can examine how Alice interacts with them as exhibiting the role of emotions in the encounters the narration presents. The predominant expression of negative emotions in the *Alice* books is notable, and all the characters Alice encounters are either rude to her (consider the Caterpillar, the Duchess, the Mad Hatter and the March Hare, the Queen of Hearts, the living Flowers, or Humpty Dumpty) or she is unconsciously rude to them (with the Mouse, the animals in the Caucus-Race, the Mock-Turtle, the White King). This preponderance of negative interactions shapes the story's development and structure, giving it specific meanings and substance: it points out how dreams work (often as embodied representations of fears and concrete negotiations of abstract conflicts); and, by presenting a threatening scenario in a story for children, it offers a sort of cathartic experience and a light representation of how to deal with adverse situations and troublesome feelings. As Morton Cohen (1995) recognises, "the theme of survival echoes all through Charles's work [...] if the *Alice* books are symbols of his own struggle to survive, they are also formulae for every child's survival" (144).

The fact that the emotional components of the interactions described in Carroll's narration play a fundamental role in structuring the story itself can be further investigated by taking into account what Hogan (2010) calls "the analysis of story structure in relation to emotion systems" (20). The pervasiveness of emotional drives affects Alice's actions, Alice's interactions and Alice's story – this last being shaped in order to follow an emotional path: starting from boredom, to the relief from it through curiosity and craving for new experiences, until the end of the story, the end of Alice's vicissitudes both in Wonderland and on the

Fig. 23: Dominic Murphy, *The Queen Cutter*, from his *Alice in Wonderland Art*. The characters merge together as different embodiments of different emotions of the same mind.

other side of the Looking-Glass, which is marked by anger and a sudden burst of rage. Alice's dreams end because of the force of her fury, which translates respectively into throwing away the living cards and into shaking the red queen into a kitten. Thus, both the *Alice* books start with Alice being bored and entering a sort of sleepy or dreamy state; all their subsequent events are determined by Alice's desire to discover new things and to visit lovely gardens, and their conclusions are provoked by Alice's rebellious anger, which throws her out of her own story. Emotions are inextricably bound into the core of the narration and to the life of its main agent.

4.2.2 Alice's Actions

Palmer stresses the relevance of actions, as well as behaviours, dispositions and emotions in the shaping of a character's mind:

> Constructions of fictional minds are inextricably bound up with presentations of action. Direct access to inner speech and states of mind is only a small part of the process of building up the sense of a mind in action. (2005, 210–211)

Actions never occur independently, but as with thoughts, they are always interconnected – and this means that the representation of a character's mind involves not only "private inner speech", but also the intentions, goals, purposes manifested by a character's actions. If emotions play an essential part in structuring Alice's character and Alice's story, they are continuous with her actions, the description of which is another key component in the process of her characterisation. The essential link between emotions and actions is the concept of embodiment: embodied emotions translated into actions, actions can be in part thought of as embodied emotions.

Alice's experiences in Wonderland do not happen because she suddenly finds herself in a strange parallel reality, with no control over it; they start because she consciously decides to follow a talking white rabbit into a rabbit hole: "her ardent pursuit of the rabbit is active, in contrast to her sister's passive engrossment in a book" (Beer 2016, 174). It is her own resolution that makes her jump into the rabbit hole, and this specific act, which makes all her story possible, is a significant sign of Alice's character – it is a manifestation of her curiosity, which, being a permanent state for Alice, comes to form her more stable disposition. Alice's actions in Wonderland are very often displays of her more constant traits: curiosity, childish changes of mood, irresponsibility, anger. There is a sort of purpose behind them (getting to have a closer look at the lovely garden she first glimpses after her fall into the rabbit hole) but this goal is not very well defined or shaped, because Alice is the fictional representation of a little girl, and, as such, she very often changes her emotional inclination and her actions follow accordingly.

The consequences of Alice's erratic emotional state in Wonderland are reflected in her erratic actions and in the very nature of her surroundings. Wonderland's chaos is just a direct result of Alice's mental environment. Wonderland *is* Alice's mind, and it too exhibits qualities of unstable mood and sudden anger. There is a strong correspondence and interconnection between the anarchic configuration of Wonderland, Alice's actions and Alice's emotions.

Contrastingly, Alice in the Looking-Glass Land has grown up somewhat; her own character is more stable and structured. In the second book her emotions are less violent, and she does not burst out crying and almost drown herself in her own tears (she cries once, but only for a moment, she immediately regains self-control and "brushes away her tears" –*TTLG*, 198). She also more successfully masters her predatory instincts towards the creatures she encounters; and she has a clear, well-defined goal (reaching the end of the chessboard and becoming a queen). As an externalisation of Alice's lucid purpose, the world around her is constructed in a more coherent and logical way than Wonderland was: the world on the other side of the Looking-Glass is a huge chessboard, the creatures living in it, although being often as rude and irrational as Wonderland's inhabitants, nevertheless have quite well-defined identities as chess pieces and commensurate roles. Alice's own sense of identity is stronger than in Wonderland, where her shifting emotions had corresponding shifting actions and shifting identities (she even often changes her own physical form); here she knows what she wants from the outset, she never changes size, and she proceeds until she reaches her final destination, the end of the chessboard and her golden crown.

If at the beginning of *Alice's Adventures in Wonderland* Alice *falls*, and therefore, even if she has decided to fall, it is still a not completely controlled move, because falling, as with falling asleep and falling in love, is something that is only partially mastered, in *Through the Looking-Glass* she goes through the mirror and jumps "lightly down into the Looking-glass room" (149). The dramatic fall into the deep interminable tunnel leading to Wonderland has been substituted by a light little jump. The internal implications of Alice's actions are clearly expressed by the space surrounding them, and this space is an emotional space. In the first book we find a colourful, confused, childish and unrestrained emotional flow, while the Looking-glass's black and white surface reflects one main emotion – Alice's ambition to become a queen (with all the possible metaphorical meanings related to it, the most evident being her own growing up) – and it is constructed accordingly.

Alice's main goal in the Looking-Glass world, which informs all her subsequent actions, shows her to the readers as a quite different character from the little girl lost in Wonderland. Here we face a determined person, who wants to get control over her dream, who does not want to be "just a sort of thing" (198) in someone else's dream, and who will not be trapped in a never-ending temporal circle: time, in the Looking-Glass dimension, surprisingly goes ahead, and Alice proceeds, overcoming the eternal return which the first book's narration uses to confine her forever in Wonderland.[7]

4.2.3 Alice's Body

As Wojciehowski and Gallese observe, "a new scientific approach to the study of the human condition is gaining momentum: it is the so-called 'embodied cognition' approach" (2011, 13), supported by scholars in cognitive science such as Damasio (1999) and Ramachandran (2003). Lakoff had already pointed out this direction in 1987, saying that "thought is embodied, that is, the structures used to put together our conceptual systems grow out of bodily experience and make sense in terms of it" (xiv). Many literary scholars developing a cognitive narratological outlook on fictional texts have embraced embodied cognition as a richer and more complex understanding of the dynamics of fictional minds. According to this theoretical perspective, fictional minds and real minds are regarded as equivalent and share common features. The embodied mind approach enables both a deeper understanding of fictional minds and a more insightful reader-response theory. Young's declaration in the introduction of her *Imagining Minds* testifies to this double significance:

> the more purely cognitive mind-brain models [...] cannot themselves *perform* what I call the novel's more fully integrated because embodied and emotionally stimulating 'mind work' – mind work that prompts us to better know our own minds. (2010, 4)

The focus on emotions in this chapter is strictly connected to the view of the mind as embodied: emotions, which are seen as intertwined with thought processes, usually present a bodily counterpart, a corporeal manifestation, a connected physical change. This perspective upon an "integrated mind" offers a holistic view of cognition as being inextricably interrelated with emotions, actions, bod-

---

[7] The ending of *Alice's Adventures in Wonderland* takes her back to the beginning, the tale of Wonderland repeating itself in her sister's imagination and marking Alice's dreamy steps towards her tea – and seems also to define her future (her sister picturing her as a grown woman still talking about Wonderland).

ily sensations. The consequences of this theoretical viewpoint for cognitive narratology can be seen, first, in our interpretation of characters' minds.

Alice's case is again especially significant for this kind of analysis, in the way it makes the representation of her body, and of the changes it undergoes an essential component in the depiction of her character. Moreover, as William Cohen argues in *Embodied: Victorian Literature and the Senses* (2009), the focus on the body and on the mind as embodied is a particular feature of Victorian texts, which very often deal with "the depiction of physical substance, interaction and incorporation" (xii). Alice's dream is "a very physical dream", and "all the senses are put in play in Carroll's 'universe of discourse' " (Beer 2016, 222). Alice is an extremely corporeal entity, and the problem of whether or not her body fits with its surroundings is a constant issue in Wonderland (in the Looking-Glass land this topic is less pervasive, since Alice has more stability, both in her mind and in her body).

Alice's growing and shrinking perfectly represents what William James (1890) recognised as "the general law that no mental modification ever occurs which is not accompanied or followed by a bodily change" (I, 4–5). Alice is curious and precipitous in wanting to get through the little door, and she shrinks too quickly; she is angry at herself and shows an excessive childish desperation, and she grows too big; she cries hopelessly, and she becomes so small again that she is in danger of drowning in her own tears. Again, Alice is annoyed at the White Rabbit ordering her about and she grows so big that she nearly destroys the Rabbit's house; after having discussed with the Caterpillar her concerns about growing, she finds her neck as long as a serpent and exhibits predatory attitudes towards the Pigeon – after having been scolded by the same Pigeon, she again returns to the normal height of a little girl – and so on. All the transformations Alice's body goes through are reflections of her unstable emotional state and of the complex process of her growing up, affecting both her identity and her body.

Beer (2016) writes "perversely, all this is a description of growing: that experience of intransigent change lost beneath consciousness in each of us, because absolutely beyond the control of consciousness" (212). She also quotes, as a further manifestation of Carroll's own preoccupation with the mysteries of the transformation from childhood to adulthood, a passage from his diaries describing a dream in which the same person ("Polly", alias Marion Terry, one of Carroll's former child friends who then became an actress) appears at the same time as both a child and a grown-up woman (214). Alice's experience of discomfort and unpleasant loss of control of her body, in conjunction with the revelation of new, latently aggressive aspects of her personality, amplifies upon the complex process of a little child confusedly confronting with the prospect of

4.2 "What Are Little Girls Made of? Sugar and Spice and All That's Nice" — 135

Fig. 24: Trevor Brown, *Eat Me*, From *Alice*, 2010. Trevor Brown's interpretation of Alice is often a grotesque, disturbing, provocative one, and one in which Alice's body plays an essential role. In this particular illustration the connection among eating, a body out of control and extreme puzzling discomfort is powerfully exasperated and highlighted.

adulthood. Carroll's approach presents the embodied mind of a child in relation to her surroundings and to her transformations, and through the means of such narrative representations presenting readers with an integrated mind, always interconnected with the body.

In this sense we cannot avoid touching also upon the subject of eating, so omnipresent in the *Alice* books that critic Sara Guyer calls Alice "the girl with the open mouth" (2004). It is not an overstatement to say that the *Alices* are constantly dealing, in one way or another, with eating and drinking. The eating and drinking form an essential and integral part of the presentation of Alice's interrelated mind and body: indeed Greenacre (1974), analysing some of Carroll's letters, states that for him "our bodies and hence our identities are determined by what we eat" (378).

Alice, in Carroll's own words, "always takes a great interest in questions of eating and drinking" (*AAIW*, 78) and she knows that "something interesting is sure to happen" whenever she eats or drinks anything (*AAIW*, 39). Alice's world is "a world animated by the foods and eating processes that might otherwise function as background, symbols, or structuring devices" (Lee 2014, 489). There is no point in listing all the passages in the books concerned with food and drink, because that would mean quoting almost *every page* of them. Alice's very first act while falling down the rabbit hole is catching a jar of marmalade and being disappointed in finding it empty, and she subsequently reflects upon cats eating bats and the other way around; most of her dialogues with the inhabitants of the two fantastical worlds of her dreams are either about what they eat, or about being eaten. The Mock-Turtle is an embodiment of a traditional soup; the trial in Wonderland is about stealing tarts; all the poems in the Looking-Glass Land deal with fish; there are kitchens and cooks, tea-parties, plum-cake banquets and dinner feasts; and the last scene in the Looking-Glass world, as a sort of grotesque exasperation of all that came before it, shows the guests becoming their own meals ("several of the guests were lying down in the dishes", 279).

Eating and drinking in the *Alices* functions as another physical manifestation of inner contradictions and impulses and thus conveys a host of different semantic ramifications. On the one hand there is the preoccupation with starving and, even, eventually dying: the jar of marmalade is empty, the bread-and-butterfly can very rarely find its tea and cream and so it always dies, the rule is "jam tomorrow, and jam yesterday – but never jam today" (*TTLG*, 206), and no one in the end can manage to taste the Looking-Glass plum cake (244). Children are often extremely hungry, and food may appear to be never enough for them: Alice's distorted childish perception of her recurring need for food is portrayed in several tragicomic passages.

On the other hand, there is the strong connection between excess, lust, cruelty and eating: as Empson remarks,

> Dodgson was well-informed about food, kept his old menus, and was wine taster to the College; but ate very little, suspected the High Table of overeating, and would see no reason to deny that he connected overeating with other forms of sensuality. (1974, 409)

Hence, references to base, animalistic instincts are often associated with food-related episodes in Carroll's stories: the consequences of eating and drinking are unpredictable and often lead to dangerous transformations. Carrollian food, like the fruits of lust the goblins sell in Rossetti's *Goblin Market*, is a constant temptation to Alice, who always succumbs to it, and, although the consequences of eating are not as tragic as for Rossetti's Laura, they are often unpleasant and often reveal Alice's predatory and violent side. Her association with the biblical serpent in her encounter with the Pigeon happens immediately after Alice has eaten a mushroom, and the association is validated by the fact that "little girls eat eggs quite as much as serpents do" (*AAIW*, 57).

The voracity of the Walrus and the Carpenter in eating the human-like little oysters makes their act almost a cannibalistic display of eating children alive, and Alice returns to these two characters when, at the end of her adventures, she tells her kitten that she will sing the Walrus and the Carpenter's song to make her imagine that she is eating oysters. She does not then appear anguished at all by the cannibalistic and perverse aspects of eating; on the contrary, she embraces them. In fact she has done so since the beginning of her stories, when she identifies with her cat Dinah's passion for eating mice and birds, precisely when she is in the presence of mice and birds; or when, a little later, she has to restrain herself from telling the Mock-Turtle that she has actually already tasted the soup made from him. Alice's shifts of identity are overtly linked with food: Michael Lee (2014) states that "Alice's journey through Wonderland thus develops a model of being in which identity is less a fixed essence than a position on a food chain that varies through association and diet" (503–504).

The Mock-Turtle is probably the most emotional creature in the *Alices*, constantly moaning and weeping, and he is at the same time the personification of a dish's (supposed) ingredient, making him a narrative emblem of this deep association between food and emotions. If recent scientific studies have highlighted the connections between gut bacteria and moods (Mayer 2016, Schmidt 2015, Knight 2016), the Mock-Turtle's tears are a visual fictional representation of this relation. Beer (2016) stresses the fact that the Mock-Turtle's account of his schooling turns traditional subjects into "activities and emotions" (237): he studied Ambition, Distraction, Uglification, Derision, Laughing and Grief, Reeling and Writhing, Drawling, Stretching and Fainting in Coils (*AAIW*, 102), which "all reach a zenith of *affect*" (Beer 2016, 238).

Conclusively, in the *Alice* books it is not possible to disentangle fears, violence, processes of growing up, aggressiveness, eating, drinking, growing and shrinking, moods and guts: they are all represented as tangible parts of the same narrative scenario concerning Alice's embodied mind and its puzzling and vast ramifications.[8]

---

[8] W. Cohen (2009) writes, referring to Victorian fictions in general, "they present a fluid exchange between surface and depth, inside and outside – a type of materialism that understands the organs of ingestion, excretion and sensation not simply to model but to perform the flow of matter and information between subject and the world" (xii).

4.3 "What Is the Use of a Book, without Pictures or Conversations?": The Readers

In the first chapter of *Empathy and the Novel* (2007, 1–35) Keen introduces contemporary theoretical perspectives on the term "empathy", in order to offer a working definition helpful for the rest of her study. I would like to rely upon this definition as well, which is going to guide my subsequent analysis of the special relationship between Carroll's nonsense and readerly empathetic reactions. As Keen writes, then, empathy can be defined as

> a vicarious, spontaneous sharing of affect, (which) can be provoked by witnessing another's emotional state, by hearing about another's condition, or even by reading [...] more complex cognitive responses to others' mental states layer atop this initial spontaneous sharing of feelings. (2007, 4)

The scholar points out that "empathy is thought to be precursor to its semantic close relative, *sympathy*", in the sense that the word empathy refers to a more spontaneous, instinctive sharing of feelings, while with sympathy we allude to a "more complex, differentiated feeling for another" (4).

Starting with this definition in mind, Keen subsequently explores various forms of empathetic attachment raised by novels, including identification, sympathy, ethical agreement, imitation and enrichment of the emotional spectrum. In this last part of the chapter I consider the empathetic reactions the *Alice* books entail, both from a historically situated perspective and from a more universal one, addressing the specific issue posed by Sewell, in *The Field of Nonsense* (1952), of the relationship between reading nonsense and experiencing emotional reactions. As pointed out in the previous section, an important theoretical premise of this analysis is the claim that real and fictional minds are susceptible of analogous treatment. An important connection with the previous character section is the concept of embodiment as operating in the character's construction and in the readers' relationship with the text. As emphasised by Lee

> Alice's consumption of other actors simultaneously moves the story along and quite literally transforms her. Undoing distinctions between eating and reading, the sequence also stands as a particularly self-reflexive instance of the text's participation in the mid- to late-nineteenth-century conceptualizations of reading as a bodily experience discussed by recent criticism concerned with the relationship between aesthetics and corporeality. (2014, 493)

4.3.1 The *Feel* of Nonsense: Do We Weep for Alice?

In the first chapter of *Empathy and the Novel* (3–35), Keen gives a general account of the current debate on the different elements (cognitive, emotional, environmental, dispositional, inherited) influencing empathy and addresses the core questions of her subsequent theoretical elaboration, which concern the sort of empathetic reactions fictional scenarios trigger in readers' minds, their causes and their consequences.[9] My focus here on the relationship between reading and experiencing empathy will consider the latter as neither purely emotional nor merely cognitive: as Keen says,

> the acts of imagination and projection involved in empathy certainly deserve to be labelled cognitive, but the sensations [...], deserve to be registered as feelings. Thus, [...] I do not quarantine narrative empathy in the zone of either affect or cognition: as a process, it involves both. (2007, 28)

The possible causes and implications of our reacting empathetically to a fictional situation and to fictional characters have been studied and hypothesised by several narratologists. There are different theoretical approaches to several aspects of the relationship between reading fiction and empathy, focussed upon, for instance: the similarity or dissimilarity with real-life experience (Prentice et. al. 1997; Batson 1991; Keen 2007, 2011); the sort of fictional representations which better elicit empathetic reactions (Bortolussi and Dixon 2003; Green 2004; Keen 2007, 2011, 2013; Nünning 2015; Hogan 2010); or the possible ethical significance attributable to empathy caused by fiction (Nünning 2015; Keen 2007, especially 146–168; Habermas et al. 2010). One crucial point many scholars acknowledge is the special status of fictions in relation to empathetic responses: Keen (2007) claims that it is precisely the fictionality of novels that boosts their empathic effects, by freeing the readers from any "demand on real-world action" (4). Nünning (2014) adds that the complexity of interactions and empathetic stimulations to be found in a novel is rarely matched by real-life situations (193–194); Feagin (1996) explores the concept of appreciation as a complex emotional response, involving empathy, specific to the reading of novels; and Herman (2013a) highlights the essential role of fictional narratives and poetry in shaping and developing a particular culture's "emotionology" (221–224).

---

[9] I am not going to inquire here into the details of scientific findings and hypotheses about human empathy, its connection with mirror neurons or its link with psychopathologies. For more information on the subject, see Keen 2007, 4–28).

I would here like to explore the sort of empathetic reactions that the *Alice* books can evoke in readers – and the universality versus the culturally situated nature of these reactions. Nonsense texts clearly offer a theoretical challenge for a theory of affective narratology. Theories of empathy bearing on realistic modes of representation are called into question if nonsense texts, with their anti-mimetic fabric, are able to generate empathetic responses. Moreover, if, as Keen (2007) herself underlines, in the Victorian period "novelists' success or failure in rendering characters that could invoke sympathetic reactions played a significant role in reviewers' responses [...] fictional characters either garner sympathy or they fail" (53), what could be the place of the *Alice* books' success, *if*, on the other hand, as Sewell (1952) and Tigges (2013) claim, "Nonsense can admit of no emotion [...] it is a game, to which emotion is alien" (Sewell, 129)?

I consider Carroll's nonsense not in opposition to the emotional discourse going on among Victorian writers, but as another, alternative way of dealing with it. Sewell (1952) points out several times that Carroll's more "sentimental" works like *Sylvie and Bruno* are to be considered "failures" (175), and that the *Alices* are masterpieces of nonsense precisely because they banish all emotions from their narrative tissue. More specifically, Sewell claims that nonsense has to keep its distance from the dimensions of dreams and madness and, that even if the *Alice* books apparently deal with both dreams and madness, they do so in a way that prevents any emotional involvement, by focusing on words and depriving them of meaning, or transforming people into things, since "the mind in the Nonsense universe, be it the mind of the maker or the guest, must not be acted upon by any of the emotive words that may be employed" (131). As I have already demonstrated throughout this chapter, the *Alice* books are full of representations of emotions, and their narrative often deals with emotional states. As Sewell herself recognises, they do portray emotions in an extremely peculiar way, mixed up with puns, strange interactions, parodies and unsympathetic characters. However, the atypicality of these representations does not entail that emotions are not there. Emotions are not banished *at all* in the *Alices*, and I would like now to show that their representation invites the readers' emotional engagement as well.

Keen (2007) states that "the most commonly nominated feature of narrative fiction to be associated with empathy is character identification", encouraged by "particular techniques of characterization" (93). Relying on this connection between empathy and characterisation, I suggest that Alice's complex characterisation differs from Victorian literary stereotypes, and that there is no contradiction, from the perspective of empathetic involvement, between this quality and the nonsense of Alice's surroundings. The different narrative methods used in the process of Alice's characterisation (such as perspective taking, indirect implication of traits and mode of representation of consciousness) demonstrate more specifically that nonsense doesn't impair the empathy-boosting capacity of such narrative techniques.

It is true that Alice is not Little Nell, her character being, as Elsie Leach notes

> a bit puzzling, even to the modern child, because it does not fit a stereotype. How much more unusual she must have seemed to Victorian children, used to girl angels fated for an early death [...] or to impossibly virtuous little ladies, or to naughty girls who eventually reform in response to heavy adult pressure. (1974, 123)

However, we can identify with Alice, possibly even more because she's *not* a stereotype, and this identification fosters our involvement. Alice is "neither naughty nor overly nice" (E. Leach, 123), and the puzzlement related to her more ambiguous and less idealised features makes readers (especially Victorian readers, but to some extent also contemporary ones) confront a more nuanced picture of a child's nature; less suited to inspiring immediate tears, perhaps, but certainly capable of evoking more complex emotions, doubts, perplexities, reflections.

If the more nuanced and elaborated rhetorical[10] result of Alice's characterisation can be seen as encouraging identification, this effect should nevertheless not be conflated with realism. Identifying with a character and her situation, her feelings and her reactions, as several empirical studies have shown (see Keen 2007, 69–70), is not necessarily connected with a realistic representation. There are narrative techniques and specific narrative scenarios which obviously invite identification; however, firstly, many of them work differently according to the cultural and historical context and personal sensitiveness of the reader; secondly, non-realism has been repeatedly shown not to interfere with identification processes. Identification and emotional involvement are not a result of mimetic representation conceived as a sort of confusion between real life and fiction: as Walsh (2007) points out "emotional response should be understood not as an effect of illusion, but as a corollary of the fundamental processes of textual comprehension" (157).

In the context of Alice's characterisation, such a view opens up other fictional ways of building identification and empathy:

> the character, viewed from a rhetorical perspective, is in fact no more than characterization itself [...] the emotional significance is grounded in textual meaning, or the semiotic means of representation, rather than the conceptual product of representation. (Walsh 2007, 158)

---

10 I am here relying on Walsh's idea of understanding the process of character representation as rhetorical, as outlined in *The Rhetoric of Fictionality* (2007), 156–159.

Several textual strategies can cooperate in order to strengthen this emotional significance. I am considering here identification as a rhetorical result of the "perspective taking" mental activity described by Nünning (2015). The scholar suggests different factors which can influence a stronger identification with a fictional character, and "perspective taking" works as one of them: "perspective taking," in relation to fiction, is understood here to be the compound mental activity enabling one to imagine adopting a character's viewpoint, feelings and beliefs, which may lead to identification and, as we have seen, to empathy.

The fictional devices Nünning mentions as helpful in realizing the mental process of perspective taking are, for instance, focalisation, which she understands as "the narrative technique which enables readers to simulate characters' thoughts and feelings" (2015, 196). The characterisation of Alice is informed by her function as the main focaliser in the stories: we share her mental processes, her thoughts and her emotional responses. Another narrative way of encouraging perspective taking, mentioned by Nünning, is the presence of narratorial commentary upon the character's situation, enhancing readers' understanding of the character. Carroll inserts several comments to describe Alice, telling us how curious she is, how she likes to pretend to be two people, how polite she tries to remain, and so on, and such narratorial remarks give us a better picture of Alice, even if this picture is not always a flattering one. According to Nünning,

> this mode of narration bridges the gap between reader and character by explicitly referring to and explaining the characters' personality traits, motives, wishes and beliefs. It often includes explicit characterisation by the narrator. (2015, 200)

Another narrative tool used to evoke readers' interest is to put the character in a dangerous and uncertain situation (Nünning 2015, 202; Keen 2007, 71–72), in which we do not know what might happen to them. Uncertainty and potential danger are two constant traits in Alice's stories, also highlighted several times throughout the narration: "never once considering how in the world she was to get out again"; "to wonder what was going to happen next" (*AAIW*, 12); "What *will* become of me?" (*AAIW*, 40); "I wonder what they'll do next!" (*AAIW*, 43); "she was a good deal frightened by this very sudden change" (*AAIW*, 55); "How it happened, Alice never knew, but exactly as she came to the last peg, she was gone" (*TTLG*, 176); "so she went on, wondering more and more at every step, as everything turned into a tree the moment she came up to it, and she quite expected the egg to do the same" (*TTLG*, 217). Alice's situation is repeatedly depicted as an uncertain one in which she finds herself always surprised and puzzled, and where numerous queer, strange and unexpected events happen; the specific nonsense narrative framework is one which triggers the presence of the unusual and the unpredictable. This strengthens our involvement with her vicissitudes since "characters' involvement in a suspenseful situation provokes physiological responses of arousal in readers" (Keen 2007, 94).

Morton Cohen, however, suggests that what the *Alice* books ultimately represent for children of all times is somewhat different:

> In the end, however, the books are not mainly about fear and bewilderment. Once readers have associated with Alice and wandered with her through Wonderland, they are together on a survival course ... they offer encouragement, a feeling that the author is sharing their miseries and is holding out a hand, a hope for their survival as they pass from childhood into adulthood. (1995, 139–140)

In this sense, a strong identification with Alice offers guidance to children, especially Victorian children oppressed by a severe environment, through the puzzlements and uncomfortable feelings related to the world of adults and education.

In the *Alices* there are two other rhetorical strategies that work in a complementary way, encouraging identification on the one hand and keeping the narration accessible and pleasant for children on the other hand. Firstly, going with Alice through unpleasant feelings, awkward interactions and dangerous scenarios not only functions as a survival guide, in M. Cohen's terms, but also as a cathartic exaggeration of real-life trials and complexities. Through identification with Alice and the empathetic reactions connected to it, we experience purification, in the Aristotelian sense, of the uncomfortable emotions she has to deal with. In the service of this same idea, the characters (as Carroll himself explained in "Alice on Stage", 1887) are often embodiments of one single strong emotion: the Queen of Hearts embodies "ungovernable passion", the White Rabbit cowardice and feebleness, the Red Queen pedantry and severity, the White Queen gentle imbecility and helplessness, the Mad Hatter lunacy, the Dormouse is "the embodied essence of Sleep", and so on. All the characters Alice meets in her journeys can be thought of as exaggerated fictional representations of specific emotional conditions or states. In this way, too, Carroll leads his readers, and especially the child readers, to a cathartic recognition of passions and unruled emotions, a sort of narrative guide through the emotional spectrum.

However (and here I introduce the second rhetorical tool, complementing the cathartic aspect), Carroll maintains a light touch: the heavy emotional baggage of these unsettling encounters, with their related affective responses of fear and uncertainty, is usually alleviated by the introduction of funny elements – the readers can often pause, relax and laugh. Laughter is a narrative tool Carroll uses to convey in a more pleasant way his otherwise too intense messages. When the Mock Turtle talks about learning "Laughing and Grief" (parodying the lessons of Latin and Greek, *AAIW*, 103), he also manages to highlight the essence of the *Alices* themselves, where comic and tragic elements are mixed together in order that one works as a relief from the other, in a subtle and carefully calibrated alternation of tones. The identification with Alice which leads to catharsis is also attenuated by laughter.

Readers' identification with Alice, then, as a result of her characterisation and specific connected rhetorical techniques leading to empathetic responses, stands as evidence against Sewell's depiction of the *Alice* books as intellectual exercises deprived of any emotional dimension from either the author's or the reader's side. In the next section I focus on the possible implications of empathetic responses to the *Alices* and on the cultural and historical repercussions of readers' involvement in Carroll's innovative books, both in Victorian times and in the modern day.

4.3.2 "Tut, Tut, Child! Every Thing's Got a Moral, if only You Can Find It"

Keen (2011a) recognises how the connection between involvement in fictional worlds and consequent modification of mental attitudes in readers was widely explored precisely in the Victorian age. She emphasises several questions posed and investigated by Victorian thinkers, such as inquiry into "novelists' efforts to stimulate development of novel-readers' sympathetic imagination", or research on "physiological responses to reading" or attention to "empathy and *Einfühlung* and the malleability of the reading mind, especially as regards readers' morals" (3). Carroll's *Alices* were inserted into this particular cultural environment, when attention to the effects of novel-reading was at its peak: Dickens was consciously using his huge cultural influence to raise awareness about specific social issues; Elizabeth Gaskell utilised perspective mobility and evocation of feeling to reach across social barriers; Hardy's work shows his knowledge of empathetic narrative strategies studied by his contemporaries and his intention of using them to arouse specific altruistic feelings (Keen 2011b) and for George Eliot "the cultivation of the reader's sympathetic imagination lay at the center of her art" (Keen 2007, 53).

In this respect, the *Alice* books again present an exceptional case. It is precisely their amorality which constitutes their moral and empathetic appeal to the reader. They intentionally banish the overt didacticism of other Victorian books for children (like Kingsley's *The Water Babies*, 1863; Barlee's *Three Paths of Life: A Tale for Girls*, 1872; MacDonald's *At the Back of the North Wind*, 1871; Craik's *The Little Lame Prince and his Travelling Cloak*, 1875; Thomas Hughes' *Tom Brown's Schooldays*, 1857) and, in doing so, they imply criticism of that didacticism. Readers' identification with Alice makes the nonsense of her surroundings a further rhetorical projection of their own surroundings: the depiction of nonsensical and absurd situations and characters stresses the absurdity of the world outside of the book that has generated those scenarios. Wonderland and the Looking-Glass Land function as fictional mirrors, giving back to Carroll's readers their own Victorian rules and morals, ridiculed and parodied.

Empathy works as both a recognition of the other and as a projection of the self: Alice represents both a self-projection for different readers in different times and a fostering of sympathy for specific categories. So, in the Victorian era, Victorian conceptions of childhood appeared challenged in the *Alices:* Alice is a potential sinner, not a completely pure and innocent creature, but she is also a living human being surrounded by incomprehensible challenges and experiencing doubts, fears, anger. Carroll's success, unlike anyone before him, was "to make the adult reader sympathise with the child Alice, the victim of the unpredictable, undependable world of adults into which she has accidentally fallen" (M. Cohen 1995, 144). Victorian England's morality and education is highlighted in its nonsensical and ridiculous features, children are finally shown as complex beings who can't be reduced to one absolute conception: "what, then, does it all add up to besides art? [...] it goes far beyond Charles's original purpose: it reaches beyond Victorian Oxford into the wide world" (138). If the *Alice* books are on the one hand in a constant rhetorical dialogue with the Victorian world where they were born, on the other hand there's a universal quality in them which challenges and inspires readers of any time. As Lowrie (2008) puts it, referring precisely to the *Alices*, "part of the beauty of memorable myths and works of art is not only the manner in which they are 'constructed', but also the manner in which they never stop making us question ourselves and our world" (218).

The affective relationship readers are able to experience with the *Alice* books is an ever-lasting one, and the continuous re-interpretations and re-adaptions of Carroll's masterpieces over time are a proof of the constantly proliferating expansion of this relationship. It is not certain to what extent novels "are ethically meaningful to disseminate values, emotional dispositions, and cognitive practices" (Nünning 2015, 1),[11] but the multiple different connections established over time between the *Alices* and their readers exemplify the deeply affective and involving meaning that a relationship with a literary text can generate. If empathy may be understood as both projection and recognition, that is apparent in the way the *Alice* books have been interpreted: as travellers' books meant to support

---

11 Keen also discusses the practical moral impact of fiction broadly in *Empathy and the Novel* (2007), 145–168.

the spirit of exploration (Douglas-Fairhurst 2015, 360); as social satires applicable to many different historical scenarios (among the most recent, representations of characters from the *Alices* have been used to parody Brexit and to caricature Donald Trump's political actions); as feminist inspirations (after all, Alice is one of the few fairy-tale female characters who does not meet any Prince Charming and who manages to both initiate her adventures and to escape dangers all by herself); as a perennial "reference point in arguments about the dangers of growing up too fast" (Douglas-Fairhurst 2015, 372); and in discussions about all the controversial and difficult stages of childhood. Even if the *Alice* books have not determined a recognizable specific social reaction, their huge, world-wide cultural influence is definitely a proof of the powerfulness of the empathetic effects they have had upon readers, of all times.

Chapter 5
Unnatural Alice

> Why, sometimes I've believed as many as six
> impossible things before breakfast.
> (*TTLG*, 209–210)

The aim of this chapter is to find a theoretical balance between a cognitive perspective upon the *Alice* books and "unnatural narratology." Unnatural narratology is a fairly new paradigm in narrative theory that offers, in the words of Richardson (2012), "to provide a conceptual framework for works that refuse to follow the conventions of ordinary storytelling" (22). According to unnatural narratologists, unconventional storytelling does not have an appropriate corresponding narrative theory: the so-called mimetic model has been used for describing the settings, situations and characters of novels mainly with reference to real-world parameters. Such a model neglects the enormous corpus of antimimetic novels that exploit antirealist modes of narrative representation, "playing with, exaggerating, or parodying the conventions of mimetic representation" and "often, foreground narrative elements and events that are wildly implausible or palpably impossible in the real world" (Richardson 2012, 20). The ways in which unnatural narratologists try to overcome what they call the "mimetic bias" of traditional narrative theory are multiple, because their theoretical approaches are quite differentiated from each other: different interpretative strategies have been proposed for analysing unnatural texts, and indeed the definition of the term "unnatural" itself is contested: "the distinctiveness of unnatural narratology, then, is in the object, aims and approach rather than any specific theoretical framework" (Alber et al. 2010, 5).

Given the various anti-mimetic aspects of the *Alice* books, this chapter proposes a cognitive analysis of them as "unnatural nonsense texts", in which I explore the theoretical connections between the "unnatural" and "nonsense": their differences and similarities, and the extent to which they can complement each other. My approach retains a cognitive outlook throughout, providing an inclusive frame for the elaboration of the concepts. As has been already recognised "ideas from cognitive narratology help illuminate the considerable, sometimes unsettling interpretative difficulties posed by unnatural elements" (Alber et al. 2010, 7); moreover, Alber asserts that "a cognitive approach does not only help us define the unnatural; it also helps us explain what the unnatural does to recipients and how we can try to make sense of it" (Alber 2016, 435).

However, I also seek to overcome some limitations of the unnatural approach: specifically, the risks of dichotomizing the natural and the unnatural and the ambiguous notion of what the unnatural actually is. In the latter respect there are two antithetical risks to be avoided: the risk of simplifying and trivializing the unnatural through a cognitive outlook and the risk of leaving it as an unintelligible mystification, defined only by its almost "transcendent" unnatural essence (see Alber and Heinze 2011, 11).

5.1 "You May Call It 'Nonsense' if You Like [...] but *I've* Heard Nonsense, Compared with Which That Would Be as Sensible as a Dictionary!": The Author

The authorial section of this chapter begins with the parallelisms between the concepts of unnatural and nonsense, and specifically Carroll's nonsense in the *Alice* books. I situate the different meanings attached to the concept of the unnatural in relation to Carroll's interests in the supernatural and the abnormal – but also show that this same link may expose some limitations of the term "unnatural". I consider whether the term "unnatural" is appropriate to all the complex qualities of unnatural narratives cited by unnatural narratologists, grounding this critique upon Monika Fludernik's article "How Natural is 'Unnatural Narratology'?" (2012). Taking Fludernik's suggestion, I then introduce the "fantastic" as a possible mediating concept. The section concludes by examining some "unnatural" features of the Carrollian narrative worlds and exploring the creative procedures for the literary invention of nonsensical/unnatural scenarios, ultimately linking them with processes of multi-disciplinary counter-factual thinking.

5.1.1 Is Nonsense Unnatural?

When they present the features of anti-mimetic fiction, unnatural narratologists offer quite broad definitions, suggesting that the unnatural elements can be found in the fictional worlds and in the characters that inhabit them, as well as in the form of the narration itself: in this sense, however, many formal characteristics of "natural" narratives, such as omniscient narration or paralepsis, turn out to be unnatural.[1] Unnatural texts, according to unnatural narratolo-

---

[1] The extreme consequences of this perspective are presented in Maria Mäkelä "Realism and the

5.1 "You May Call It 'Nonsense' if You Like [...] but *I*'ve Heard Nonsense — **149**

Fig. 25: Andrea D'Aquino, illustration from *Alice's Adventures in Wonderland*, 2015. Beautiful and colourful illustration by Andrea D'Aquino provides an idea of the nonsensical tissue of the *Alice* books as something which can be re-interpreted in a more abstract, post-modernist fashion, confirming the idea that "the Victorian genre of nonsense literature [...] emerges at the beginning of a far-reaching break with the mimetic tradition" (Schwab 1996, 49).

Unnatural" (2013), where she argues that *any* narration, by the simple fact of being a narration, i.e. a fictional representation, is unnatural.

gists,[2] include not only post-modern fictions (like many Ballard or Pynchon novels, Roth's *The Breast*, O' Brien's *The Third Policeman*, Coover's "The Babysitter" …) but also Shakespeare's plays and works by Rabelais, Aristophanes and Apuleius. There is a striking similarity between unnatural narratology's compendium of unnatural fictions and the general canon of nonsense texts, as presented in theoretical accounts of the nonsense genre (Lecercle 1994; Haughton 1988; Holquist 1999; Tigges 2013; Stewart 1979). Exactly the same literary works are cited, for their use of nonsense-related devices; such a correspondence between instances of nonsense and instances of the unnatural suggests that the two concepts can be viewed as very close to each other.

Are the concepts of nonsense and the unnatural defining the same kind of texts? Nonsense can be considered as having a more historically situated position, since its most representative examples (works by Carroll and Lear) are literary products of a specific period, the Victorian Age. Nevertheless, if nonsense assumes its most characteristic literary form in Victorian England, many of its features are common to other previous (and subsequent) narratives.[3] These manifestations of nonsense qualities in novels, poems and plays outside the Victorian era give the term a scope broadly comparable to that of unnatural fiction.[4] This does not in itself entail a complete correspondence between the two, but the common elements provide a basis for narratologically fruitful theoretical comparison.

In their programmatic article "Unnatural Narratives, Unnatural Narratology: Beyond Mimetic Models" Alber, Iversen, Nielsen and Richardson (2010) identify the different possible aspects of unnatural narratives as the depiction of unnatural storyworld settings, the representation of unnatural minds and the use of unnatural acts of narration. The distinction between these three aspects can be linked to my own logical division, in addressing the *Alice* books from a cognitive perspective, between issues pertaining to the author, the characters and the reader's mind.

All these features of unnatural fiction are to be found also in theoretical conceptualisations of nonsense texts. Lecercle (1994) gives an account of nonsense narrative elements in which he repeatedly mentions the *unusual* as a narrative device, evidenced in fictional strategies such as the use of paradoxes, contradictions, uncommon linguistic structures, impossible representations and abnormal

---

[2] See Alber et al., *A Poetics of Unnatural Narrative*, *Unnatural Narratives- Unnatural Narratology* (2013), and "Unnatural Narratives, Unnatural Narratology: Beyond Mimetic Models" (2010).
[3] See, for example, Lecercle (1994) on the *achrony* and *diachrony* of nonsense (165–222).
[4] "Broadly" since the definition of an unnatural text is not unequivocally established, the emphasis changing for different unnatural narratologists.

minds. The fact that "nonsense or madness not only subvert, they also disclose and construct" (6) is a claim unnatural narratologists also raise in relation to unnatural texts, understood as narratives depicting "situations and events that move beyond, extend, challenge, or defy our knowledge of the world" (2013, 2), so "taking us to the most remote territories of conceptual possibilities" (Alber et al. 2010, 114).

Therefore, if we consider the two terms "nonsense" and "unnatural" in a broad manner (that is, the only way of considering the unnatural, since it only entails a broad definition; and one of two correlated ways – synchronic and diachronic – to look at nonsense), we can observe how they entail a very similar set of narrative features. It is true that if we take the unnatural as being defined exclusively in an anti-mimetic way, nonsense is not circumscribed only by that opposition; and some specific aspects of nonsense, like the focus on wordplay, are not emphasised in definitions of unnatural narrative. However, my purpose here is not only to highlight specific aspects of the *Alices*' nonsense that can be considered "unnatural," but also to avoid a rigid dichotomy between the mimetic and the anti-mimetic.

Taking for granted the privileged status of the *Alices* as nonsense masterpieces, we find they also fit many of the general features of unnatural novels: they present non-human and impossible characters (often linked with the personifications of linguistic behaviours and concepts – in this sense wordplay is incorporated as being *also* unnatural); they offer endings which are just new beginnings; they adopt peculiar ways of representing the progression of events (in *Through the Looking-Glass*, for example, events are organised following the moves of a pawn in a chessboard) and even challenge the idea of a progression of events; they depict unnaturally functioning minds; they continuously propose parodies of conventional genres and critiques to moral rules (this latter aspect is another one which, as mentioned previously, is highlighted as a frequent feature of unnatural texts by Richardson 2012, 2016).

More fundamentally, Fludernik (2012) points out that unnatural texts are a combination of two different narrative discourses: "the discourse of fable, romance, before-the-novel narrative; and the discourse of postmodernist anti-illusionism, transgression, and meta fiction" (363); the distinctive generic status of the *Alice* books positions them in precisely such a complex position between the fairy tale and postmodern anti-mimetic creations. According to Schwab,

> we might well argue that Carroll marks the beginning of those far-reaching challenges to our cultural notions of mimesis and representation which culminate in what we have come to call the simulacra of postmodernism. (1996, 49)

This peculiar place of the *Alices* as literary staging posts between the fantastic and fairy tale heritage and postmodern fiction makes them an ideal case study mediating between the two different narrative traditions to which the unnatural is linked.

Moreover Fludernik (2012), in her constructive critique of the unnatural approach, stresses the fact that the recovery of the fantastic and of anti-mimetic techniques related to it can be considered one of the most interesting aspects of the unnatural narratology programme:

> one of the most important *practical* consequences of discovering the "unnatural" in the deceptively realist or familiar text is therefore this recuperation of the fabulous, magical, fantastic or supernatural. Since narratology was so strongly focused on the realist novel and therefore tended to neglect pre-eighteenth-century narratives, it has devoted comparatively little attention to the supernatural. (363)

This attitude is one I would like to embrace, since the *Alice* books display "anti-mimetic" narrative techniques in relation to the fantastic. The theoretical goal, then, is to position the fantastic[5] as a possible conceptual tool defining nonsense and the unnatural in a broader, more complex and not dichotomous fashion. What Prickett writes about Victorian fantasy is worth quoting here, since it emphasises two important aspects of this approach:

> Over the last two hundred years fantasy has helped us to evolve new languages for new kinds of human experience; it has pointed the way towards new kinds of thinking and feeling. [...] it has also created far other worlds and other seas. By them we have been able to hold a mirror to the shadowy and more mysterious sides of our own, and see reflected in a glass darkly mysteries not otherwise to be seen at all. (3)

On the one hand, there is the connection between the fantastic and the idea of the unnatural; and, on the other hand, the impossibility of disentangling this concept from our own reality.

In what follows I further link nonsense and the unnatural through the specific fantastical tissue of the *Alice* books and through the figure of Lewis Carroll

---

5 I am using here the concept of the "fantastic" in a broad manner, in a different way from Todorov's definition of it – my definition can be considered closer to what Todorov calls marvellous tales and supernatural tales (1975, 41–57). I refer here to instances of Victorian fantasy, contemporary fantasy, and fairy tales, taking the peculiarity of the *Alice* books' genre as a case in point (about the definition of the *Alices*' genre, see also Demurova 1982). The term "fantastic", because of its long conceptual history, might not be the ideal one: however, it is the specific meaning I attach to it the real innovative theoretical approach, not the term itself, which can in future be replaced with a more original word.

himself, who can be considered a sort of ideal example of natural author of unnatural texts. I also analyse in more depth the features of the *Alices*' unnatural landscapes and the creative methods the author uses to depict this unnaturalness. I keep using the term "unnatural", not to create confusion, instead of "fantastic": however, as a relevant indication for further research, I aim to propose a specific new term to indicate my distinctive perspective on what the "fantastic", as a third, negotiating term between the natural and the unnatural, means and entails.

5.1.2 Carroll's Interest in the Supernatural, Unnatural, Hypernatural

Carroll was not only interested in how our minds work in general, but also developed a specific preference for the study of mental phenomena on the threshold of the supernatural. From the peculiar tissue of the dreamscape to the strange psychological state that makes it possible to see fairies, Carroll studied, and depicted in his narrative works, the most uncommon possible (and impossible) scenarios.[6] The specific declination of Carrollian nonsense proves once again to have features of the unnatural as enunciated by unnatural narratologists, and a sense "equivalent to a variety of meanings that include the fabulous, the magical, and the supernatural besides the logically or cognitively impossible" (Fludernik 2012, 362).

To recapitulate the different manifestations of Carroll's scholarly penchant for unnatural phenomena, as discussed in the first chapter: first, in spite of his more traditional professional approach in the fields of mathematics, geometry and logics (see Throesch 2009), in his fictional work Carroll continuously plays with ideas of different space and time dimensions,[7] concepts of "mysterious negative numbers" (M. Gardner 2001, 103), suggestions on the existence of anti-matter, representations of paradoxes and depictions of non-existent entities (like the non-existent being par excellence, the Unicorn). As Beer says

> In his professional life, Dodgson relied wholly on Euclid; as Lewis Carroll, exploring possible worlds in fantasy, however, he could play freely with all the non-Euclidean elements newly available for thought. Rather than just making fun of them, he is engaged in a dance

---

[6] See chapter one for the list of books Carroll owned on the subject of the supernatural.
[7] It can be also worth recollecting that he owned a first-edition copy of *Flatland* and that he read Zollner's *Transcendental Physics: An Account of Experimental Investigations* (see Lovett 2005, 370).

of ideas that takes him far from land: turning a somersault in the sea, as in the Lobster-Quadrille. (2016, 47)

Secondly, Carroll's interest in psychic phenomena and in the studies of the Society for Psychical Research demonstrates his concern with another aspect of the "unnatural". In this sense, dreams and dreamy states have profound meanings, abnormal psychic incidents are connected with the exploration of supernatural realities and phenomena such as clairvoyance and ESP are considered worthy of intellectual exploration. The possible existence and substance of ghostly entities and the phenomenon of telepathy were also frequent topics in Carroll's reading (Lovett 2005).

It is also true, and significant for the present argument, that many of the phenomena in which Carroll was interested *cannot* actually be defined as completely unnatural: while unicorns and fairies are unreal creatures (though still they can stand for something less unreal!), the explorations of anti-matter and alternative dimensions of space-time, as well as the enigmatic power recognised in dreamy states, all establish a continuity with the natural. The impossibility of establishing an absolute boundary between the natural and the unnatural confirms Fludernik's point, that "all these dichotomies […] can be deconstructed in numerous ways" (2012, 359).

A further element of Carroll's exemplary fit with "unnatural" concerns, and also one that demolishes rigid oppositions, is the "unnaturalness" of his writing identity itself: as a nonsense novelist the Reverend Charles Ludwig Dodgson adopted the invented name of Lewis Carroll, mirroring the "unnatural" substance of his narrative writings with the creation of a parallel identity, an unreal name under which to pursue his narrative exploration of the mysterious, the surreal and the unusual. Nevertheless, while a *nom de plume* may assert two distinct identities, Charles Dodgson and Lewis Carroll, it does so only to acknowledge them, at the same time, as the same person, two sides of the same coin.

5.1.3 The "Unnaturalness" of the Carrollian Worlds

The unusual narrative scenarios of the *Alices* can elucidate in more detail the peculiarities of the Carrollian fictional worlds. Unnatural narratologists emphasise the immense potentiality of the creation of imaginary landscapes with unrealistic features, a quality well-articulated by Italo Calvino (1988) in his *Six Memos for the Next Millennium*, where he describes imagination as "the repertory of what is potential, what is hypothetical, or what does not exist and has never existed, and perhaps will never exist but might have existed" (91). At the same time however,

Calvino calls attention to the problematic aspects of an oppositional definition of the unnatural: he mentions "what might have existed", using thus a mimetic criterion, alongside his reference to "what has never existed". As Fludernik rightly underlines, especially in her discussion of "Binary Opposites and Conceptions of the Natural" (2012, 358–362) a binary opposition between natural and unnatural does not do justice to either of the two dimensions, neutralizing their mutual connections and interdependencies in favour of a blind hypostatisation:

> what "unnatural" narratology sets out to do is to escape from mimeticism. However, quite ironically so, by setting itself in opposition to the natural (what is *un*natural must be the opposite of "natural" or mimetic), it falls into the trap of having to acknowledge the reality of the natural in the shape of the mimetic, even if the idea is to trace the non-mimetic underside of the mimetic. (365)

The multiple possibilities connected to the imaginary worlds of fantasy emphasised by Calvino are the very ones made possible by narrative creations of the "unnatural" – they often play with what could be possible but is not actual, or, when representing the impossible, they blend realistic and fantastic elements in new combinations, creating multi-faceted representations where oppositions like "natural" and "unnatural" are much less appropriate than a term that would "signify a third space or position from which to analyse the negotiations between the mimetic and its various contraventions. (Perhaps *impossible* or *phantasmal* [...] could work)." (Fludernik 2012, 366).[8]

In this sense the *Alice* books can offer a practical demonstration that the definition of "unnatural" as "anti-mimetic" is inadequate. The constant inter-play of realistic and unrealistic elements, a prominent feature of Victorian fantasy (see Prickett), receives a complex and meaningful elaboration in the narrative scenario of the *Alices*, where "natural" and "unnatural" are so interconnected as to be inseparable from each other. The polite Victorian Alice finds her way to parallel realities through magical passages – the rabbit hole and the "bright silvery mist" of a mirror – and in these new dimensions she has to deal with a puzzling mixture of Victorian conventions and absurd, nonsensical elements. However, this is precisely the point: the two dimensions intermingle to produce a composite universe, where the fantastic and the real are merged together in a seamless

---

8 It is worth mentioning that Alber, Iversen, Nielsen and Richardson (2012), in their reply to Fludernik, acknowledge the necessity of avoiding dichotomies: "each of us believes in a gradual spectrum of narrative possibilities rather than a system of binary oppositions" (374).

ensemble,[9] where actually there is no such thing as the unnatural on one side and the natural on the other: they participate in the same, multi-sided scenario.

Elements of conventional Victorian culture are projected into the phantasmagorical lands down the rabbit hole and on the other side of the mirror: the British ceremony of afternoon tea; the game of croquet (very popular in Alice's time); the prominence of royalty (Wonderland and the Looking-Glass land are full of duchesses, queens and kings); and more specific things, like the proverb "to grin like a Cheshire cat", or the habit of eating mock-turtle soup. Carroll's outlandish landscapes are populated by impossible beings such as talking cards, gryphons, unicorns, living flowers, looking-glass insects, or fabulous monsters like the Jabberwocky. Yet these marvellous creatures are always somehow connected to Alice's Victorian reality: for example, the flowers are a parody of Tennyson's *Maud*; the insects represent a reflection about current debates on the meaning of language; and the Jabberwocky is a medieval beast like the ones painted by the Pre-Raphaelites.

The degree to which unnatural and natural, as well as *sense and nonsense*, are juxtaposed in the *Alice* books reaches an extreme and sometimes puzzling complexity – yet nonsense itself, as the paradigm of paradox and of the coexistence of multiple identities, is the perfect way to express it.[10] As Haughton (1988) emphasises, "the 'sense' of nonsense has something to do with its opposition to what is normally considered 'sense'. It defies sense, and yet works in implicit dialogue with it, as if setting a diction against its contradictions" (2). I would like to suggest that the "unnatural" can be regarded in the same light: as a way to deconstruct boundaries in favour of a multi-faceted and multi-signifying interpretative landscape.

I have thus linked nonsense with the unnatural, and, in turn, nonsense with the fantastic – in this respect the idea of the fantastic in Victorian literature plays a relevant role in this renegotiation of the unnatural: the Victorian fantastic entails that

---

9 Florence Becker Lennon recognises the importance of this aspect of the *Alices*, by saying that "to *Alice* and its calm transference of the preposterous and magical into the everyday, can be traced such books as David Garnett's *Lady into Fox*, Christopher Morely's *Thunder on the Left*, James Hilton's *Lost Horizon* [...] Gertrude Stein and James Joyce were Carrollian adepts" (1962, 104).

10 In turn the exploration of the fantastic in the *Alice* books is also linked to what Prickett (1979) calls "the internalization of the fantastic" (38), which Alber defines as one of the ways to make sense of the unnatural, a "naturalization of the unnatural." I deal with this in the reader section of this chapter.

the extraordinary and ordinary both have a place in fantasy and reality. The Victorian fantasy authors began to become conscious of this and began experimenting with the relationship between elements of the everyday and the unfamiliar in order to produce new fantasy worlds. [...] Because they consist of the same elements, fantasy and reality are never really that far apart, but exist right next to each other, as close as England and Elfland. (Harding 2009)

The Carrollian fictional worlds elaborately represent these elements in an evident subversion of such rigid oppositions and well-defined boundaries as those between the mimetic and anti-mimetic, the real and unreal: "Lewis Carroll personifies this fantastical mixture of the ordinary and the extraordinary" (Harding).[11]

The very concept of mimesis, after all, is not really apt to define a merely realistic fictional approach, given that the Aristotelian definition of mimesis refers to a much more multi-faceted concept: mimesis is an essential poetical device illuminating the profound meaning of human existence through artistic practice. Aristotle's [350 BCE] mimesis is the representation and imagination (not necessarily realistic) of existential complexities, unfathomable feelings, mysterious passions, recondite worlds. He explicitly allows for the supernatural to be a part of this representation (he mentions for instance the episode of the statue of Mitys at Argos, Halliwell 1998, 1452a) on the basis that seeming plausibility, not strict possibility, should be the criterion for mimesis. Therefore, it is possible to say that Aristotle's mimesis actually includes the concept of the unnatural. As Fludernik (2012) states "not only is realism illusionary, but the mimetic reproduces both that which is natural and fictional scenarios that are non-natural" (368).[12] This brings us back to Calvino's description of the fantasy writer's imaginative processes, in which the "natural" and "unnatural" are both included as parts of his idea of artistic creation:

---

[11] This happy coexistence of multiple elements of reality is also a typical trait of the Victorians because of their new, extraordinary scientific discoveries, which contribute in building up this cultural tissue where what was possible and what was impossible were no more clearly defined and divided (see Armstrong 2010 about the technological developments leading to a new vision of a world constantly changing and without boundaries).

[12] In response to this, Alber, Iversen, Nielsen and Richardson (2012) say that their concept of anti-mimetic is constructed in relation to Plato's conception of mimesis as the artistic attempt to reproduce reality through imitation, and not in relation to Aristotle's, which they acknowledge to be a much more comprehensive concept related to representation, projection and understanding of the world through imaginative processes. Nevertheless, it is Aristotelian mimesis, as elaborated in the *Poetics*, that has most centrally informed narrative theory and fiction studies and which immediately comes to mind when the mimetic is mentioned.

> let us say that various elements concur in forming the visual part of the literary imagination: direct observation of the real world, phantasmic and oneiric transfiguration, the figurative as it is transmitted by culture at its various levels, and a process of abstraction, condensation and internalization of sense experience, a matter of prime importance to both the visualization and verbalization of thought. (1988, 95)

The next section is dedicated to the specific creative strategies for the creation of unnatural scenarios.

5.1.4 Creating the Unnatural: Authorial Strategies and Scientific Connections

The writer's creation of nonsense, or unnatural, or impossible narrative landscapes, merits analysis in a little more depth. Stewart in her *Nonsense: Aspects of Intertextuality in Folklore and Literature* (1979) mentions five procedures characterizing the creation of nonsense scenarios: 1) reversals and inversions, 2) play with boundaries, 3) play with infinity, 4) uses of simultaneity, 5) arrangement and rearrangement within a closed field (58–195). Similar strategies are listed by Sewell (1952), who states that all of them are marked by an inclination for "re-patterning", "dislocating", giving "glimpses of other orders beyond and through our usual perspectives" (41). These procedures highlight, in a general sense, the inter-textual nature of nonsense poetical discourse, in which different domains are at play with and against each other, and the limits of rigid categories and boundaries are constantly shown to be mere conventions. The unnatural or nonsensical tissue of Carroll's creations makes manifest the arbitrariness of "beginnings, middles and ends employed as markers in art and everyday life" (Lindhal 1983, 72), a distinctive feature of unnatural narratives also explored by Richardson (2012, 57–83).

This prominent tendency of the *Alice* books in particular and of nonsense and the unnatural in general can be connected to the mental processes of counterfactual thinking. I am here using the concept as outlined in *Counterfactual Thinking-Counterfactual Writing*, where the enormous potential of counterfactual thinking in literary works is emphasised, stating

> how productively literary texts employ the interplay between fictionality and counter-factuality in order to involve the reader in their fictional world [...] as a consequence, from the perspective of literary studies there are many ways of looking at counterfactual thinking as an 'imagination of alternatives to reality'. (Birke at al. 2011, 11)

In the section of the book dedicated to literary theory, different counterfactual literary scenarios (from time travel to post-modernist retellings of well-known literary works) are explained as tools to convey a host of diverse meanings (social critique, scientific exploration, meta-fictional discourse, psychological study on the effects of emotions).

I relate this notion of the counterfactual to the unnatural, in that both accommodate impossible or unrealistic alternatives to the actual, and in turn I would highlight the extreme counterfactual scenarios at play in the *Alices*, as products of elaborated anti-realistic narrative structures, which can be understood with reference to Stewart and Sewell's lists of authorial procedures for creating nonsense, as well as in terms of Spolsky's process of "transfiguration" (2007, 79), indicating "the ways in which artists may represent the abstract, the unfamiliar, or the non-representable" (Wojciehowski and Gallese 2011, 24). This transfiguration process, used to depict extreme counterfactual subjects, entails that writers (or visual artists) focus upon engaging the human cognitive ability to move between different sources of knowledge (from perceptive to abstract ones) and different structures of information, so playing with cognitive boundaries. As Wojciehowski and Gallese put it

> through techniques of embodied representation, the artist enables readers (or viewers) to find partial matches between their own sensory experiences or memories on the one hand and, on the other, the abstract concepts that the artist also wishes to convey; the audience, in turn, produces representations within their own minds of things that might otherwise seem impossible to imagine. (2011, 24)

These creative operations, which Carroll uses to make readers think and visualise the impossible, are also linked to the exploratory task of playing with new scientific frameworks and new philosophical approaches. Beer (2016), in her significant chapter "the faculty of invention" (45–73), quotes Carroll's mathematician friend J.J. Sylvester, who wrote that "the doctrine of the imaginary and the inconceivable" is very useful in seeking to quicken the mind of a student of mathematics (46). Carroll's work provocatively foregrounds the instability of "assumptions of a secure hierarchy" (51) and takes the reader on a phantasmagorical journey incorporating impossible worlds, unusual temporal and spatial narratives, non-existent beings and contradictory physical laws, taking advantage of counterfactual scenarios "to make him or her think about the state of his or her actual world, or about the way in which texts themselves shape out thinking about 'reality'" (Birke et al. 2011, 11). Elbert, also quoted by Beer (2016), rightly asserts that "Lewis Carroll was the first to take a character out of the containing walls of Euclidean space and put her into the non-Euclidean world of a landscape of shifting fields" (19–20).

Carroll's scientific narrative investigations take him (and his readers) towards extremely experimental realms (for his time at least): negative numbers, flat or infinite spaces, concepts of anti-matter. For instance, Alice wonders about the reversal of matter's particles on the other side of the looking-glass "how would you like to live in a Looking-glass House, Kitty? I wonder if they'd give you milk in there. Perhaps Looking-glass milk isn't good to drink" (*TTLG*, 148). Or again, she pops into other space-time dimensions, through infinite holes or dissolving glass, resembling what may happen in going through an Einstein-Rosen bridge. [13] Carroll further amplifies these scientific suggestions in his later narrative work, the *Sylvie and Bruno* books [1889; 1893], where he develops concepts already introduced in the *Alices* into even more scientifically elaborated representations, like the Fortunatus Purse, an extended multi-sided Moebius stripe (2010, 106), or the Outlandish Watch, which can make the time go backward, and, also, through its "Reversal Peg", make the events proceed in a reversed way (1988, 345–360). [14]

Daniel Brown, in his *The Poetry of Victorian Scientists: Style, Science and Nonsense* (2013), has pointed out the strong links between Victorian scientists, poetry and nonsense; similarly, according to Stewart (1979), authorial strategies for creating nonsense landscapes often play with a cross-disciplinary approach, merging disciplines and erasing boundaries. In the context of unnatural narratology, Alber (2013, 64) recognises the role the unnatural may play in new scientific theories, as a theoretical tool for the formulation of new hypotheses. This perspective leads us back again to Calvino, in whose *Six Memos for the Next Millennium* the parallelisms between scientific speculations and literary creations and their unusual harmony, are constantly discussed, emphasizing their mutual imaginative processes:

> So, then, I believe that to draw on this gulf of potential multiplicity is indispensable to any form of knowledge. The poet's mind and at a few decisive moments the mind of the scientist, works according to a process of association of images that is the quickest way to link and choose between the infinite forms of the possible and the impossible. The imagination is a kind of electronic machine that takes account of all possible combinations and chooses the ones that are appropriate to a particular purpose, or are simply the most interesting, pleasing, or amusing. (1988, 91)

---

13 See Rucker 2014, 113–131, and 2009, 54–55.
14 The episodes related to the peculiar working of the Outlandish Watch are in fact "the second earliest known instances in fiction of time-travel made possible by a machine (H.G. Wells's *The Time Machine* had appeared a year earlier in a magazine)"; the Reversal Peg provides the first fictional scene "in which time goes the wrong way" (M. Gardner 1988, xiii).

5.2 "… But There's one Great Advantage in It, That One's Memory Works Both Ways": The Character(s)

Fig. 26: Salvador Dalí, *A Mad Tea Party*, 1969. Dalí's illustrations for *Alice in Wonderland* highlight the numerous connections that can be found between surrealism and Carroll's nonsense – such as automatism in writing and drawing, collages and portmanteau, interest in madness and the unconscious (see Burstein 2015). An even more significant connection is Dalí's interest in mathematics and obsession with the topic of time, which make him the ideal postmodern interpreter of the *Alices*.[15]

---

[15] Art historian Victoria Sears Goldman describes the image in the following way: "his Mad Tea Party is not an intelligible image at first glance. But slowly the individual images come together and the scene becomes apparent. The Tea Party floats ambiguously and is interspersed with dots and oversized insects; the latter are, curiously, the only realistically rendered images. The pocket watch, central to the Tea Party in the text, is cleverly conceived by Dalì as an oversized drooping clock, thus surely alluding to his Persistence of Memory" (7).

Under the heading of Characters in this chapter I consider the representation of unnatural minds, following Iversen's suggestions about the topic, and treating in particular the "unnatural" depiction of memory and perceptions of time in the *Alices*. I explore the different senses in which the characters' minds in the *Alice* books can be seen as unnatural, and, in doing so, I further develop my argument about the status and definition of the unnatural.

My starting point is the experience of time in the *Alice* books: time is circular, changeable and paradoxical in Carroll's worlds. How the characters mentally interact with such temporality is a key aspect of their "unnaturalness", but ultimately shows that this definition is not a satisfying one. The paradoxical nature of time in the *Alices* does not merely entail unnaturalness, it also inspires reflections and conjectures on the "real" nature of time. As Ryan puts it, discussing the paradoxical representations of time in literature:

> By accompanying the author on the climb, readers are compelled to take a glance into the vertiginous philosophical abyss of the nature of time. But if the projects are to succeed, the paradox must be more than pure exploration of the possible – in other words, more than experimentation for its own sake – it must also present an expressive dimension, which means that it must shed light on some aspect of human experience. (2009, 159)

5.2.1 Unnatural Minds in the Alices: It's Always Tea-Time

Stefan Iversen (2013) points out how tools taken from cognitive narratology may be helpful in dealing with what he calls "unnatural minds" in narrative (94–112). Under this term Iversen gathers the "subversive, arresting, strange, and odd minds that one encounters in narratives" (94) and suggests a number of possible theoretical approaches. On the one hand he agrees with Alber's perspective (see Alber 2009) according to which many unnatural minds can actually be understood by conventionalizing them (more on this later in the chapter); on the other hand he aligns himself with Abbott's (2008) idea that there exist narrative minds which resist any kind of naturalisation and which "work best when we allow ourselves to rest in that particular combination of anxiety and wonder that is aroused when an unreadable mind is accepted as unreadable" (448).

Cognitive narratology can be invoked, Iversen suggests, to deal both with unnatural minds that can be naturalised and with unnatural minds that remain cognitively impossible. He writes that

> cognitive narratology offers invaluable help in explaining what happens on the level of structure and reception. Nonetheless [...] cognitive concepts will not save us from the unknown, will not undo the haunting feelings some narratives produce. (2013, 110)

I shall appeal to the example of the *Alice* books in order to both agree and disagree with Iversen: I would like to argue, with regard to the *Alices*, that an unnatural mind is defined as unnatural because it can *at the same time* be understood within naturalizing conventions *and* as a cognitive impossibility. In order to illustrate this idea in clearer fashion, I shall examine how Carroll depicts his characters' relation with time in Wonderland and in the Looking-Glass Land. The peculiar connection between Carroll's fictional minds and concepts of time helps to clarify the specific meaning of unnatural minds in the *Alice* books. The *Alice* books offer help in conceiving of the unnatural through the characters' experiences of temporality, from the circular never-ending time of the tea-party to the mystery of a memory that works "both ways" and through Alice's own efforts to cope with this strange temporal environment. As Beer (2016) says, "the sense of the monstrous that haunts the *Alice* books derives from the doubling of the thinkable and the unthinkable" (48).

There is little doubt that "Time and its troubling haunt both the *Alice* books" (Beer 2016, 28). Time is a constant preoccupation in the *Alices:* it is even possible to state that Time, personified in the Mad Hatter's fashion, is one of the main characters of the two books. At the beginning of *Alice's Adventures in Wonderland*, Alice is not particularly shocked by the appearance of a talking rabbit: "it's the *watch* that startles her" (29) and that initiates all her adventures (*AAIW*, 11–12). Likewise, in *Through the Looking-Glass and What Alice Found There*, the first strange thing Alice notices in the looking-glass room where she finds herself (as is foregrounded in Tenniel's famous illustration), is the clock: she could only see the back of it before, since she was on the other side of the mirror, but it has "the face of a little old man, and grinned at her" (150). Again, Time is personified and he is making fun of Alice's previous conception of it (him), which here in the Looking-Glass Land will be comprehensively challenged.

Going back to Wonderland, we can gain a better understanding of the narrative representation of unnaturally functioning minds from Carroll's peculiar depictions of the mysteries and conundrums of time that Alice encounters there. These representations of unnaturally experienced time can be read as experimental scientific speculations, representations of madness or, simply, as *impossible* mental scenarios. Philosophers and thinkers from St Augustine to Kant have speculated upon the possibility that time is only in our minds: the nonsense of the *Alices* offers a playful narrative version of these speculations, where the different possible (and impossible) ways in which the mind can construct, or deconstruct, time's flow and features are portrayed through the eccentric behaviour of many Carrollian characters. As Stewart (1979) states, nonsense "stands in direct contradiction to the [...] three laws of Husserl's lived experiences of time"

(146).¹⁶ In the same way unnatural texts defy real-world assumptions about the nature of time, as listed in Alber's chapter about unnatural temporalities (2013, 149–184).

The first Wonderland character dealing with time is the White Rabbit. His main concern is his being always late: during his first appearance he is anxiously checking the pocket watch and notoriously repeating "Oh dear! Oh dear! I shall be too late!" (11), and he is similarly obsessed and always handling his watch, every other time Alice meets him. It is as if he is perennially engaged in a useless effort to catch up with a Time that is continuously escaping him and his watch. Carroll underlines the impossibility of his quest: he wants to defeat time by running fast through space: but this is not how it works.¹⁷ Bergson [1922] states that thinking spatially is not the right way to conceive time: yet the measurement of time reduces it to a spatial conception. Bergson's *durée* happens at a mind-level regardless of the actual movements happening in space. It is thus impossible to stop change or time by moving (or not moving) through space, as the White Rabbit tries to do: it would need an enchanted crystal forest like the one described by Ballard (1988) in his *The Crystal World*, which is a kind of "ancestral paradise where the unity of time and space is the signature of every leaf and flower" (88), where a crystalline and beautiful anti-time is realised by the immobilisation of trees, flowers, birds, crocodiles, butterflies and in the end human beings, in an illuminated universe of petrified jewels. But Wonderland is not a petrified crystal forest, and the White Rabbit's obsession with time stresses our misleading conception of it and emphasises time's relativity and its paradoxes.

Another instance of Carroll's fictional dealings with time, maybe the most emblematic, is the famous "Mad Tea-Party". The Cheshire Cat tells Alice that if she goes on walking in one direction she will find a Hatter, while in the *other* direction there will be a March Hare: actually, Alice finds *both* in the same direction, her choice of which, indeed, is not an unequivocal one (the two senses simultaneously, the two directions at the same time, are characteristics of the paradox realised by nonsense, Deleuze 1969, 77). Puzzled by the nonsensical conversations of the two characters, Alice advises them "I think you might do something better with the time, than wasting it in asking riddles that have no answers" (*AAIW*, 75). From this point, starting with a linguistic misunderstanding about time, the conversation goes on to address the substance of

---

16 The laws are: 1) different times can never be conjoint, 2) their relation is a non-simultaneous one 3) there is transitivity, for to every time belongs an earlier and a later (Stewart 1979, 145–149).
17 Carroll also speaks ironically about Zeno of Elea's paradox of Achilles and the Tortoise, in his "What the Tortoise said to Achilles" (1895), challenging Zeno's conception of space.

time: the boundaries between linguistic features and physical substance are thus blurred and indistinguishable.[18]

Alice's previous conception of time as something impersonal, linear and continuous (a conception shared by most readers)[19] rapidly turns into a strange, elusive realisation of time as something (or *someone*) personified, chaotic and modifiable. If one is kind with time, the Mad Hatter explains to Alice, it is possible to bend his will, but if contrarily one treats him badly, he revolts against you, as has happened in their case. The Hatter was reciting a poem (a parody, obviously), but in doing so he was "murdering the time" (77): consequently, from that moment the time has refused to listen to their requests. The result is: "it's always tea-time."[20] The Mad Hatter and the March Hare have killed what we normally consider the present, that now "no longer subsists except in the abstract moment, at tea-time" (Deleuze 1969, 79). It is an absolute present which repeats eternally itself, where the two mad men go on drinking tea and turning around the table changing their place, in "a kind of never-ending game of musical chairs" (Rackin 1991, 55), since they have "no time to wash the things between whiles" (*AAIW*, 77). Alice, with her idea of time as a meaningful continuum, asks "but what happens when you come to the beginning again?" (77) and nothing is replied to her, as always in Wonderland when she asks something following the logic of the "upper world". Alice is not able to understand an idea of time as illogical and cyclical, in which the "turn" is eternally repeated in a reiteration without progress nor sense. This is a kind of Nietzschean eternal recurrence of the same ante-litteram, a cyclical pattern of infinite time and space meaninglessly repeating itself. Maybe it is precisely Alice's mental inability to conceive the mad time of the tea party that makes it possible for her to escape it. She can in fact walk away, "she is not imprisoned in their eternal loop" (Beer 2016, 41), and her mind is only temporarily trapped in between "natural"

---

18 This interpretation of sentences in a literal way, linked also to the concretisation of metaphors, as highlighted in my second chapter "Virtual Alice", demonstrates the broken connection between an unnatural mind and the common mental recognition of abstractions and conceptual metaphors. I return to this topic below.
19 "If readers insist that time flows, is linear and mono-directional, then a narrative that breaks with these assumptions will be considered unnatural, regardless of the fact that it might actually be true to physical law" (Heinze 2013, 34).
20 M. Gardner cites scholars who have compared the Mad Tea-Party to a portion of De Sitter's model of the cosmos in which time stands eternally still (2001, 80), while Deleuze cites Boltzmann, for whom the clock's hand can apply only to a present circumscribed to individual worlds or systems, and consequently for the entire universe it is impossible to distinguish time's directions, or to establish an up and a down position (1969, 77).

and "unnatural" perceptions of time: it is Alice's mind then, which functions as a mediating term, showing the impossibility of drawing well-defined boundaries.

The time of the Mad Hatter's watch, which is filled with butter and then dipped into a cup of tea, is tea-dependent: it is petrified, always telling six o'clock. The Dormouse, probably, symbolises this sense of (tea-) time: a time perennially asleep, motionless in a delirium of no-meaning, or repeating always the same thing. The linguistic repetitions of the sleepy Dormouse correspond to the infinite hour of six-o'clock tea. The Dormouse is the time ill-treated by the two mad men: when Alice arrives, they are using him as a cushion, then they try to put him in the teapot. This quality of stillness is the contrary of Alice's previous conception of time as something flowing frenetically and relentlessly: here time is a Dormouse that sleeps, and which sometimes tells absurd stories while drowsing.

The way the March Hare and the Mad Hatter experience time illustrates the peculiar unnaturalness of Carrollian minds: on the one hand, the eternal present perceived by the two characters exhibits Carroll's interest in the malleable dimension of dream-time, as well as different perceptions of time-space, their incongruities and their complex relation to infinity. In this respect the *Alices* work as reflections of Victorian theoretical changes in the fields of mathematics and physics: "space and time were during Carroll's lifetime coming to be understood more and more as being in intricate and shifting relations" (Beer 2016, 30). On the other hand, the tea-time of the Mad Hatter and the March Hare serves Carroll's interest in the working of mad or hallucinating minds. Nonsense and madness are often recognised as alike: as Stewart emphasises "the procedures by which the schizophrenic or aphasiac 'fails' to make sense are often the same procedures by which others succeed in making nonsense" (1979, 32).

Carroll's interest in ill-functioning minds is evident from his vast collection of studies on madness and mental disturbance as well as books on mind-distortions produced by certain substances. Carroll's uncle Skeffington Lutwidge (his "favourite uncle", Seiberling and Bloore 1986, 135) was a barrister and a commissioner in lunacy, and there are records proving that Carroll himself went to visit asylums in company of his uncle because of his intellectual curiosity about madness. Tenniel's illustration of the Mad Hatter (or Hatta, his alternative name in *Through the Looking-Glass*) in jail is a quite faithful reproduction of the photography of a lunatic. As Franziska Kohlt highlights, one of the new entertainments offered to patients in Victorian asylums were tea-parties:

> Carroll's Mad Tea-Party mirrors not only numerous popular beliefs about insanity, but also more specific peculiarities of professional practice at Victorian pauper lunatic asylums, and was conceived in a period of increased exposure to Skeffington's work. (2016, 156)

The time-related deficiencies clearly experienced by the Mad Hatter and the March Hare (who are the most striking examples, although many other characters in the *Alice* books are characterised by their unusual perception of time, as we shall see) can also be thought of as a depiction of schizophrenic minds, or hallucinating minds. The absence of a time-structure "properly" working in the brain is often connected to mental disorders or drug-induced distortions: "distortions in timing are induced by narcotics such as cocaine and marijuana or by such disorders as Parkinson's disease, Alzheimer's disease, and schizophrenia" (Eagleman 2009, 159–160). Apparently, the brain has to work in order to create a temporal binding, since the temporal flow is not given readymade to the human mind, but it is a difficult mental construction that has to be done by processing and harmonizing different temporal stimuli coming from different neural devices (see again Eagleman 2009). It is possible, then, that these separate neural mechanisms may not agree with each other: such circumstances can be induced to provoke time illusions, or can be symptomatic of a neural disturbance. Furthermore, damages to the time-construction systems of the brain are also connected with language and reading disorders (see for instance Toplak et al. 2003, Glezerman and Balkoski 2002, Indefrey and Gullberg 2008): linguistic confusions and failures are one of the most prominent traits of Carrollian characters (the Mad Hatter and the March Hare *in primis*), as also is a tendency to literalise abstract concepts (a typical schizophrenic trait).

If the unnaturalness of the Mad t^{21} Party can be understood in terms of either Carroll's speculations on the topic of new scientific approaches, or his well-documented interest in mad and abnormally working minds, it is also true that it is not possible to reduce its effects to these causes entirely: the weirdness, the anomaly and the defamiliarizing atmosphere created in the nonsense landscapes of the *Alice* books always retain something inexplicable, which defies any attempt at normalisation. When the Mad Hatter asks Alice (and the readers) "why is a raven like a writing-desk?":[22] there is *no* possible definitive answer to that. Equally, the minds of the Mad Hatter and the March Hare (and with theirs, also many others from the *Alice* books) are by no means readily explainable.

---

[21] It is quite significant that the word "tea" is pronounced like the scientific abbreviation for time, *t*. This further emphasises the inter-changeability of time and tea in the chapter – the eternal time is tea time – and the madness which characterises it.

[22] Beer (2016) points out "such a riddle also lacks closure, ebbing discomfitingly outward through time without stop. The question is launched. No answer responds. Boundaries vanish. Time is stayed but trickles pointlessly" (38).

How to imagine a mind without time? Carroll tries the impossible: representing in a narrative, and thus a time-dependent framework, the absence of precisely this attribute. As Heinze (2013) remarks, "time and narrative appear to be both fundamental and inherently inseparable and interdependent concepts" (31). The logical and ontological impossibility of Time imprisoned in a teapot is sketched in the peculiar, illogical, dream-like structure of the *Alices*, but it exemplifies a recurrent effect of the books, which is the persistence of an unfathomable quality, something which escapes the narrative itself. Nonsense (understood as I have proposed, as another way to name the unnatural) can never be completely captured and encapsulated through an explanatory reading: the slippery nature of nonsense always leaves something beyond our cognitive grasp, some unanswerable question, a sort of constant reference to nothingness, a persistent sense of *horror vacui*.

5.2.2 "… And the Rule Is, Jam Tomorrow and Jam Yesterday – Never Jam Today"

In *Through the Looking-Glass and What Alice Found There* Carroll represents time as an eccentric chessboard, where past and future are inextricably confused: going back in order to go ahead, running to preserve the past, going to jail before committing the crime, crying before being hurt, handing round a cake in order to have it cut into slices. The form of time in the Looking-Glass world is defined only by past and future, the present is continually absorbed by these two complementary and infinite dimensions: "an unlimited past-future rises up here reflected in an empty present which has no more thickness than the mirror" (Deleuze 1969, 171). The White Queen explains this complex time-dimension to Alice with a practical example, by saying that she surely would enjoy eating a very good jam, only "the rule is, jam tomorrow and jam yesterday – but never jam today" (*TTLG*, 206). Martin Gardner (2001) points out that in Latin the word *iam* means "now", but it is only used in past and future tenses, while in the present tense the word for "now" is *nunc* (206). Hence, Alice's present in the Looking-Glass Land is a past-future moment, a non-existent floating instant.[23]

Memory is a fascinating faculty in the Looking-Glass world: here, in fact, it is possible to remember things *before* they actually happen. The White Queen

---

[23] Mark Currie (2007) addresses the issue of the philosophical paradox of the present, recognising that "as long as the present has duration, any duration at all, it can be divided into the bits of it that have been, and so are not, and the bits of it that are to be, and so are not yet, so that the very duration of its existence consigns it to nonexistence" (8).

knows that the week after the next the King's Messenger (none other than the Mad Hatter himself) will be imprisoned, then there will be the trial and "of course the crime comes last of all" (*TTLG*, 207). Memory is linked to the future: no present is included. Again, finding a solid, univocal explanation for the narrative representation of a memory "working both ways" is an interpretative task which can never be fully accomplished. It is possible to conjecture about mind and time-related phenomena: "our consciousness lags 80 milliseconds behind actual events. When you think an event occurs, it has already happened" (Eagleman 2009, 160). Consequently, just as "for the Queen the present is never realised" (Gray 1995, 81), we are actually never really in the present moment: our brains fall behind, even as our minds project beyond. Furthermore, as Young emphasises, "the neural networking of memory and imagination (past and future) is almost identical" (2010, 42): in this sense, the Looking-Glass time and the White Queen's bizarre memory can be understood as comical but effective representations of how the mind actually works, going always both ways[24] and making sense of the mutual interdependence of the past and future.

Nonetheless, as Stewart (1979) rightly recognises, nonsense (or/and the unnatural) is "an overlapping of two or more disparate domains" (35): the unusualness of the Looking-Glass Land's time construction can be also thought of as a layering of different possible meanings, which ultimately also leads to the nullification of any definitive, all-encompassing significance. Looking-Glass time and memory appear to have different possible explanations, none of which excludes the others and none of which imposes itself as definitive. The characteristic paradox of nonsense involves the coexistence of a multitude of meanings at the same time and nonsense shows itself to be "the most multiply-meaningful of fictions" (Stewart 1979, 34). Considering Carroll's nonsense as extremely close to the concept of the unnatural, this multiplicity of representations and meanings emphasises how a fixed, stabled definition of the unnatural is not advisable.

Consequently, the reflections on unnatural time and memory characterizing *Through the Looking-Glass* are simultaneously conjectures on the working of the human mind, scientific approaches to the possibility of backwards universes and emotional reverberations of Carroll's own perceptions of Alice's growing up (the simultaneous and contradictory presence of her being trapped in her childhood in the past-celebrating dimension of the Looking-Glass Land and her capability of proceeding in a world which can only go back). Different times, different mem-

---

[24] Young emphasises that brain-injured people with amnesia are kept from experiencing *both* past and future: when the hippocampus, the neural device responsible for the acts of memory, is damaged, the capacity of imagining the future is also inhibited (2010, 189–194).

ories and different perceptions are set in play constantly in the *Alices*, where Carroll explores "the giddying vacillations that time performs within us" (Beer 2016, 43).

5.2.3 What Happens in the Minds of Flowers, Cards, Chess Pieces

Abbott (2008) lists three different ways in which one can try to make sense of unnatural minds: 1) linking them to madness and insanity 2) seeing them as functional to the characterisation of another fictional mind 3) reading them as symbols of specific concepts, thus as allegories or metaphors. While the first method entails a naturalisation of the unnatural, the other two are figurative interpretations, which leave part of the unnaturalness intact. As seen, the Mad Hatter and the March Hare can be read as depictions of abnormal, schizophrenic minds, and the connection with madness can account for several narrative passages in the *Alices*. I would like now to apply the two other possible readings suggested by Abbott to some of the minds in the *Alice* books, ultimately to reaffirm what Abbott himself states: the existence of narrative minds which escape a complete and univocal naturalisation.

In the previous chapters, I have often dealt with the representation of Alice's mind as featuring some specific attributes of a child's mind (for example, some characteristics of her curiosity impulse, her dreaming state and her volatility). More specifically, in "Mirrored Alice", especially in section 3.2.3, I have addressed the topic of Alice's reading of the other characters' minds, concluding that, if on the one hand Carroll's characters can be read as inexplicably unreadable, on the other hand the internal focalisation encourages us to interpret the other fictional minds as seen from Alice's perspective, i.e., the point of view of a child who has not yet developed a proper mind-reading mental system. This latter interpretation can be linked to the second of Abbott's proposed readings of impossible minds, but does not exclude other possible readings; it therefore illustrates the coexistence of seemingly contradicting connotations in the nonsense unnatural landscape of Carrollian minds.

If it is plausible to regard the inaccessibility of the minds Alice encounters in Wonderland and in the Looking-Glass Land as a means to construct Alice's own mind (that is, her childish inability to grasp what is going on in others' minds), it is also true that this impenetrability can also stand as a symbol for other layers of meaning (and this is Abbott's third interpretative strategy for the understanding of unnatural minds). The obscurity of the Carrollian creatures' minds may for instance represent the absurdity of rigid Victorian norms and behaviours: among the many likely examples are the senseless obsession the Duchess has with finding morals in everything and the constant, incomprehensible preoccupation with nonsensical rules exhibited by the inhabitants of both Wonderland and the Looking-Glass world. Or, the impossibility of understanding what the characters Alice meets are thinking can also symbolise more generally the distance between the world of adults and the world of children: retaining Alice's viewpoint through the two books, our experience of the mental inaccessibility of other creatures' thoughts may represent the difficulty children have grasping the meaning of the remote and puzzling world of adults. This latter option also re-connects with the second way unnatural minds can be understood, as projections and means of constructing another character.

Another possible symbolic implication of the unreadability of minds in Alice's worlds can be a more existentialist inquiry on the nature and essence of human communication itself: the constant misunderstanding, the impossibility of establishing any empathetic connection and the inapplicability of ToM in the Carrollian worlds would then serve to highlight the solitude of human existence, the final unattainability of any real exchange of thoughts between individuals. Here nonsense would reveal its dark side, its *humour noir*, its hidden sadness: the apparently humorous nonsensical dialogues with the foolish creatures of Wonderland would actually convey that Beckettian truth, that "nothing is funnier than unhappiness" (2009, 1, 194).

Unnatural fictional minds can thus be understood as mad minds, as minds functional in the understanding of another character and as minds standing for a symbolic, metaphorical or allegorical meaning. Nevertheless, as both Iversen and Abbott remark, "there is value in not allowing default responses to override the immediate experience of an unreadable fictional mind" (Abbott 2008, 148). Minds in the *Alices*, as recognised by Douglas-Fairhurst (among others), are "flat" (2015, 149), so no mind-reading strategy is applicable to them; they *do not function* as real minds. Often, when characters in a book are not people but, say, animals or objects or bizarre creatures, they still tend to be represented with human-like mental mechanisms. In the case of the *Alice* books, almost all the characters but Alice are not only not human, they defy any human-like way of reasoning. As Beer (2016) states "in these worlds anything may turn out to have a mind and will of its own: puddings, unicorns, mice, bottles, mutton, gnats, candles, shawls" (51) and their parameters of thought are inaccessible and mysterious. They do not act as we, from our perspective, would expect them to act: cards do not methodically and logically follow game rules, but rather seem to be chaotic beings, engaged in painting flowers, exploiting animals, beheading everyone and organising absurd trials. Flowers are always quarrelling with each other and they judge creatures around them according to their own standards, so Alice has "untidy petals" and is "beginning to fade", while the Red Queen (actually a chess piece) has "petals done up close, almost like a dahlia" and is "one of the thorny kind" (*TTLG*, 169). Chess pieces are not moving strategically on the chessboard seeking to win, they are occupied in apparently pointless activities, illogical dialogues and senseless fights.

Unnatural minds in the *Alice* books, then, present the coexistence of possible different explanations of their unnaturalness, but at the same time these explications themselves coexist, with an irreducible resistance to definitive elucidation of their sense and nature – which is the result of this same coexistence. As I shall further argue in the next section, cognitive reflections can help us inspect the working of unnatural fictional minds, but "their unnaturalness remains resistant to being fully translated, normalised, or recognised" (Iversen 2013, 110).

5.3 "It Always Makes One a Little Giddy at First": The Readers

In this last section of the chapter, I address the different ways in which readers cognitively make sense of the unnatural or nonsense-related literary devices of the *Alice* books. I do so by invoking Alber's proposed navigational interpretative tools and applying them to the *Alices*. As Alber states, "I am primarily interested in the question of what the human mind does to come to terms with phenomena that transcend real-world possibilities" (Alber 2016, 435); this is the main theoretical purpose of this third part, aiming to elucidate the cognitive challenges posed by impossible and unusual literary scenarios.

5.3.1 How Do We Grasp the Unnatural?

Alber (2013) lists seven reading strategies readers may adopt to make sense of the different unnatural features a fictional text can present: 1) the blending of scripts/frame enrichment 2) generification 3) subjectification 4) foregrounding the thematic 5) satirisation 6) reading allegorically 7) positing a transcendental realm. These methods can be connected to the second and third ways Abbott (2008) suggests unnatural minds can be interpreted (that is, as being functional to the characterisation of another fictional mind and as symbols or metaphors), but they have a more explicit cognitive orientation. Alber acknowledges Doležel's (1998) argument that in order to understand denaturalised narrative spaces "the actual-world encyclopaedia might be useful, but it is by no means universally sufficient" (181) and suggests different methods that can be applied to the decoding of unnatural storyworlds. These reading strategies are particular-

Fig. 27: Max Ernst, *Alice in 1941*, painting, 1941. Max Ernst repeatedly comes back to the *Alice* books with his painting, Alice being a special symbol pointing to a different, unconscious psychical dimension where the imagination has more pervasive power. Alice was an important figure for the surrealist movement; Marcel Duchamp said that "I am convinced that, like Alice in Wonderland, [the young artist of tomorrow] will be led to pass through the looking-glass of the retina, to reach a more profound expression" (189).

ly interesting from my perspective, since they deal with the cognitive processes and the cognitive effects involved in readers' responses to unnatural fictions.

Alber's first proposed reading strategy is conceptual blending, which allows readers to enrich their cognitive frames in order to include the new scenarios depicted in unnatural fictions. In my second chapter I highlight the way Carroll's narratives have introduced new conceptual metaphors, modifying our standard cognitive mapping (in particular, I explore the most striking example, the Rabbit-Hole); such metaphorical innovations offer complex blending spaces, combining together different, apparently unrelated inputs. Our cognitive parameters are especially stimulated by the ways the *Alice* books put together different elements in new, powerful combinations.

Beyond conceptual blending, however, all the reading strategies proposed by Alber can potentially be used to interpret the unnaturalness of the *Alices* (and many of them have already actually been applied). In relation to Alber's second strategy, "generification" (in which the unnatural elements of a specific fictional context are recognised as marking features of a particular literary genre), the *Alice* books stand as a quite peculiar case, since they make this strategy effectively continuous with the first one, conceptual blending. When we try to understand certain unnatural characteristics of the *Alices* as belonging to a specific genre (for instance, the talking animal as an index of the fairy-tale), we are soon forced to reconsider this assignation, because the next unnatural feature follows the rule of an altogether different genre. Thus, our generic frame of reference itself keeps shifting in the course of the narration, requiring a constant cognitive effort to catalogue and re-catalogue the unnatural under shifting literary conventions. The resultant conceptual blending at a generic level helps us in mapping the diverse possible genre-related sources of the *Alices*' unnatural traits, building up a complex cross-genre texture. To reiterate a point from my second chapter, the more cognitive shifts a text obliges the readers to make, the more cognitively challenging and difficult to categorise it becomes. To anticipate a little, in the case of the *Alice* books this issue connects to the fifth navigational tool proposed by Alber, satirisation, in that their genre often seems to have a satirical function, in which the unusual and grotesque serves to mock Victorian cultural and literary conventions (as for instance with the nonsensical parody-poems, or "The Garden of Live Flowers" as a parody of Tennyson's *Maud*).

The third strategy, "reading as internal states" (or subjectification), applies to the ways in which the *Alice* books can be understood as depictions of mental landscapes, portraying various enigmatic aspects of mind-related processes. They are dream-narratives, dwelling on the mechanisms of dreams; or they can be read as explorations of madness, or descriptions of altered perceptions;

or they may be representations of the cognitive perspective of a child's mind. Here, the unnaturalness of the *Alices* works also as a means to articulate complex mental states. Here, too, there are connections between Alber's strategies, and his sixth strategy, reading allegorically, is also applicable – Alber himself states that "several cognitive mechanisms are layered on top of each other simultaneously during the reading process" (2013, 62). Different reading approaches can be at work together at the same time: unnatural mental states in the *Alices* can be interpreted as representations of general communication-related issues (like the distance between adult and child-like ways of looking at the world); or, unnatural components and characters in the Carrollian stories can be interpreted allegorically, as when the Looking-Glass Insects are read as symbols of the impossible link between names and things (an allegory of the realist conception of language); when Alice's elongated serpent-like neck is taken to imply an allegory of Eve, Sin and sexual temptations; when Humpty Dumpty is read as an allegory of the figure of the writer; when the nonsensical chessboard in which Alice is trapped allegorises life as a game with incomprehensible rules in which people are pawns in the hands of unseen players.

In relation to reading strategy number four, Alber mentions that "unnatural spaces may be seen as exemplifications of particular themes that the narrative addresses" (2013, 48); in this sense the unnatural landscapes and characters Alice encounters in her adventures are also ways of representing her growing up process, with all the puzzling, insidious, seductive and dangerous elements that characterise it. Her frequent changes of proportions and dimensions suggests her struggle with her changing identity (from both a bodily and a mental perspective).

The seventh navigational tool Alber suggests, making sense of impossible narrative spaces by understanding them as transcendental realms, may seem more problematic in relation to the *Alices*. However, this interpretative approach is exactly the one undertaken by Josephine Gabelman, in her *A Theology of Nonsense* (2016), which advances the hypothesis that the nonsense tissue of Carroll's books can be grasped as an example of "the theological validity of unreason" (35). Gabelman uses "nonsense literature as a point of comparison with the religious imagination" (35) and through this link promotes an apprehension of Carroll's nonsense as both cognitively significant and theologically meaningful. For instance, the paradoxical aspects of the *Alice* books, expressed in paradoxes of speech, paradoxes of sense and paradoxes of time (41–45), can be connected to the numerous paradoxes that characterise the Christian faith and the conception of divine substance and attributes: she writes that

> within the sphere of the imagination, one of the effects of this type of paradoxical play is that it nurtures a cognitive flexibility. The presence of paradox within nonsense requires the imagination to perform the critical role of envisaging the 'impossible' or thinking outside the parameters of logic. (Gabelman 2016, 45)

Emphasizing how an "imaginative traversing of logical boundaries" (46) can work as a powerful juncture between Christian and nonsense theoretical approaches.

I hope to have demonstrated that all the reading strategies put forward by Alber prove to be useful analytical tools for dealing with the *Alices*' unnaturalness; nevertheless, as I have asserted in relation to Iversen's account of unnatural minds, I think that the peculiarity of nonsense lies in the coexistence of different explanations and of no explanation at all: nonsense is "a genre of narrative literature which balances a multiplicity of meaning with a simultaneous absence of meaning" (Tigges 2013, 47). Alber claims that

> we as readers are ultimately bound by our cognitive architecture (even when we try to make sense of the unnatural). Therefore, the only way we can respond to narratives of all sorts (including unnatural ones) is on the basis of cognitive frames and scripts. (2013, 63–64)

and I agree; however, I also find the nature of nonsense to be in tune with the state of "anxiety and wonder" mentioned by Abbott (2008, 448), as a cognitive puzzlement provoked by the unnatural which cannot be completely reabsorbed by our reading strategies. The interpretation of the *Alice* books' unnaturalness is in this sense a sort of mental heterotopia, to invoke Foucault's concept metaphorically, involving a cognitive juxtaposition "in a single real place of several spaces, several sites that are in themselves incompatible" (1986, 24).

5.3.2 The Slippery Nature of the Impossible: Unicorns, Little Girls and Other Fabulous Monsters

This heterotopic interpretative landscape, which is necessary in order to deal with the unnatural tissue of the *Alice* books, also has a literary mirror in Carroll's narratives themselves, where Alice is so often confronted with impossible creatures and events, and where her reaction to them, as well as the nature of these impossibilities themselves, is always changing and never contained by a fixed, pre-determined conceptual order. "The slippery nature of the impossible" is repeatedly revealed in the *Alice* books, where the narration of paradoxical scenarios involves cognitive manipulation, contradictory impressions, philosophical implications and meta-fictional observations. By affirming this link between impossible narrative scenarios and the unnatural, I mean to stress once again the slippery nature of the unnatural itself, which the mere label "unnatural" cannot really capture.

Fig. 28: Maxim Mitrofanov, illustration for *Alice's Adventures in Wonderland*, 2013. This colourful illustration effectively shows the multi-faceted meanings of the impossible/unnatural beings depicted in the *Alices*. The delight of the cognitive appraisal of the unnatural can be read in Alice's expression, while the simultaneous existence of contrasting elements (such as sadness and happiness), together with the sense of a comic masquerade, are evident in the representation of the Gryphon and the Mock-Turtle and the other little weird creatures surrounding the scene.

How do we consider impossible things? The huge and complex topic of the status of non-existent beings and objects in logic is a controversy that has interested many philosophers, before and after Carroll, and the writer of the *Alice* books, as a logician, was not unaware of the implications of talking about unicorns. Even in this field (as in mathematics and geometry) officially Carroll was a strict traditionalist. However, he was famous for the funny creativity of his examples: "his syllogisms are peopled with sharks dancing the minuet, green-eyed kittens and wise young pigs that fly in balloons"; however, "these examples only appear in universal negatives [...] which do not make any ontological claims" (Lecercle 1994, 201). Do the impossible landscapes of the *Alice* books have any ontological status then? Peter Alexander, as quoted by Lecercle, argues that all the impossible vicissitudes narrated in *Alice's Adventures in Wonderland* can be treated as "the logical consequences of the first narrative proposition expressed in the tale" (Lecercle 1994, 199), which is the appearance of a talking white rabbit with a waistcoat pocket. The same thing is true for Alice's adventures in the world on the other side of the mirror: "by the false postulate – that little girls do climb through mirrors into other worlds – any other proposition [...] is materially implied" (Gray 1995, 77). This first proposition being manifestly false and anti-mimetic, all the other impossible events could be seen just as legitimate consequences of this first assumption.

Nonetheless, Carroll's narration indulges quite extensively in the description of these subsequent impossibilities. It is possible to see Carroll's nonsensical representations as protracted sorites, "each sorite is an incipient Wonderland" (Lecercle 1994, 201); so that while, in theory, Carroll's logical position denies true existence to impossible entities, his fictional worlds are nonetheless a continuous reflection on the substance of these non-existent elements. The implications of Carroll's impossible fictional worlds are numerous: connected considerations about the status of fictional creations and of logical impossibilities; scientific inquiries into the nature of the null class and the non-existent; philosophical conjectures about Non-Being.

The representation of things which contain in themselves violations of the principle of non-contradiction cannot but be contradictory itself, inspiring puzzling cognitive readings: in the *Alices* the nature of Nothing, No-one and the impossible, shifts from being ridiculed to becoming an exaltation of relativity. The Mad Hatter talks about "the nothing" inside Alice's cup of tea (*AAIW*, 78), offering her some wine, even if "there isn't any", giving thus real substance to the term, in the same way as he personifies Time. Humpty Dumpty celebrates un-birthdays, emphasizing the anti-Parmenidean fact that what is not is just as real and existent as what is, giving the topic a more philosophical turn (*TTLG*, 223). Mathematical implications arise during Alice's encounter with the Gryphon and the Mock-Turtle, when the Gryphon, a fabulous creature, talks about the null-class, the execution of Nobody and the possibility of mysterious negative numbers.[25] The Cheshire Cat works as an embodiment of the logical problem of impossible beings: the attribute existing without the substance, *the grin with-*

---

25 The strange lessons taking place at "the school in the sea" the Mock-Turtle and the Gryphon attend have the peculiar characteristic that the hours of lessons per day decreases progressively: ten hours the first day, nine the next and so on. The eleventh day is holiday and Alice asks the Gryphon "and how did you manage on the twelfth?" a question to which the Gryphon decides not to answer, because it would introduce the possibility of the existence of negative numbers, a concept which still puzzled many mathematicians in Carroll's time (*AAIW*, 103).

out the cat, represents the conceivability of impossibility. Moreover, the applicability of actions to impossible beings like the Cheshire Cat is provoked by "the phenomena of the cat's head without its body, the possibility of which brings about a heated disputation between the king and the executioner" (Ben-Zvi, 2002).

Reading fiction is an elaborate mental process which itself touches upon this metaphysical and aesthetical problem of impossible entities. I follow here Kendall Walton's perspective on reading fiction and make-believe in *Mimesis as Make-believe* (1990): entering the fictional world, we suspend our evaluation of the truth value of sentences and we engage in a process of make-believe. Sainsbury (2010) states that "a fictive intention is one in which the utterer intends a potential audience to make believe something": if the content of an uttered sentence, *s*, is that *p*, then an audience should, on encountering *s*, make believe that *p* (7–8). If the make-believing defines the main feature of readers' mental approach to fiction, however, a special kind of make-believing has to be put in place when dealing with unnatural storyworlds. On the other hand, unnatural fiction may also be considered as an extreme case of what fiction of any kind actually is: as Maria Mäkelä points out, "many realist conventions are peculiarly balanced between the cognitively familiar and the cognitively estranging" (2013, 145). Carroll's fictional representation of non-existent and impossible beings, then, can also be read as a meta-fictional reflection on the nature of fictional statements. Gryphons and unicorns are extreme cases of what any fictional being is: non-real entities whose status logicians, philosophers and narratologists have extensively debated about.

The Meinongian solution to the problem of thinking, imagining and believing in non-real objects is, notoriously, the distinction between having the properties of being and existing. Pegasus is a flying horse – does this mean that there are flying horses? Yes, but they do not exist: they belong to the class of non-existent objects. "Il principio di Indipendenza meinonghiano dice che il *Sein* di un oggetto, ossia il suo status esistenziale, è indipendente dal suo *Sosein*, ossia dal suo avere proprietà" (Berto 2010, 65).[26] Of all the related controversies and debates, I would like to focus in particular on Priest's proposed solution, embraced and enriched by Berto (and which he calls his own peculiar evolution of Meinong's theory). Non-existent beings, says Priest, exist not in the actual world, but in other possible or impossible worlds. In particular, in *impossible worlds*,

---

[26] "The Meinongian principle of Independence entails that the *Sein* of an object, which is its existential status, is independent from its *Sosein*, which is its having properties" (my translation).

things such as the round square (or a grin without a cat, or a head without a body to be beheaded) can exist, because the principle of non-contradiction does not hold. This solution, embraced by some logicians, can easily be reconnected to the case of fictional discourse: imagining and making believe are the necessary and sufficient acts for the conception of impossibilities.

Although Carroll often deals with controversies related to non-real scenarios, it is in particular in the seventh chapter of *Through the Looking-Glass* ("The Lion and the Unicorn") that he extensively explores the problematic of representations of the impossible and non-existent. He does so in a fictional scenario, which collocates the issue with that specific frame of reference. The chapter, in fact, could have been called "Impossible Creatures and How to Deal with Them," being entirely devoted to the description of Nothing, Nobody and impossible beings. Nobody walks along the road, and he goes faster or slower than the King's Messenger. The King's response, when Alice sees "nobody on the road", is: "I only wish *I* had such eyes, the King remarked in a fretful tone, to be able to see Nobody! And at that distance too! Why, it's as much as *I* can do to see real people, by this light!" (*TTLG*, 237) – thus Nobody is not a real person, but nevertheless he can walk fast or slow.

In this chapter there is also a Unicorn, the non-existent object *par excellence*, and he lives in a world where he is real and alive and able to wonder about the actual presence of, from his perspective, an impossible being: Alice herself! When he sees the child, the Unicorn reacts with disgust and perplexity: " 'I always thought they (i.e., children) were fabulous monsters!' Said the Unicorn. 'Is it alive?' 'It can talk', said Haigha solemnly" (*TTLG*, 241). Thus, Alice is not an existent being, but she can talk: in a Meinongian sense, she has properties even without having an existential status, at least in the Looking-Glass world. The way by which Alice and the Unicorn can address their mutual presence is explained by the latter: " 'well, now that we *have* seen each other,' said the Unicorn, 'if you'll believe in me, I'll believe in you. Is that a bargain?' " (241). Alice's status as a fictional being is in itself problematic: what exactly are her individual properties? It is interesting to notice how Alice herself embodies paradoxes in her character: as Auerbach (1982) puts it, she is "simultaneously Wonderland's slave and its queen, its creator and destroyer as well as its victim" (49); she is at the same time a child and a fabulous monster.

Even if Hume stated that everything that is thinkable is possible, Meinong and his followers clearly show that impossibility is thinkable: conceiving something does not mean that it has to necessarily follow the logical rules of our world. Again Carroll puts it better, in the narrative universe of the little Alice: Alice remarks to the White Queen "one *can't* believe impossible things", but the Queen immediately replies: "I daresay you haven't had much practice, [...]

when I was your age, I always did it for half an hour a day. Why, sometimes I've believed as many as six impossible things before breakfast" (*TTLG*, 209–210). As Meinong affirms, the totality of beings which exist, have existed and will exist, has a number infinitely smaller than the totality of the objects of knowledge. Impossible things which do not exist in the actual world may be equated with fictions, fantasies, desires and beliefs, which could be events not realised in this world, that may have happened in an impossible world, or that *will* happen in an impossible world. In the second chapter, "Virtual Alice," I deal with the application of possible worlds theory to fictionality, pointing out how the approach can be expanded in a more cognitive fashion, in order to provide a better explanation for the kinds of fictional worlds that set themselves the farthest away from real-world parameters. How we deal with the unnaturalness of these story worlds, then, can be better understood within a more cognitively-oriented approach, which, as I have argued, can also help in the definition of unnaturalness itself.

In conclusion, on the one hand Carroll's impossible storyworlds inspire reflections on the relationship between readers and fictional entities in general and on how to cognitively access the narrative worlds; on the other hand they represent an extreme case of dealing with fictionality, by their constant portrayal of paradoxical elements. The make-believing enacted by readers who encounter a specific narrative has a more composite and elaborate nature when we are dealing with unnatural fictional scenarios. As recognised by Alber's proposed reading strategies, unnatural narratives entail distinctive kinds of cognitive activity, and the *Alices*' discourse on impossible beings functions as a poetical and often comical meditation on their philosophical, cognitive and logical implications. As Gabelman (2016) remarks, comparing Tolkien's worlds to the Carrollian ones, "although both Carroll and Tolkien require from their reader an imaginative acceptance of the impossible, the nonsensical imagination seems to demand the *persistent* practice of accepting impossibilities" (46): this is what the White Queen says to Alice, speaking about her habit of believing six impossible things before breakfast, which, however, requires "practice", and has to be done "for half an hour a day" (209).

Conclusion

The main argument of this book is launched by the epigraph to chapter two, "Virtual Alice," a quotation from *Through the Looking-Glass* about the puzzlement the Unicorn experiences in front of Alice, having always believed that children were "fabulous monsters" (241). The last section of my last chapter concerns "little girls, unicorns and other fabulous monsters" (247). The book, then, enacts a circular movement, returning to the point from which it started: my cognitive study of the *Alices*' virtual realities in chapter two ultimately reappears in my analysis of the specific impossible/unnatural scenarios these realities entail.

However, this return to the beginning does not nullify what lies on the circuit in between, but rather is only possible as the outcome of the intervening process. Before examining these Carrollian storyworlds from an "unnatural" perspective, it was necessary to work through an understanding of several relevant cognitive concepts and relate them to the *Alice* books. How Carroll's virtual realities are constructed, what they are made of, how we grasp them, what the conceptual cornerstones are to their narrative form, what their emotional aspects are; these are all necessary steps towards a complete cognitive study of the *Alices*. These theoretical steps lead us, finally, to a cognitive conceptualisation of the relation between nonsense and the unnatural.

In the introduction I propose the idea of the *Alice* books as cognitive playgrounds, and this book itself can be interpreted in a similar way, progressively elaborating the cognitive complexities of its subject matter. It begins with basic conceptual metaphors, their creative development by the author and interpretation by the reader (chapter two); it then goes into detail with the cognitive metaphor of the mirror (chapter three); it then pursues the emotional ramifications of the *Alices*' cognitive games, in relation to the author, characters and readers (chapter four); finally it addresses the cognitive challenge of unnaturalness, presented by the more extreme aspects of the narratives and the more complex mental games initiated by Carroll's scenarios (chapter five).

These stages of my analysis are all interconnected: they do not offer a sequential progression through discrete phases of argument, but rather the various elements of the discussion relate reciprocally to each other. The circularity of the ending, where the impossible worlds of the unnatural are conceived in dialogue with the *possible* world theory introduced at the beginning, is merely the final demonstration of this reciprocity. This same interconnected structure can be found within each chapter, in the relation between the sections on the author, the characters and the readers. The connections across these separately treated frames of reference also highlight the anti-dichotomous principles that permeate the whole book, which advocates for the coexistence of complementary perspectives and a synthetic view of antitheses.

My methodological approach, too, sustains an interplay between diachronic and achronic premises; my attention to Carroll's biography and to the specific Victorian cultural and social environment coexists with universal claims and theoretical models that transcend particular historical junctures, or make broad connections among different periods. In this respect the book opens out some possibilities for future research, hinted towards in the final chapter: the *Alices'* peculiar genre, a complex situated conceptually and historically between the fairy tale tradition and the postmodern text, itself invites further cognitive inquiry, connecting Carroll's works with a broader idea of the fantastic.

Gillian Beer, in the introduction to her *Alice in Space* (2016), points out that her chapters work together in revealing "particular patterns", rather than "proceeding irreversibly from stage to stage", and that "by this means I respect the picaresque nature of Alice's travels and resist seeking a moral progress or an apotheosis that would falsify Lewis Carroll's achievement" (25). This attitude is precisely the one I maintain in my own structural order: there is a progressive elaboration of cognitive complexity and enrichment of the argument, but at the same time, there is continual cross-reference between connecting passages from different parts of the overall architecture.

Both cognitive narratology and the *Alice* books require this approach, I believe, which is one of the reasons they are so conceptually compatible: cognitive narratology is a flexible and malleable field, mirrored by the picaresque multi-facetedness of Alice's stories. I demonstrate in this book how a "soft", metaphorical, cognitive perspective can lead to fruitful results for narrative studies and so contribute to the dialogue between disciplines that is the intellectual cornerstone of both cognitive narratology and Carroll's masterpieces.

Bibliography

Abbott, H. Porter. 2008. "Unreadable Minds and the Captive Reader." *Style* 42.4: 448–466. url: https://www.jstor.org/stable/10.5325/style.42.4.448
Acheta Domestica. 1879. *Episodes of Insect Life*. London: G. Bell and Sons.
Ackerman, Sherry L. 2008. *Behind the Looking-Glass: Reflections on the Myth of Lewis Carroll*. Newcastle: Cambridge Scholars Publishing.
Alber, Jan. 2009. "Impossible Storyworlds – and What to Do with Them". *StoryWorlds: A Journal of Narrative Studies* 1: 79–96. doi: 10.1353/stw.0.0008
Alber, Jan. 2013. "Unnatural Spaces and Narrative Worlds". In *A Poetics of Unnatural Narrative*, edited by Jan Alber, Henrik Skov Nielsen and Brian Richardson, 45–66. Columbus: The Ohio State University Press.
Alber, Jan. 2016a. *Unnatural Narrative: Impossible Worlds in Fiction and Drama*. Lincoln: University of Nebraska Press.
Alber, Jan. 2016b. "Gaping before Monumental Unnatural Inscriptions? The Necessity of a Cognitive Approach". *Style* 50.4: 434–441. doi: 10.5325/style.50.4.0434
Alber, Jan, and Monika Fludernik. Eds. 2010. *Postclassical Narratology: Approaches and Analyses*. Columbus: The Ohio State University Press.
Alber, Jan, and Rüdiger Heinze. Eds. 2011. *Unnatural Narratives – Unnatural Narratology*. Berlin: Walter de Gruyter.
Alber, Jan, Stefan Iversen, Henrik Skov Nielsen and Brian Richardson. 2010. "Unnatural Narratives, Unnatural Narratalogy: Beyond Mimetic Models". *Narrative* 18.2: 113–136. doi: 10.1353/nar.0.0042
Alber, Jan, Stefan Iversen, Henrik Skov Nielsen and Brian Richardson. 2012. "What Is Unnatural about Unnatural Narratology? A Response to Monika Fludernik". *Narrative* 20.3: 371–382. doi: 10.1353/nar.2012.0020
Alighieri, Dante [1472]. 1999a. *Divina Commedia: Inferno*, edited by Anna Maria Chiavacci Leonardi. Bologna: Zanichelli.
Alighieri, Dante [1472].—. 1999b. *Divina Commedia: Paradiso,* edited by Anna Maria Chiavacci Leonardi. Bologna: Zanichelli.
Armstrong, Isobel. 2008. *Victorian Glassworlds: Glass Culture and the Imagination 1830–1880*. Oxford: Oxford University Press.
Asimov, Isaac. 1992. *The Complete Stories. Vol. 2*. New York: Foundation.
Auerbach, Nina. 1973. "Alice and Wonderland: A Curious Child". *Victorian Studies* 17.1: 31–47. url: http://www.jstor.com/stable/3826513
Auerbach, Nina. 1982. "Falling Alice, Fallen Women, and Victorian Dream Children". *English Language Notes* 20.2: 46–64.
Baker, Kenneth. 1999. "Elaine Scarry's Dreaming by the Book". *San Francisco Chronicle*. Review quoted in Scarry, Elaine. *Dreaming by the Book*. Princeton (NJ): Princeton University Press.
Bakewell, Michael. 1996. *Lewis Carroll: A Biography*. Toronto: Random House of Canada.
Ballard, James Graham. 1988. *The Crystal World*. New York: Farrar, Straus and Giroux.
Banfield, Marie. 2007. "From Sentiment to Sentimentality: A Nineteenth Century Lexicographical Search". *19* 4: 1–11. doi: 10.16995/ntn.459
Batson, Daniel C. 1991. *The Altruism Question: Towards a Social-Psychological Answer*. Hillsdale (NJ): Erlbaum.

Beckett, Samuel [1957]. 2009. *Endgame*. London: Faber & Faber.
Beer, Gillian. 2016. *Alice in Space*. Chicago and London: The University of Chicago Press.
Bernini, Marco, and Marco Caracciolo. 2013. *Letteratura e Scienze Cognitive*. Roma: Carocci Editore.
Bernini, Marco. 2014. "Supersizing Narrative Theory: On Intention, Material Agency and Extended-Mind Workers". *Style* 48.3: 349–366. url: www.jstor.org/stable/10.5325/style.48.3.349
Berta, Luca. 2010. "Death and the Evolution of Language". *Human Studies* 33.4: 425–444. doi: 10.1007/s10746-011-9170-4
Berto, Francesco. 2010. *L'esistenza non è logica: dal quadrato rotondo ai mondi impossibili*. Roma, Bari: Laterza.
Birke, Dorothee, Michael Butter and Tilmann Koppe. Eds. 2011. *Counterfactual Thinking/ Counterfactual Writing*. Berlin and Boston: Walter de Gruyter.
Blom, Jan Dirk. 2016. "Alice in Wonderland Syndrome: A Systematic Review". *Neurology Clinical Practice* 6.3: 259–270. doi:10.1212/CPJ.0000000000000251
Bohm, David. 2004. *On Dialogue*. New York: Routledge.
Borges, Jorge Luis. 2001. Ed. and Trans. Tommaso Scarano. *Nove Saggi Danteschi*. Milano: Adelphi.
Bortolussi, Marisa and Peter Dixon. 2003. *Psychonarratology: Foundations for the Empirical Study of Literary Response*. Cambridge: Cambridge University Press.
Bown, Nicola. Ed. 2007. "Rethinking Victorian Sentimentality". *19* 4
Brown, Daniel. 2013. *The Poetry of Victorian Scientists: Style, Science and Nonsense*. Cambridge: Cambridge University Press.
Bruhn Mark J. 2011. "Introduction: Exchange Values: Poetics and Cognitive Science". *Poetics Today* 32.3: 404–460. doi: 10.1215/03335372-1375243
Bruner, Jerome. 1986. *Actual Minds, Possible Worlds*. Cambridge (MA) and London: Harvard University Press.
Burstein, Mark. 2015. "Dodgson and Dalì". In *Alice's Adventures in Wonderland: 150th Anniversary Edition Illustrated by Salvador Dalì*, vii–xvii. Princeton and Oxford: Princeton University Press.
Calvino, Italo. 1988. *Six Memos for the Next Millennium*. Cambridge (MA): Harvard University Press.
Cappelletto, Chiara. 2009. *Neuroestetica: l'Arte del Cervello*. Bari: Editori Laterza & Figli Spa.
Carroll, Lewis (Charles Lutwidge Dodgson). [1887]. 2011. "Alice' on the Stage". *The Theatre* 1. In Alice's Adventures in Wonderland, edited by Richard Kelly. Peterborough (ON): Broadview Press. 223–227.
Carroll, Lewis. 1894. "A Logical Paradox". *Mind: A Quarterly Review of Psychology and Philosophy:* 436–438.
Carroll, Lewis. 1895. "What the Tortoise Said to Achilles". *Mind: A Quarterly Review of Psychology and Philosophy:* 278–280.
Carroll, Lewis. [1889]. 1988. *Sylvie and Bruno*. New York: Dover Publications.
Carroll, Lewis. 2000. *Alice nel Paese delle Meraviglie e Attraverso lo Specchio*. Edited and translated by Milli Graffi. Milano: Garzanti.
Carroll, Lewis. [1865]. 2001. "Alice's Adventures in Wonderland". *The Annotated Alice: The Definitive Edition*. Edited by Martin Gardner. London: Penguin Books.

Carroll, Lewis. [1871]. 2001. "Through the Looking-Glass and What Alice Found There". *The Annotated Alice: The Definitive Edition*. Edited by Martin Gardner. London: Penguin Books.
Carroll, Lewis. 2003. *Alice's Adventures in Wonderland and Through the Looking-Glass*. Edited by Hugh Haughton. London: Penguin Classics.
Carroll, Lewis. 2003. *The Mathematical Recreations of Lewis Carroll: Pillow Problems and a Tangled Tale*. New York: Dover Publications.
Carroll, Lewis. 2004. *Alice's Adventures Underground*. Whitefish (MT): Kessinger Publishing.
Carroll, Lewis. 2004. "Bruno's Revenge". Edited by Dennis Denisoff. *The Broadview Anthology of Victorian Short Stories*. Peterborough (ON): Broadview Press.
Carroll, Lewis. [1876]. 2006. *The Hunting of the Snark*. Edited by Martin Gardner. New York and London: W.W. Norton and Company.
Carroll, Lewis. [1893]. 2010. *Sylvie and Bruno Concluded*. Charleston (SC): NabuPress.
Changeux, Jean-Pierre. 2008. *Du Vrai, du Beau, du Bien. Une Nouvelle Approche Neuronale*. Paris: Odile Jacob.
Claeys, Gregory and Lyman Tower Sargent. Eds. 1999. *The Utopia Reader*. New York and London: New York University Press.
Clark, Andy. 1998. *Being There: Putting Brain, Body, and World Together Again*. Cambridge (MA): The MIT Press.
Clarke, Anne. 1979. *Lewis Carroll: A Biography*. London: Dent.
Clarke, Anne. 1982. *The Real Alice: Lewis Carroll's Dream Child*. New York: Stein and Day.
CogniFit. 2020. "Neural Plasticity and Cognition". Last accessed: April 2020. url: https://www.cognifit.com/brain-plasticity-and-cognition
Cohen, Daniel J. 2007. *Equations from God: Pure Mathematics and Victorian Faith*. Baltimore: John Hopkins University Press.
Cohen, Morton N. 1989a. *The Selected Letters of Lewis Carroll*. London and New York: Palgrave Macmillan.
Cohen, Morton N. 1989b. *Lewis Carroll: Interviews and Recollections*. London: Palgrave Macmillan.
Cohen, Morton N. 1995. *Lewis Carroll: A Biography*. New York: Alfred A. Knopf.
Cohen, William A. 2009. *Embodied: Victorian Literature and the Senses*. Minneapolis: The University of Minnesota Press.
Collingwood, Stuart D. 1898. *The Life and Letters of Lewis Carroll*. Woking and London: Unwin Brothers the Gresham Press.
Cosmides, Leda, and John Tooby. 2000. "Consider the Source: The Evolution of Adaptations for Decoupling and Metarepresentations." In *Metarepresentations: A Multidisciplinary Perspective*, edited by Dan Sperber, 53–116. New York: Oxford University Press.
Cotton, Nathaniel [1794]. 2010. *Poems by Nathaniel Cotton M.D. with the Author's Life*. London: Gale Ecco Print Editions.
Currie, Mark. 2007. *About Time: Narrative, Fiction and the Philosophy of Time*. Edinburgh: The Edinburgh University Press.
Dällenbach, Lucien. 1977. *Le récit spéculaire. Essai sur la mise en abyme*. Paris: Seuil.
Damasio, Antonio, 1994. *Descartes' Error: Emotion, Reason and the Human Brain*. New York: G.P. Putnam's Sons.
Damasio, Antonio. 1999. *The Feeling of What Happens: Body and Emotion in the Making of Consciousness*. New York: Harcourt Brace.

Davis, Richard Brian. 2010. Ed. *Alice in Wonderland and Philosophy, Curiouser and Curiouser.* New Jersey: John Wiley and Sons.
De La Mare, Walter. 1932. *Lewis Carroll.* London: Faber and Faber Limited.
Deleuze, Gilles. 1969. *The Logic of Sense.* Translated by Mark Lester. New York: Columbia University Press.
Demurova, Nina. 1982. "Toward a Definition of Alice's Genre: The Folktale and Fairy-Tale Connections". In *Lewis Carroll: A Celebration*, edited by Edward Guiliano, 75–88. New York: Clarkson N. Potter.
Doležel, Lubomir. 1998. *Heterocosmica: Fiction and Possible Worlds.* Baltimore: The Johns Hopkins University Press.
Domhoff, William G. 2010. "The Case for a Cognitive Theory of Dreams". *DreamResearch.*
Douglas-Fairhurst, Robert. 2015. *The Story of Alice: Lewis Carroll and the Secret History of Wonderland.* London: Harvill Secker.
Driver, Julia. 2007. "Dream Immorality". *Philosophy* 82.1: 5–22. doi: 10.1017/S0031819107319013
Duchamp, Marcel. 1975. "Where Do We Go from Here". *Studio International:* 189.
Duchan, Judith F., Gail A. Bruder and Lynne E. Hewitt. 2005. *Deixis in Narrative: A Cognitive Science Perspective.* Hillsdale (NJ): Lawrence Erlbaum Associates.
Eagleman, David M. 2009. "Brain Time". In *What's Next? Dispatches on the Future of Science: Original Essays from a New Generations of Scientists*, edited by Max Brockman, 155–169. New York: Vintage Books.
Eco, Umberto. 1979. "Lector in Fabula". In *The Role of the Reader: Explorations in the Semiotics of the Texts*, 200–260. Bloomington: Indiana University Press.
Eco, Umberto. 1985. *Sugli specchi e altri saggi. Il segno, la rappresentazione, l'illusione, l'immagine.* Milano: Bompiani.
Endsley, Mica R. 1995. "Toward a Theory of Situation Awareness in Dynamic Systems". *Human Factors* 37: 32–64. doi: 10.1518/001872095779049543.
Empson, William. 1974. "Alice in Wonderland: The Child as Swain". In *Aspects of Alice: Lewis Carroll's Dream Child as Seen Through the Critics' Looking-glasses, 1865–1971*, edited by Robert Philips, 400–435. London: Penguin.
Feagin, Susan L. 1996. *Reading with Feeling: The Aesthetics of Appreciation.* Ithaca and London: Cornell University Press.
Fensch, Thomas. 1970. *Alice in Acidland.* New York: A.S. Barnes and Company.
Finke, Ronald A., Thomas B. Ward, and Steven M. Smith. 1992. *Creative Cognition: Theory, Research, and Applications.* Cambridge, MA: The MIT Press.
Fisher, John. 1973. *The Magic of Lewis Carroll.* London: Nelson and Sons.
Fludernik, Monika. 2009. "The Cage Metaphor". In *Narratology in the Age of Cross-Disciplinary Narrative Research*, edited by Sandra Heinen and Roy Sommer, 109–128. Berlin and New York: Walter de Gruyter.
Fludernik, Monika. 2011. Ed. *Beyond Cognitive Metaphor Theory: Perspectives on Literary Metaphor.* New York: Routledge.
Fludernik, Monika. 2012. "How Natural Is 'Unnatural Narratology'; or, What Is Unnatural about Unnatural Narratology?". *Narrative* 20.3: 357–370. doi: 10.1353/nar.2012.0019
Foucault, Michel. 1986. "Of Other Spaces". Translated by Jan Miskowiec. *Diacritics*, 16.1: 22–27.

Foulkes, David. 1999. *Children's Dreaming and the Development of Consciousness*. Cambridge (MA): Harvard University Press.
Freeman, Margaret H. 2000. "Poetry and the Scope of Metaphor: Toward a Cognitive Theory of Literature". In *Metaphor and Metonym at the Crossroad: A Cognitive Perspective*, edited by Antonio Barcelona, 250–281. Berlin: Mouton de Gruyter.
Freeman, Margaret. 2012. "Blending and Beyond: Form and Feeling in Poetic Iconicity". In *Cognitive Literary Studies: Current Theme and New Directions*, edited by Isabel Jaén and Julien Jacques Simon, 127–144. Austin: University of Texas Press.
Gabelman, Josephine. 2016. *A Theology of Nonsense*. Eugene, Oregon: Wipf and Stock Publishers.
Gallese, Vittorio. 2009. "Mirror Neurons, Embodied Simulation, and the Neural Basis of Social Identification". *Psychoanalytic Dialogues* 19.5: 519–536. doi: 10.1080/10481880903231910
Gallese, Vittorio, and Alvin Godman. 1998. "Mirror Neurons and the Simulation Theory of Mind-Reading". *Trends in Cognitive Sciences* 2.12: 493–501. doi:10.1016/s1364-6613(98)01262-5.
Gardner, Howard. 1984. *Art, Mind and Brain: A Cognitive Approach to Creativity*. New York: Basic Books.
Gardner, Martin. 1988. "Introduction to the Dover Edition" of *Sylvie and Bruno* by Lewis Carroll, x–xxxi. New York: Dover Publications.
Gardner, Martin. 2001. Ed. *The Annotated Alice: The Definitive Edition*. London: Penguin Books.
Gavins, Joanna. 2005. "Text World Theory in Literary Practice". In *Cognition and Literary Interpretation in Practice*, edited by Harri Veivo, Bo Pettersson and Merja Polvinen, 89–104. Helsinki: Yliopistopaino (Helsinki University Press).
Gerrig, Richard J., and Giovanna Egidi. 2003. "Cognitive Psychological Foundations of Narrative Experiences". In *Narrative Theory and the Cognitive Sciences*, edited by David Herman, 33–55. Stanford (CA): CSLI Publications.
Glezerman, Tatiana, and Victoria Balkoski. 2002. *Language, Thought and the Brain*. New York: Kluwer Academic Publishers.
Goldman, Victoria S. 2007. "Evolution of a Dream-Child: Images of Alice and Changing Conceptions of Childhood, Part V: The Late Nineteen Sixties". *Knight Letter* 79: 7.
Gordon, Jan B. 1974. "The Alice Books and the Metaphors of Victorian Childhood". In *Aspects of Alice: Lewis Carroll's Dream Child as Seen Through the Critics' Looking-glasses, 1865–1971*, edited by Robert Philips, 127–150. London: Penguin.
Gottlieb, Jacqueline, Pierre-Yves Oudeyer, Manuel Lopes, and Adrien Baranes. 2013. "Information-Seeking, Curiosity and Attention: Computational and Neural Mechanisms. *Trends in Cognitive Science*, xx: 1–9. doi: 10.1016/j.tics.2013.09.001
Graffi, Milli. 2000. "Introduzione", in *Alice nel Paese delle Meraviglie e Attraverso lo Specchio*, edited and translated by Milli Graffi, vii–xxxiii. Milano: Garzanti
Gray, Christopher. 1995. "Alice in Wittgenstein: Inside the Great Mirror". *The Journal of Value Inquiry* 29.1: 77–88. doi:10.1007/BF01079063
Green, Melanie C. 2004. "Transportation into Narrative Worlds: The Role of Prior Knowledge and Perceived Realism". *Discourse Processes* 38.2: 247–266. doi: 10.1207/s15326950dp3802_5

Greenacre, Phyllis. 1974. "The Character of Dodgson as Revealed in the Writings of Carroll". In *Aspects of Alice: Lewis Carroll's Dream Child as Seen Through the Critics' Looking-glasses, 1865–1971*, edited by Robert Philips, 369–386. London: Penguin.

Gregory, Horace. 1974. "On Lewis Carroll's Alice and her White Knight and Wordsworth's 'Ode on Immortality' ". In *Aspects of Alice: Lewis Carroll's Dream Child as Seen Through the Critics' Looking-glasses, 1865–1971*, edited by Robert Philips, 164–177. London: Penguin.

Grice, Paul H. 1989. *Studies in the Way of Words*. Cambridge (MA): Harvard University.

Groth, Helen. 2013. *Moving Images. Nineteenth-century Reading and Screen Practices*. Edinburgh: Edinburgh University Press.

Gurney, Edmund, Frederic William Henry Meyers and Frank Podmore. 1886. *Phantasms of the Living*. London: Rooms of the Society for Psychical Research.

Guiliano, Edward. 2019. *Lewis Carroll: Worlds of His Alices*. Brighton: Edward Everett Root Publishers.

Guyer, Sara. 2004. "The Girl with the Open Mouth Through the Looking-Glass". *Angelaki: Journal of the Theoretical Humanities* 9.1: 159–163. doi: 10.1080/0969725042000232469

Habermas, Tilman, and Verena Diel. 2010. "The Emotional Impact of Loss Narratives: Event Severity and Narrative Perspectives". *Emotion* 10.3: 312–323. doi:10.1037/a0018001

Halliwell, Stephen, trans. 1998. *Aristotle's Poetics*. Chicago: University of Chicago Press.

Hanks, William F. 2005. "Deixis". In *The Routledge Encyclopaedia of Narrative Theory*, edited by David Herman, Manfred Jahn and Marie-Laure Ryan, 99–100. Oxon: Routledge.

Harding, Olivia. 2009. "The Ordinary and The Extraordinary". *VictorianWeb*. http://www.victorianweb.org/genre/harding.html

Hatch, Evelyn. 2006. *A Selection from the Letters of Lewis Carroll to His Child Friends*. Montana: Kessinger Publishing.

Haughton, Hugh. Ed. 1988. *The Chatto Book of Nonsense Poetry*. London: Chatto and Windus.

Haughton, Hugh. 2003. "Introduction". In *Alice's Adventures in Wonderland and Through the Looking-Glass*, edited by Hugh Haughton, ix–lxv. London: Penguin Classics.

Heinze, Rüdiger. 2013. "The Whirligig of Time". In *A Poetics of Unnatural Narrative*, edited by Jan Alber, Henrik Skov Nielsen and Brian Richardson, 31–44. Columbus: The Ohio State University Press.

Herman, David. 2002. *Story Logic. Problems and Possibilities of Narrative*. Lincoln: University of Nebraska Press.

Herman, David. 2003a. "Stories as a Tool for Thinking". In *Narrative Theory and the Cognitive Sciences*, edited by David Herman, 163–192. Stanford (CA): CSLI Publications.

Herman, David. 2003b. "How Stories Make Us Smarter: Narrative Theory and Cognitive Semiotics". *Recherches en Communication*, 19: 133–153. doi: 10.14428/rec.v19i19.48463

Herman, David. 2005a. "Narrative as Cognitive Instrument". In *The Routledge Encyclopedia of Narrative Theory*, edited by David Herman, Manfred Jahn and Marie-Laure Ryan. Oxon: Routledge.

Herman, David. 2005b. "Storyworld". In *The Routledge Encyclopaedia of Narrative Theory*, edited by David Herman, Manfred Jahn and Marie-Laure Ryan, 569–570. Oxon: Routledge.

Herman, David. 2007. "Cognition, Emotion, and Consciousness". In *The Cambridge Companion to Narrative*, edited by David Herman, 245–259. Cambridge: Cambridge University Press.

Herman, David. 2009. *Basic Elements of Narrative*. Chichester: John Wiley & Sons.

Herman, David. 2013a. *Storytelling and The Science of the Mind*. Cambridge (MA): The MIT Press.

Herman, David. 2013b. "Cognitive Narratology". In *The Living Handbook of Narratology*, edited by Peter Hühn et al., paragraph 36, 1–43. Hamburg: Hamburg University Press. Last access: October 2015.

Hogan, Patrick C. 2003. *Cognitive Science, Literature, and the Arts*. New York: Routledge.

Hogan, Patrick C. 2010. "A Passion for Plot: Prolegomena for Affective Narratology". *Symploke* 18.1–2: 65–81. doi: 10.1353/sym.2011.0030

Hollingsworth, Cristopher. Ed. 2009. *Alice Beyond Wonderland: Essays for the Twenty-First Century*. Iowa City: University of Iowa Press.

Holquist, Michael. 1999. "What is a Boojum? Nonsense and Modernism". *Yale French Studies* 96: 100–117. doi: 10.2307/3040720

Holt, Jonathan. 2001. "Deconstructing the Mirror: The Crisis of Logic in the Looking-Glass World". *Lore Journal*, Issue N. http://www.lorejournal.org/2001/03/deconstructing-the-mirror-the-crisis-of-logic-in-the-looking-glass-world-by-jonathan-holt/

Iakimova, Galina et al. 2006. "The Understanding of Metaphors in Schizophrenia and Depression. An Experimental Approach". *Encephale* 32.6: 995–1002. doi: 10.1016/s0013-7006(06)76279-0.

Indefrey, Paul and Marianne Gullberg. Eds. 2008. *Time to Speak: Cognitive and Neural Prerequisites of Time in Language*. Hoboken (NJ): Blackwell.

Iversen, Stefan. 2013. "Unnatural Minds". In *A Poetics of Unnatural Narrative*, edited by Jan Alber, Henrik Skov Nielsen and Brian Richardson, 94–112. Columbus: The Ohio State University Press.

Jaén, Isabel and Julien J. Simon. Eds. 2012. *Cognitive Literary Studies: Current Themes and New Directions*. Austin: University of Texas Press.

James, William. 1890. *The Principles of Psychology. Vols. I and II*. New York: Dover.

James, William. 1986. "Essays in Psychical Research". In *The Works of William James, Vol. 16*, edited by Frederick Burkhardt, xiii–xxxvi. Cambridge (MA): Harvard University Press.

Jepma, Marieke, et al. 2012. "Neural Mechanisms Underlying the Induction and Relief of Perceptual Curiosity". *Frontiers in Behavioural Neuroscience* 6.5: 5. doi: 10.3889/fnbeh.2012.00005

Johnson, George. 2006. *Dynamic Psychology in Modernist British Fiction*. London: Palgrave MacMillan.

Johnston, Adrian. 2016. "Jacques Lacan". In *The Stanford Encyclopaedia of Philosophy*, edited by Edward N. Zalta. Stanford University: Metaphysics Research Lab.

Kang, Min Jeong et al. 2009. "The Wick in the Candle of Learning: Epistemic Curiosity Activates Reward Circuitry and Enhances Memory". *Psychological Science* 20.8: 963–973. doi: 10.1111/j.1467-9280.2009.02402.x

Karlsson, Jenny. 2009. "Alice's Vacillation between Childhood and Adolescence in Lewis Carroll's *Alice's Adventures in Wonderland*". PhD diss., Karlstads University.

Keen, Suzanne. 2007. *Empathy and the Novel*. Oxford: Oxford University Press.

Keen, Suzanne. 2011a. "Introduction: Narrative and the Emotions". *Poetics Today* 32.1: 1–53. doi: 10.1215/03335372-1188176

Keen, Suzanne. 2011b. "Empathetic Hardy: Bounded, Ambassadorial and Broadcast Strategies of Narrative Empathy". *Poetics Today* 32.2: 349–389. doi: 10.1215/03335372-1162695

Keen, Suzanne. 2013. "Narrative and Empathy". *The Living Handbook of Narratology*, edited by Jan Christoph Meister. https://www.lhn.uni-hamburg.de/node/42.html. Last access: April 2020.

Keene, Melanie. 2015. *Science in Wonderland: The Scientific Fairy Tales of Victorian Britain*. Oxford: Oxford University Press.

Kimmel, Michael. 2011."Metaphor Sets in The Turn of the Screw: What Conceptual Metaphors Reveal about Narrative Functions". In *Beyond Cognitive Metaphor Theory: Perspectives on Literary Metaphor*, edited by Monika Fludernik, 196–223. New York: Routledge.

Kintgen, Eugene R. 1983. *The Perception of Poetry*. Bloomington: Indiana University Press.

Kittay, Eva F. 1987. *Metaphor: Its Cognitive Force and Linguistic Structure*. Oxford: Clarendon Press.

Klauk, Tobias and Tilmann Köppe. 2013. "Reassessing Unnatural Narratology: Problems and Prospects". *Storyworlds: A Journal of Narrative Studies* 5: 77–100.

Knapp, Krister Dylan. 2001. "WJ, Spiritualism and Unconsciousness 'Beyond the Margin". *Streams of William James* 3.2: 1–5.

Knight, Rob. 2016. *Follow Your Gut: The Enormous Impact of Tiny Microbes*. Ted Books.

Kohlberg, Lawrence. 1984. *The Psychology of Moral Development: The Nature and Validity of Moral Stages (Essays on Moral Development, Volume 2)*. New York: Harper & Row.

Kohlt, Franziska. 2016. "'The Stupidest Tea-Party in All My Life': Lewis Carroll and Victorian Psychiatric Practice". *Journal of Victorian Culture* 21.2: 147–167. doi: 10.1080/135555502.2016.1167767

Korkmaz, Baris. 2011. "Theory of Mind and Neurodevelopmental Disorders of Childhood". *Pediatr Res* 69: 101–108. doi:10.1203/PDR.0b013e318212c177

Kunka, Andrew. 2007. "Dynamic Psychology in Modern British Fiction (Review)". *Modern Fiction Studies*, 53.4: 905–909. doi: 10.1353mfs.2008.0015

Lakoff, George. 1987. *Women, Fire, and Dangerous Things: What Categories Reveal about the Mind*. Chicago: University of Chicago Press.

Lakoff, George, and Mark Johnson. 1980. *Metaphors We Live by*. Chicago and London: University of Chicago Press.

Lakoff, George, and Mark Turner. 1989. *More than Cool Reason: A Field Guide to Poetic Metaphor*. Chicago: The University of Chicago Press.

Langdon, Robyn, Richard J. Siegert, John McClure, and Leigh Harrington. 2005. "Schizophrenia, Theory of Mind, and Persecutory Delusions". *Cognitive Neuropsychiatry* 10.2: 87–104. doi: 10.1080/13546800344000327

LaPlante, Eve. 1993. *Seized: Temporal Lobe Epilepsy as a Medical, Historical, and Artistic Phenomenon*. New York: Harper & Collins.

Leach, Elsie. 1974. "Alice in Wonderland in Perspective". In *Aspects of Alice: Lewis Carroll's Dream Child as Seen Through the Critics' Looking-glasses, 1865–1971*, edited by Robert Philips, 121–126. London: Penguin.

Leach, Karoline. 1999. *In the Shadow of the Dreamchild: The Myth and Reality of Lewis Carroll*. London: Peter Owen.

Leach, Karoline. 2000. "Lewis Carroll: A Myth in the Making". *VictorianWeb.* http://www.victor ianweb.org/authors/carroll/dreamchild/dreamchild1.html

Lecercle, Jean-Jacques. 1994. *Philosophy of Nonsense: The Intuitions of Victorian Nonsense Literature.* London: Routledge.

Lee, Michael Parrish. 2014. "Eating Things: Food, Animals, and Other Life Forms in Lewis Carroll's Alice books". *Nineteen Cent Lit* 68.4: 484–512. doi: 10.1525/ncl.2014.68.4.484

Leekam, Susan R., and Josef Perner. 1991. "Does the Autistic Child Have a Metarepresentational Deficit?". *Cognition* 40: 203–218. doi: 10.1016/0010-0277(91)90025-Y

Lehrer, Jonah. 2008. *Proust Was a Neuroscientist.* New York: First Mariner Books edition.

Lehrer, Jonah. 2010a. "The Itch of Curiosity". *Wired.*

Lehrer, Jonah. 2010b. "Psychopaths and Rational Morality". *Science Blogs.*

Lennon, Florence Becker. 1962. *Victoria Through the Looking-Glass.* New York: Collier.

Lepore, Jill. 2012. *The Mansion of Happiness: A History of Life and Death.* New York: Alfred A. Knopf.

Levin, Henry. 1974. "Wonderland Revisited". In *Aspects of Alice: Lewis Carroll's Dream Child as Seen Through the Critics' Looking-glasses, 1865–1971*, edited by Robert Philips, 217–242. London: Penguin.

Lindahl, Carl. 1983. "Reviewed Work: Nonsense: Aspects of Intertextuality in Folklore and Literature by Susan Stewart". *Western Folklore* 42.1:71–73.

Lovett, Charlie. 2005. *Lewis Carroll Among His Books: A Descriptive Catalogue of the Private Library of Charles L. Dodgson.* Jefferson (NC): McFarland & Company.

Lowrie, Joyce. 2008. *Sightings: Mirrors in Texts – Texts in Mirrors.* Amsterdam and New York: Editions Rodopi B.V.

MacDonald, George [1858]. 2008. *Phantastes.* Milton Keynes and London: Paternoster.

Mäkelä, Maria. 2013. "Realism and the Unnatural". In *A Poetics of Unnatural Narrative*, edited by Jan Alber, Henrik Skov Nielsen and Brian Richardson, 142–166. Columbus: The Ohio State University Press.

Mandler, Jean M. 1984. *Stories, Scripts, and Scenes: Aspects of Schema Theory.* New Jersey: Lawrence Erlbaum Associates.

Marcus, Leonard S. 1984. "Alice's Adventures, the Pennyroyal Press Edition." *Children's Literature* 12: 175–184.

Margolin, Uri. 1996. "Characters and Their Versions". In *Fiction Updated: Theories of Fictionality, Narratology, and Poetics*, edited by Calin-Andrei Mihailescu and Walid Hamarneh, 112–132. Toronto: Toronto University Press.

Marìas, Javier. 1996. *Tomorrow in the Battle Think on Me.* Translated by Margaret Jull Costa. London: Penguin Books.

Matrix. 1999. Dir. The Wachowskis. Perf. Keanu Reeves, Laurence Fishburne, Carrie-Anne Moss, Hugo Weaving, Joe Pantoliano. Warner Bros. Film.

Mayer, Emeran. 2016. *The Mind-Gut Connection: How the Hidden Conversation Within Our Bodies Impacts Our Mood, Our Choices and Our Overall Health.* New York: Harper Wave.

McGee, American J. 2011. *Alice: Madness Returns.* Microsoft Windows, PlayStation 3, Xbox 360.

McHale, Brian. 2006. "Cognition en Abyme: Models, Manuals, Maps". *Partial Answers: Journal of Literature and the History of Ideas* 4.2: 175–189. doi: 10.1353/pan.0.0105

McLeod, Saul. 2013. "Kohlberg". *SimplyPsychology.Org.*

McVee, Marie B., Kailonnie Dunsmore, and James R. Gavelek. 2005. "Schema Theory Revisited". *Review of Educational Research* 75.4: 531–566. doi: 10.3102/00346543075004531

Miall, David S. 1989. "Beyond the Schema Theory: Affective Comprehension of Literary Narratives". *Cognition and Emotion* 3.1: 55–78. doi: 10.1080/02699938908415236

Morton, Lionel. 1978. "Memory in the Alice Books". *Nineteenth-Century Fiction* 33: 285–308. doi: 10.2307/2933016

Mullane, Harvey. 1965. "Moral Responsibility for Dreams". *Dialogue* 4.2:224–229. doi: 10.1017/s0012217300033576

Murphy, Gardner, and Robert Ballou. 1960. *William James on Psychical Research*. New York: Viking Press.

Nabokov, Vladimir. 2000. *The Annotated Lolita*. Ed. Alfred Appel. London: Penguin Classics.

Nünning, Vera. 2014. *Reading Fictions, Changing Minds: The Cognitive Value of Fiction*. Heidelberg: Universitätsverlag Winter.

Nünning, Vera. 2015. "The Ethics of (Fictional) Form: Persuasiveness and Perspective Taking from the Point of View of Cognitive Literary Studies". *Arcadia* 50.1: 37–56. doi: 10.1515/arcadia-2015-0004.

Ovidio, Publio Nasone [8 AD]. 2015. *Le Metamorfosi*. Milano: Einaudi.

Palmer, Alan. 2005. *Fictional Minds*. Lincoln: University of Nebraska Press.

Peirce, Charles Sanders. 1966. *Selected Writings: Values in a Universe of Chance*. Ed. Philip Wiener. New York: Dover Publications.

Petersen, R. Calvin. 1979. "'To Sleep, Perchance to Dream': Alice Takes a Little Nap". *Jabberwocky* 8.2: 27–37.

Pettersson, Bo. 2011. "Literary Criticism Writes Back to Metaphor Theory: Exploring the Relation between Extended Metaphor and Narrative in Literature". In *Beyond Cognitive Metaphor Theory: Perspectives on Literary Metaphor*, edited by Monica Fludernik, 94–112. New York: Routledge.

Piaget, Jean. 1997. *The Moral Judgement of the Child*. New York: Free Press Paperbacks.

Pinhas, Ben-Zvi. 2002. "Lewis Carroll and the Search for Non-Being". *The Philosopher* LXXXX.1. http://www.the-philosopher.co.uk/2002/03/

Pinker, Steven. 1997. *How the Mind Works*. New York and London: W.W. Norton & Company.

Plato [369 BCE]. 1987. *Theaetetus*. London: Penguin Classics.

Podoll, Klaus, Holger Ebel, Derek Robinson and Ubaldo Nicola. 2002. "Obligatory and Facultative Symptoms of the Alice in Wonderland Syndrome". *Minerva Med*, 93.4: 287–293.

Prentice, Deborah A., Richard J. Gerrig and Daniel S. Bailis. 1997. "What Readers Bring to the Processing of Fictional Texts". *Psychonomic Bulletin & Review* 4.3: 416–420. doi: 10.3758/BF03210803

Prickett, Stephen. 1979. *Victorian Fantasy*. Hassocks, Sussex: The Harvester Press Limited.

Prioleau, Elizabeth. 1975. "Humbert Humbert Through the Looking-Glass". *Twentieth Century Literature* 21.4: 428–437. doi: 10.2307/441056

Proceedings of the Society for Psychical Research. 1882. London: Trübner and Co.

Rabbit Hole. By David Lindsay-Abaire. Dir. David Sullivan. Perf. Cynthia Nixon, John Slattery, Tyne Daly, John Gallagher, Mary Catherine Garrison. Biltmore Theatre, Broadway, Manhattan. January-April 2006. Performance.

Rabbit Hole. 2010. Dir. John Cameron Mitchell. Perf. Nicole Kidman, Aaron Eckhart, Dianne Wiest, Miles Teller. Lionsgate. Film.
Rackin, Donald. 1982. "Love and Death in Carroll's Alices". In *Soaring with the Dodo: Essays on Lewis Carroll's Life and Art*, edited by Edward Guiliano and James Kincaid, 26–45. Michigan: The Lewis Carroll Society of North America.
Rackin, Donald. 1991. *Alice's Adventures in Wonderland and Through the Looking-Glass. Nonsense, Sense and Meaning*. New York: Twayne.
Ramachandran, Vilayanur, S. 1998. *Phantoms in the Brain: Human Nature and the Architecture of the Mind*. London: Fourth Estate.
Ramachandran, Vilayanur, S. 2003. *The Emerging Mind*. The Reith Lectures.
Ramachandran, S. Vilayanur, and Edward M. Hubbard. 2003. "The Phenomenology of Synaesthesia". *Journal of Consciousness Studies* 10.8: 49–57.
Ranson-Pollizzotti, Sadi. 2011. *The Bedside, Bathtub & Armchair Companion to Lewis Carroll*. New York: Continuum Publish Corporation.
Revonsuo, Antti. 2000. "The Reinterpretation of Dreams: An Evolutionary Hypothesis of the Function of Dreaming". *Behavioural Brain Science* 23.6: 877–901. doi: 10.1017/S0140525X00004015
Richards, Joan. 1988. *Mathematical Visions: The Pursuit of Geometry in Victorian England*. Boston: Harcourt Brace Jovanovitch.
Richardson, Brian. 2000. "Narrative Poetics and Postmodern Transgression: Theorizing the Collapse of Time, Voice, and Frame". *Narrative* 8.1: 23–42. url: www.jstor.org/stable/20107199
Richardson, Brian. 2006. *Unnatural Voices: Extreme Narration in Modern and Contemporary Fiction*. Columbus: The Ohio State University Press.
Richardson, Brian. 2012. "Antimimetic, Unnatural, and Postmodern Narrative Theory". In *Narrative Theory: Core Concepts and Critical Debates*, edited by David Herman, James Phelan, Peter J Rabinowitz, Brian Richardson, and Robyn Warhol, 20–28. Columbus: The Ohio State University Press.
Rizzolatti, Giacomo and Corrado Sinigaglia. 2006. *So quel che fai: il cervello che agisce e i neuroni specchio*. Milano: Raffaello Cortina Editore.
Robson, Catherine. 2001. *Men in Wonderland: The Lost Girlhood of the Victorian Gentleman*. Princeton (NJ): Princeton University Press.
Roiphe, Katie. 2001. *Still She Haunts Me: A Novel of Lewis Carroll and Alice Liddell*. London: Headline Book Publishing.
Ronen, Ruth. 1994. *Possible Worlds in Literary Theory*. Cambridge: Cambridge University Press.
Rucker, Rudy. 2009. "Thoughts on Alice: An Interview with Rudy Rucker". In *Alice Beyond Wonderland: Essays for the Twenty-First Century*, edited by Cristopher Holllingsworth, 53–62. Iowa City: University of Iowa Press.
Rucker, Rudy. 2014. *The Fourth Dimension: Toward a Geometry of Higher Reality*. New York: Dover Publications.
Ryan, Marie-Laure. 1991. *Possible Worlds, Artificial Intelligence and Narrative Theory*. Bloomington: Indiana University Press.
Ryan, Marie-Laure. 2009. "Temporal Paradoxes in Narrative". *Style* 43.2: 142–164. url: https://www.jstor.org/stable/10.5325/style.43.2.142

Ryan, Marie-Laure. 2010. "Narratology and Cognitive Science: A Problematic Relation". *Style* 44: 469–495. url: https://www.jstor.org/stable/10.5325/style.44.4.469
Sacks, Oliver. 1985. *The Man Who Mistook His Wife for a Hat*. London: Duckworth Books.
Sainsbury, Richard Mark. 2010. *Fiction and Fictionalism*. Oxon and New York: Routledge.
Sartori, Leo. 1996. *Understanding Relativity: A Simplified Approach to Einstein's Theories*. Oakland: University of California Press.
Scarry, Elaine. 1999. *Dreaming by the Book*. Princeton (NJ): Princeton University Press.
Schank, Roger C., and Robert P. Abelson. 1977. *Scripts, Plans, Goals and Understanding: An Inquiry into Human Knowledge Structures*. Hillsdale (NJ): Lawrence Erlbaum Associates.
Schwab, Gabriele. 1996. *The Mirror and the Killer-Queen: Otherness in Literary Language*. Bloomington: Indiana University Press.
Schmidt, Charles. 2015. "Mental Health: Thinking from the Gut". *Scientific American* 312.3: 97–100.
Schmidt, Stanley. Ed. 1990. *Analog Essays on Science*. New York: Wiley.
Schneebeli, Célia. 2013. "Systematised Impoliteness in the Nonsense World of *Alice's Adventures in Wonderland* and *Through the Looking-Glass*", in *Aspects of Linguistic Impoliteness*, edited by Denis Jamet and Manuel Jobert, 160–172. Newcastle upon Tyne: Cambridge Scholars Publishing.
Schneider, Marcus, and Ralf Hartner. Eds. 2012. *Blending and the Study of Narrative*. Berlin and New York: Walter de Gruyter.
Scrittori, Anna Rosa. 1991. "Alice di Lewis Carroll: una fiaba vittoriana". *Annali di Ca' Foscari*, Estratto XXX: 1–2.
Scrittori, Anna Rosa. 2003. *Alice e dintorni, figure della creatività di Lewis Carroll*. Venezia: Supernova.
Segal, Erwin M. 2005a. "A Cognitive-Phenomenological Theory of Fictional Narrative", in *Deixis in Narrative: A Cognitive Science Perspective*, edited by Duchan, Judith F., Gail A. Bruder and Lynne E. Hewitt, 61–78. Hillsdale (NJ): Lawrence Erlbaum Associates.
Segal, Erwin M. 2005b. "Narrative Comprehension and the Role of Deictic Shift Theory", in *Deixis in Narrative: A Cognitive Science Perspective*, edited by Duchan, Judith F., Gail A. Bruder, and Lynne E. Hewitt, 3–18. Hillsdale (NJ): Lawrence Erlbaum Associates.
Seiberling, Grace, and Carolyn Bloore. 1986. *Amateurs, Photography and the Mid-Victorian Imagination*. Chicago and London: The University of Chicago Press.
Sewell, Elizabeth. 1952. *The Field of Nonsense*. London: Chatto and Windus.
Shaberman, Raphael B. 1973. "Lewis Carroll and the Society for Psychical Research". *Jabberwocky*, 11.1: 4–7.
Shaberman, Raphael B. 1982. "George MacDonald and Lewis Carroll". *North Wind: A Journal of George MacDonald Studies* 1.1: 10–30.
Shadwell, Thomas [1688]. 2007. *The Squire of Alsatia: A Comedy etc. (In five Acts and in Prose. With songs)*. London: British Library, Historical Print Editions.
Sinding, Michael. 2011. "Storyworld Metaphors in Swift's Satire". In *Beyond Cognitive Metaphor Theory: Perspectives on Literary Metaphor*, edited by Monica Fludernik, 239–257. New York: Routledge.
Sinding, Michael. 2012. " 'A sermon in the midst of a smutty tale': Blending in Genres of Speech, Writing and Literature". In *Cognitive Literary Studies: Current Theme and New Directions*, edited by Isabel Jaén and Julien Jacques Simon, 145–162. Austin: University of Texas Press.

Sommer, Andreas. 2012. "Psychical Research and the Origins of American Psychology: Hugo Munsterberg, William James and Eusapia Palladino". *History of the Human Sciences* 25.2: 23–44. doi: 10.1177/0952695112439376

Sommer, Andreas. 2013. "Spiritualism and the Origins of Modern Psychology in Late Nineteenth-Century Germany. The Wund-Zollner Debate". In *The Spiritualist Movement: Speaking with the Dead in America and Around the World Vol.1*, edited by Christopher M. Moreman, 55–72. Santa Barbara, CA: Praeger.

Soto, Fernando. 2004. "Mirrors in MacDonald's Phantastes: A Reflexive Structure". *North Wind: Journal of the George MacDonald Society* 23.4. url: https://digitalcommons.snc.edu/northwind/vol23/iss1/4

Spolsky, Ellen. 1994. *Gaps in Nature: Literary Interpretation and the Modular Mind*. New York: State University of New York Press.

Spolsky, Ellen. 2007. *Word vs Image: Cognitive Hunger in Shakespeare's England*. New York: Palgrave MacMillan.

Stern, Jeffrey. 1990. "Carroll Identifies Himself at Last". *Jabberwocky* 74.

Stewart, Susan. 1979. *Nonsense: Aspects of Intertextuality in Folklore and Literature*. Baltimore: John Hopkins University Press.

Stockwell, Peter. 2002. *Cognitive Poetics: An Introduction*. London and New York: Routledge.

Stoneham, Tom. 2019. "Dreaming, Phenomenal Character and Acquaintance", in *Acquaintance: New Essays,* edited by Jonathan Knowles and Thomas Raleigh, 145–168. Oxford: Oxford University Press.

Strauch, Inge. 2005. "Rem Dreaming in Transition from Early Childhood to Adolescence: A Longitudinal Study". *Dreaming*, 15: 153–161. doi: 10.1023/A:1021341732185

Swift, Jonathan. [1726]. 2010. *Gulliver's Travels*. London: Penguin Classics.

Tapiero, Isabelle. 2014. *Situation Models and Levels of Coherence: Toward a Definition of Comprehension*. Abingdon, Oxfordshire: Routledge.

Tate, Allen. 1937. "The Last Days of Alice". In *Selected Poems*. New York: C. Scribner's sons.

Taylor, Alexander L. 1952. *The White Knight: A Study of C.L. Dodgson (Lewis Carroll)*. Edinburgh and London: Oliver & Boyd.

Taylor, Marjorie, Sara D. Hodges, and Adèle Kohàni. 2003. "The Illusion of Independent Agency: Do Adult Fiction Writers Experience Their Characters as Having Minds of Their Own?". *Imagination, Cognition and Personality*, 22.4: 361–380. doi: 10.2190/2FFTG3-Q9T0-7U26-5Q5X

Tigges, Wim. 2013. *An Anatomy of Literary Nonsense*. Amsterdam: Rodopi.

Throesch, Elizabeth. 2009. "Nonsense in the Fourth Dimension of Literature: Hyperspace Philosophy, the 'New' Mathematics, and the Alice books". In *Alice Beyond Wonderland: Essays for the Twenty-First Century*, edited by Cristopher Hollingsworth, 37–51. Iowa City: University of Iowa Press.

Todorov, Tzvetan. 1975. *The Fantastic: A Structural Approach to a Literary G*enre. Ithaca, New York: Cornell University Press.

Toplak, Maggie E. et al. 2003. "Time Perception Deficits in Attention-Deficit/Hyperactivity Disorder and Comorbid Reading Difficulties in Child and Adolescent Samples". *The Journal of Child Psychology and Psychiatry* 44.6: 888–903. doi: 10.1111/1469-7610.00173

Turner, Mark. 1996. *The Literary Mind: The Origins of Thought and Language*. Oxford: Oxford University Press.

Turner, Mark. 2003. "Double-scope Stories". In *Narrative Theory and the Cognitive Sciences*, edited by David Herman, 117–142. Stanford (CA): CSLI Publications.
Van Dijk, Teun Adrianus and Walter Kintsch. 1983. *Strategies in Discourse Comprehension*. New York: Academic Press.
Vinge, Vernor. 2006. *Rainbows End*. New York: Tor Science Fiction.
Wakeling, Edward. 1993. Ed. *Lewis Carroll's Diaries: The Private Journals of Charles Lutwidge Dodgson (Lewis Carroll): The First Complete Version of the Nine Surviving Volumes with Notes and Annotations*. Maryland: The Lewis Carroll Society.
Wakeling, Edward. 2015. *Lewis Carroll: The Man and His Circle*. London: Bloomsbury.
Walsh, Richard. 2007. *The Rhetoric of Fictionality: Narrative Theory and the Idea of Fiction*. Columbus: The Ohio State University Press.
Walsh, Richard. 2016. "The Fictive Reflex: A Fresh Look at Reflexiveness and Narrative Representation". *Neohelicon* 43: 379–389. doi.org/10.1007/s11059-016-0351-z
Walton, Kendall L. 1990. *Mimesis as Make-Believe: On the Foundations of the Representational Arts*. Cambridge (MA): Harvard University Press.
Wilde, Oscar. 1997. *Collected Works of Oscar Wilde*. Ware, Herfordshire: Wordsworth Editions.
Wilson, Deirdre, and Dan Sperber. 1988. "Representation and relevance". In *Mental Representation: The Interface between Language and Reality*, edited by Ruth Kempson, 133–153. Cambridge: Cambridge University Press.
Wojciehowksi Chapelle Hanna, and Vittorio Gallese. 2011. "How Stories Make Us Feel: Toward an Embodied Narratology". *California Italian Studies* 2.1: 1–35. url: http://escholarship.org/uc/item/3jg726c2
Woolf, Jenny. 2010. *The Mystery of Lewis Carroll: Understanding the Author of Alice in Wonderland*. London: Haus Publishing.
Young, Kay. 2010. *Imagining Minds: The Neuro-Aesthetics of Austen, Eliot and Hardy*. Columbus: The Ohio State University Press.
Zsuzsa, Hetényi. 2018. "The Carroll Carroll Pattern: Nabokov and Lewis Carroll". *Toronto Slavic Quarterly* 2: 1–19. url: http://sites.utoronto.ca/tsq/63/Hetenyi63.pdf
Zunshine, Lisa. 2006. *Why We Read Fiction: Theory of Mind and the Novel*. Columbus: The Ohio State University.
Zwaan, Rolph A. 1998. "Situation Models in Language Comprehension and Memory". *Psychological Bulletin* 123.2: 162–185. doi: 10.1037/0033-2909.123.2.162

Authors Index

Alber, Jan 6–8, 147f., 150f., 155–157, 160, 162, 164, 172, 174–176, 181
Auerbach, Nina 51, 53, 110, 128f., 180

Beer, Gillian 124, 131, 134, 137, 153, 159, 163, 165–167, 170f., 183

Carroll, Lewis 1, 4–6, 9–14, 16–24, 26–40, 42, 46–53, 60f., 63–66, 68–70, 72–75, 77, 79f., 82–101, 104–107, 111, 113–127, 129, 134–136, 138, 140, 142–145, 148, 150–154, 156–164, 166–170, 174–183
Cohen, Morton 10f., 13, 18–20, 26, 36, 49, 85f., 94, 114f., 120, 124f., 129, 134, 137, 143, 145

Damasio, Antonio 113, 133
Douglas-Fairhurst, Robert 1, 48f., 61, 73, 75, 83, 91, 95, 97f., 115, 120, 122, 124, 146, 171

Eco, Umberto 54, 73f., 88

Fludernik, Monika 4, 7f., 25f., 34, 148, 151–155, 157
Freeman, Margaret 4, 25, 28, 58

Gallese, Vittorio 5, 101, 113, 133, 159
Gardner, Martin 21, 27f., 32f., 37, 39, 53, 56, 73, 77–79, 83–87, 95, 99, 119, 153, 160, 165, 168
Graffi, Milli 92
Guiliano, Edward 124

Haughton, Hugh 30, 38f., 47, 80, 83f., 87, 94–96, 106, 119, 124, 126, 150, 156
Herman, David 2f., 5, 8f., 102, 113, 127f., 139
Hogan, Patrick 1f., 4, 36–39, 113, 129, 139

Iversen, Stefan 6, 150, 155, 157, 162f., 171f., 176

James, William 14f., 17, 20, 121, 134, 156

Keen, Suzanne 5, 12, 89, 102, 113f., 138–145
Kittay, Eva 28

Leach, Elsie 124, 141
Leach, Karoline 36, 120, 122, 124, 141
Lecercle, Jean-Jacques 9f., 27, 29, 98, 118, 150, 177f.
Lehrer, Jonah 2, 42, 45
Lovett, Charlie 14, 16f., 19, 74, 153f.

MacDonald, George 33, 53, 68, 74f., 144

Nabokov, Vladimir 124, 126
Nünning, Vera 139, 142, 145

Palmer, Alan 5, 40, 90, 97f., 127f., 131
Prickett, Stephen 152, 155f.

Rackin, Donal 47, 70, 73, 95, 107, 109f., 122, 124, 165
Ramachandran, Vilayanur 5, 22f., 34f., 37, 73, 101, 113, 133
Richardson, Brian 6, 147, 150f., 155, 157f.
Robson, Catherine 125
Rucker, Rudy 12f., 37, 160
Ryan, Marie-Laure 3, 25, 54–57, 59, 101–103, 162

Scarry, Elaine 4, 61, 63–66
Schwab, Gabriele 30, 149, 151
Scrittori, Anna Rosa 88, 109
Segal, Erwin 59f.
Sewell, Elizabeth 51, 87, 94, 96, 116f., 138, 140, 144, 158f.
Shaberman, Raphael 13f., 74
Sinding, Michael 4, 25, 27f.
Sommer, Andreas 16
Spolsky, Ellen 2f., 159

Stewart, Susan 150, 158–160, 163 f., 166, 169
Stockwell, Peter 3, 8, 25, 58, 113

Throesch, Elizabeth 11, 153
Tigges, Wim 117, 140, 150, 176
Turner, Mark 4, 25 f., 30, 32, 34 f., 58

Wakeling, Edward 18 f., 23, 49, 91, 120, 124
Walsh, Richard 103, 120 f., 141

Young, Kay 5, 113, 116, 133, 169

Zunshine, Lisa 5 f., 103, 106, 110, 113

Index of Subjects

Affect   21, 32, 104, 129, 137–139
– Affective narratology   113, 127, 140
– Affective response   143
Alice   1, 3–7, 9, 11–14, 16, 18–22, 25, 29–31, 33–44, 46–53, 55–57, 60, 63–70, 76–80, 82–87, 89–99, 101, 103–107, 109f., 112, 114f., 117–129, 131–147, 151–156, 159–178, 180–183
– Alice books   3–7, 9–12, 14, 18–32, 34–40, 42, 47, 50f., 53, 55, 57, 59–61, 63, 65f., 68–70, 74f., 77, 79f., 84, 89–92, 94f., 97f., 101, 103f., 106, 111, 113f., 117–119, 124, 126, 129, 131, 135, 137f., 140, 143–152, 155f., 158, 162f., 167, 170–177, 182f.
– Alice in Wonderland   23, 28, 47, 65, 70, 90–92, 100, 130, 161, 173
– Alice Liddell   9, 36, 47f., 50, 65f., 85, 91, 120, 122–124, 126
– Alice's body   127, 133–135
– Alice's dream   48, 50f., 53, 55, 57, 88, 105, 118, 128, 130, 134
– Alice's mind   42, 53, 97f., 100, 104, 127, 132, 166, 170
– Alice's worlds   3, 61, 103, 171
– Alice through the Looking-Glass   78
– Queen Alice   91
Alice's Adventures in Wonderland   13, 16, 31, 40, 49, 69f., 74, 77, 80, 84, 92, 99f., 105, 107f., 118, 121, 124, 128, 132f., 149, 163, 177f.
Alternative worlds   37
Anger   74, 94, 130–132, 145
Author   1, 4f., 8f., 25f., 36, 55, 58, 61, 65, 68, 70, 84f., 88, 105, 114, 117f., 121, 143f., 148, 150, 153, 157, 162, 182
Authorial strategies   158, 160

Blending   34f., 58, 172
– Blending spaces   174
– Conceptual blending   4, 25f., 34, 36, 59, 174
Blue Caterpillar   20, 98f.

Body   17, 23, 87, 109, 113, 116, 118, 127, 134f., 179f.
– Body and mind   116
Boundaries   7, 22, 33, 49, 55, 74f., 96, 156–160, 165–167, 176

Cats   49–51, 60, 92, 105f., 109, 136
Character   5, 8f., 15f., 27, 29f., 34f., 40–42, 44f., 49–52, 55f., 61, 63, 79, 83–86, 89–92, 94–99, 102, 104–107, 114–116, 119–122, 127–132, 134, 137–143, 145–148, 150f., 159, 161–164, 166f., 170f., 175, 180, 182
Cheshire Cat   19, 29f., 42, 79, 92, 95, 109, 156, 164, 178f.
Children   6, 9, 29, 35, 38f., 44, 46–48, 50, 52, 59f., 80, 83, 85, 87, 96, 107, 117, 120f., 124f., 129, 136f., 141, 143–145, 171, 180, 182
Child's mind   39f., 42, 104, 170, 175
– Creative mind   36, 39
– Fictional and real minds   127
– Mind-reading skills   99
– Readers' mind   53, 58f., 63f., 66, 104, 111, 139
– Unnatural mind   6, 29f., 99, 150, 162f., 165, 170–172, 176
Cognition   1, 5, 21, 26, 30, 44, 65, 113, 127, 133, 139
– Creative cognition   4, 27
– Embodied cognition   133
Cognitive approach   1, 9, 55, 58, 147
Cognitive deixis   3, 7, 58f., 66
Cognitive metaphor   25f., 182
Cognitive narratology   1–3, 5f., 8, 24, 102f., 134, 147, 162, 183
Cognitive perspective   147, 150, 175, 183
Cognitive poetics   8
Cognitive science   1, 2, 101–103, 133, 134
Consciousness   2, 11, 13, 15, 18f., 21, 23, 83, 104, 113, 116, 127f., 134, 141, 169
Cultural context   59, 69, 110, 114, 124, 128

Culture   2, 32, 35, 69, 120, 139, 158
– Victorian culture   74, 116, 118, 120, 156

Dialogue   20, 91, 102, 109, 136, 145, 156, 171f., 182f.
Dodgson (Charles Ludwidge)   9, 16, 38, 70–73, 84f., 114, 121f., 124, 136, 153f.
Double   9, 34, 51, 68, 70, 84f., 90, 93f., 96f., 126, 133
Dream   3, 9, 13f., 16–21, 31–33, 38–42, 44, 47–53, 55f., 59f., 63f., 77, 83–85, 88, 91–94, 96, 104–106, 116, 118f., 125, 127–129, 133f., 136, 140, 154, 166, 168, 174
– Dream states   14, 19
– Dream worlds   24

Embodied emotions   131
Embodied mind   113, 133, 135, 137
Embodiment   29, 92, 99, 109, 113, 116, 127, 129–131, 136, 138, 143, 178
Emotional involvement   7f., 117f., 140f.
Emotional states   128, 140
Emotion   5, 7, 8, 21, 31, 34, 36, 45, 46, 52, 53, 101, 112–114, 116–118, 120, 122, 124, 125–134, 136–146, 159, 169, 182
Empathy   5, 45, 101, 113f., 138–142, 144f.
Euclid   11, 153
Experience   2, 5, 8, 12–16, 18, 21, 23, 25f., 31, 35, 37, 39–45, 49f., 58–60, 70, 79, 82f., 85, 91, 93f., 101, 103f., 109, 115, 121, 128f., 131, 133f., 138f., 143, 145, 152, 158f., 162f., 166, 171, 182

Fairy tale   12, 33, 35, 38, 40, 47, 59f., 70, 74f., 83, 89, 109, 151f., 183
Fantastic (the)   7, 11, 35, 53, 75, 148, 152f., 155f., 183
Feeling   13, 15, 36, 42–44, 106, 113f., 116, 122, 125, 129, 138f., 141–144, 152, 157, 162
Fiction   3, 5f., 8, 15f., 32, 54f., 57, 60, 65, 97, 114, 121, 137, 139–142, 145, 148, 150–152, 157, 160, 169, 174, 179, 181
Frame   2, 7, 39f., 59, 104, 147, 172
– Cognitive frame   65, 174, 176

– Frame of reference   3, 58, 65, 67, 97, 105, 174, 180, 182

Game   5, 10, 32f., 36, 49, 87, 92, 94f., 116f., 140, 156, 165, 171, 175, 182
– Game of chess   32, 36, 54, 106, 126
– Life (as a) game   10, 12, 17, 21, 23, 32f., 38f., 46f., 52, 64, 70, 73, 75, 84, 86, 89f., 92, 97, 99, 109, 118, 120, 131, 139, 141, 143f., 153, 158, 175
– Linguistic game   28, 50, 60, 86
– Mind game   10, 103
Garden   33f., 47f., 53, 60, 65, 67, 79, 83, 93, 107, 109f., 117, 131, 174
Genre   4, 59–61, 98, 116, 149, 151f., 174, 176, 183

Illustration   10, 15, 17, 28, 62, 65f., 69, 76, 80f., 89, 100, 108, 112, 135, 149, 161, 163, 166, 177
Imagination   4, 17, 36, 55, 58, 61, 63, 65f., 68f., 91, 101, 116f., 133, 139, 144, 154, 157f., 160, 169, 173, 175f., 181
Imitation   5, 101, 138, 157
Immersion   59, 61, 84, 101
Impossible worlds   3, 6, 9, 159, 179, 182

Jabberwocky   20f., 80, 156

Language   5, 28, 32, 70, 80, 82, 86–88, 93, 98, 109f., 152, 156, 167, 175
Literature   1f., 6, 11, 17, 24, 31, 34f., 37, 42, 77, 86, 90, 115f., 121, 158, 162, 176
– Nonsense literature   35, 116, 149, 175
– Victorian literature   70, 114, 116, 134, 156
Lolita   122, 124, 126
Looking-Glass insects   28, 52, 86–89, 175

Madness   16, 29, 31f., 79, 85, 116, 140, 151, 161, 163, 166f., 170, 174
Meaning   4–6, 13f., 21, 26–28, 30f., 34–37, 39, 44, 46f., 51–55, 61, 70, 73, 75, 77, 79f., 82, 85, 88, 92, 94, 97, 99, 103, 111, 118, 121f., 129, 132, 140f., 145, 148, 152–154, 156f., 159, 163, 166, 169–171, 176f.

Index of Subjects

Memory 9, 12, 19, 43, 45, 52, 64, 77, 79, 82, 85, 88, 91, 106, 111, 118, 120, 122, 161–163, 168 f.
Metaphor 4, 25–34, 36 f., 58, 65, 68, 84, 99 f., 103 f., 106, 111, 113, 165, 170, 172
– Cognitive metaphor theory 25
– Conceptual metaphor 4, 29 f., 32, 58, 61, 68, 84, 165, 174, 182
– Embedded metaphor 4
– Literary metaphor 26
Meta-representation 6, 9, 101, 106 f., 109–111
Mimesis 151, 157, 179
Mind 1–17, 19–26, 28–33, 36, 39–42, 44, 45, 49–53, 57–59, 61, 63–66, 68, 73, 79, 80, 84–86, 88, 90, 91, 94, 97–107, 109, 111–113, 116, 117, 120, 121, 126–128, 130–135, 137–140, 144, 150, 151, 153, 157, 159, 160, 162–172, 174–176, 182
– Characters' mind 6, 25, 97 f., 111, 134, 162, 170
Mirror neurons 5 f., 68, 99, 101–103, 113, 139
Mirror 9, 10, 12, 13, 17, 23, 32, 33, 36–38, 42, 49, 50, 56, 68–70, 72–80, 82–104, 106–108, 110, 111, 113, 125, 132, 139, 145, 152, 154–156, 163, 166, 168, 170, 174
– Mirror and language 70
Mise en abyme 68–70, 76–80, 104

Narrative 2, 4–9, 12, 14, 16, 19, 21, 24 f., 27–29, 32–35, 37–39, 47, 50–52, 54–59, 68, 70, 75, 77, 79 f., 82 f., 90, 95, 97, 99, 101–104, 107, 110, 113, 117, 119, 121, 125, 127, 129, 137, 139–144, 147 f., 150–155, 158–160, 162 f., 165, 168, 170, 174–178, 180–183
– Narrative representation 135, 147, 163, 169
– Narrative techniques 79, 141, 152
– Narrative theory 6, 8, 54 f., 147, 157
– Nonsense narrative 7, 80, 142, 150
– Unnatural narrative 7, 148, 150 f., 158, 181

Narratology 7 f., 99, 101 f., 152, 155
– Unnatural narratology 6 f., 147 f., 150, 152, 160
Nonsense 5, 9, 11, 20 f., 26 f., 29, 38–40, 49–51, 60, 69 f., 86, 88, 95 f., 98, 107, 109, 111 f., 114, 116–120, 122, 138–141, 145, 147 f., 150 f., 153 f., 156, 158–161, 163 f., 166–172, 175 f.
– Nonsense and (the) unnatural 7, 11, 30 f., 114, 138, 150, 152, 158, 166, 182
– Nonsense genre 28, 79, 150
– Nonsense texts 27, 30, 118, 120, 140, 147, 150
– Nonsense worlds 51, 99

Parody 11, 35, 65, 79–81, 89, 93, 118–120, 146, 156, 165, 174
Photography 70, 72 f., 166
Poetics 54, 69 f., 74 f., 150, 157
Possible world theory 3 f., 25, 54 f., 57 f., 65, 181 f.
Principle of minimal departure 3, 57 f., 60, 66

Queen of Hearts 32, 91–93, 98, 109 f., 129, 143

Rabbit hole 12, 27, 31–33, 37, 51, 60, 92, 131, 136, 155 f.
Reader-response theory 8, 133
Reading strategies 172, 174, 176, 181
Realism 141, 148, 157
Red Queen 32, 63, 89, 93, 95, 98, 112, 131, 143, 172
Reversal 29, 68–70, 73, 80–83, 96, 108, 110, 158, 160, 174
Rhetoric 8, 114, 116, 120 f., 141

Schema 23, 26, 30, 36
Schizophrenia 30, 167
Scripts 172, 176
Sentimentality 114, 116–118, 120
Simulation 5 f., 103, 113
Society for Psychical Research 12–14, 49, 154
Space 1–4, 7, 11, 12, 17, 19, 24, 26–28, 30, 33–37, 52, 59–61, 63, 70, 82, 101, 126,

132, 153–155, 159, 160, 164–166, 172, 174
- Blended space   27, 34–36
- Hyperspace   11f.
- Mental space   3, 34, 59
- Narrative space   61, 172, 175
- Space-time   12, 154, 160

Spiritualism   14, 16–19, 24

Story   3, 8f., 15f., 18, 34–40, 46, 49, 51, 55, 59f., 65, 68, 75, 77–80, 82–84, 92, 105, 110, 114, 118f., 122, 125, 129, 131, 138, 181

Storyworld   3f., 7, 25, 27–29, 59, 70, 91, 97, 102, 150, 172, 179, 181f.

Sylvie and Bruno   13–16, 18f., 38f., 116, 140, 160

Tea-time   12, 51, 105, 109, 165f.

Temporality   162f.

Theory of Mind   5f., 45, 68, 113, 128

Through the Looking-Glass   10f., 20, 35, 38, 47, 49, 56, 60–64, 69, 76f., 80–82, 84, 93, 99, 103, 105, 110, 118f., 122, 132, 151, 163, 166, 168f., 180, 182

Tweedledum and Tweedledee   56, 83, 88, 95f.

Unicorn   10, 25, 95f., 153f., 156, 171, 176f., 179f., 182

Unnatural (the)   3, 6f., 55, 82, 104, 147f., 150–160, 162–166, 168–172, 174–177, 179, 181f.

Unusual (the)   21, 141, 143, 150, 154, 159f., 167, 172, 174

Virtuality   25, 101

Walrus (the) and the Carpenter   52, 137

White Knight   10, 51f., 64, 69, 80, 85f., 93, 95, 119, 122, 125f.

White Queen   12, 63f., 93, 98, 111f., 143, 168f., 180f.

White Rabbit   13, 29, 31, 35, 42f., 51, 60, 107, 131, 134, 143, 164, 178

Wonderland   3f., 6, 10, 12–14, 27, 30–35, 39f., 42–44, 47, 49–53, 55, 57, 61, 66, 79, 83–85, 90–95, 97–99, 104–107, 109f., 125–127, 129, 131–134, 136f., 143, 145, 156, 163–165, 170f., 178, 180

www.ingramcontent.com/pod-product-compliance
Lightning Source LLC
Chambersburg PA
CBHW061939220426
43662CB00012B/1958